AF522652

UNDERSTANDING EUROPEAN INTEGRATION
History, Culture and Politics of Identity

UNDERSTANDING EUROPEAN INTEGRATION
History, Culture and Politics of Identity

R. PAVANANTHI VEMBULU

AAKAR BOOKS
DELHI

This publication has been produced with the financial assistance of the European Community. The views expressed herein are those of the author and can therefore in no way be taken to reflect the official opinion of the European Commission.

UNDERSTANDING EUROPEAN INTEGRATION
History, Culture and Politics of Identity

First Published, 2003

ISBN 81-87879-10-6

Published by
AAKAR BOOKS
28-E, Pocket-IV, Mayur Vihar Phase-I, Delhi-110 091
Phone : 22795505 Telefax : 22795641
E-mail : aakarb@del2.vsnl.net.in

Typeset at
Nidhi Laser Point, Shahdara Delhi-32
Ph. : 22825424

Printed in India on behalf of M/s Aakar Books by
Arpit Printographers, B-7, Saraswati Complex,
Subhash Chowk, Laxmi Nagar, Delhi-110 092

To ***Appa,*** with love

Preface

The year 1992 is in many ways a paradox. In this year, Europe celebrated the completion of five hundred years of Columbus' historical expedition and discovery of the *New World*. It was indeed a historical 'big bang', which set off the expansion of the European universe and superimposing its image onto the rest of the planet. However, in a squirm contrast, the same year witnessed the signing of the Treaty of Maastricht signifying the retreat of Europe into its medieval perimeters. This paradox of European biography requires a larger canvas to deal with.

It is not only Europe's temporality, even its present existential moment too is ruptured by a paradox: on the one hand, moves towards closure economic and political co-operations are taking place in the western part of Europe; but in the eastern part of Europe, the forces of newly awakened nationalism have rekindled all sorts of emotional identifications accompanied by ethnic warfare and violence.

There is yet another most enduring paradox of Europe around which this book develops its interest. When most of the Asian and African countries were striving to achieve their own independence through their national struggle, their colonial masters – 'the authors of nationalism' started moving towards some post-national political set up. To dramatize the event, let it be put like this: When Jawaharlal Nehru declared, at the midnight stroke, India's so-called tryst with destiny, more or less at the same time his counterpart in Britain Clement Atlee in his historical declaration proclaimed: "Europe should federate or perish". Once the conceivers of nationalism now turn to its gravediggers.

These set of paradoxes throw immense challenge to theoretical understanding of Social Sciences. Trapped in the web of ironies, all the disciplines of the Social Sciences, irrespective of their demarcation and division of methodological boundaries, started theorizing these paradoxes with surfeit of pre-suffixes such as 'post' of something, 'end' of something or emergence of some 'new' thing. International Relations too has its own terminologies such as Post-Westphalian system, New World Order, End of Cold War and even End of History. These catchwords are generally coined to emphasize the theoretical foundation of a particular approach to understand an international event or phenomenon.

One such phenomenon, which has started attracting the scholars of interdisciplinary inclination, is the European integration process. Yet, the predominating consensual opinion on European integration is: 'A regional organization for promoting economic interest and nothing more or special about it'. Most of the scholars still assume that European integration was and is an instrument of economic co-operation and a novel mechanism of pooling their collective economic interest. For some others, the European integration is exclusively a political agenda. They would reduce the matter as a political problem of having to achieve a federal set-up among some group of states in Western Europe to promote and preserve peace in this zone. Thus so far only two approaches dominate in the understanding of European integration: economic and political aspects of the integration; cultural issues so far appear to have assumed marginal role.

My engagement with the cultural aspect of integration has to be both at empirical and theoretical level: at empirical level, the focus of this book would be on how the European Union through its various cultural policy initiatives deliberately tries to transform the loyalties of people from the national limit to the much broader European horizon; at theoretical level, the intension is to understand the integration within the cultural history of Europe. Unable to accept the much circulated theoretical arguments of cold war conditions or the longing for a perpetual peace in Europe, I intend to open a new space by tracing the genealogy of integration from the cultural dualism that Europe had landed from ancient times onwards. By identifying this dualism in the catchword "Europe at the antithesis of culture and civilization", the study would further reveal that the integration was and is an act of synthesizing this dualism in which Europe caught hold of.

Having thus delineated the theoretical foundation of this book, the structure of the study could be conceptually divided into three parts: a search towards a meaning of Europe both in time and space; the European Union's efforts of culturally re-inscribing Europe; a post-colonial critic of this re-inscription. Each part will have a specific thematical question to be exclusively dealt with. However, the one continuing thread, which interconnects all these three parts, will be the issue of European integration.

Before proceeding on this line, as a ground clearance activity, the introduction will undertake an exhaustive survey of the various theories and debates that have been going on in the integration studies for over five decades. This introductory chapter has been further divide into three sections. In the first section, the focus will be on the various international relations theories that have taken up the integration as their scope of investigations. Specific focus will be given to realism / neo-realism, liberalism and neo-functionalism. In the second section, the stress will be on the political economy of European integration. Here the theories of interdependence, regimes and hegemony will be analyzed in the context of the issue of European integration. Further, Wallerstein's world-system analysis and his understanding of European integration will also be highlighted. The last and final section of this introduction will be more in critical tone. After emphasizing the inadequacy of those western theories of integration, the study will argue for the necessity of bringing the historical imperial experience of Europe as a yet another explanatory category in the understanding of the integration process.

As a first step towards envisioning such an alternative

mode of analysis, the first chapter will take up the question of defining what is Europe. Here, the study will bring into light the different modes of defining Europe: as a continent; as a civilization; and as a consciousness. After revealing the inadequacy of each mode of definition, the book will develop its own definition. Europe, it will be emphasized, is a sign of power relation. The stress will be given onto how Europe was imagined to perpetuate the power relations during the imperial phase and how this same strategy is being adopted and employed in the service of integration nowadays.

The second chapter will take up the question whether the phenomenon of European integration is a modern, more specifically the post-Second World War phenomenon? Here the focus will be to prove that the issue of integrating Europe under one political set up could be traced from the late medieval period onwards. To trace such a genealogy, this chapter shall exclusively focus on the cultural history of Europe. In this endeavor, the study will extricate one recurring phenomenon through out the history of Europe from ancient to modern periods, which will be identified in the study as "Europe at the Antithesis of Culture and Civilization". The inherent idea behind this catchword is to demonstrate that how Europe at least from the medieval period onwards caught trapped in the web of different forces pulling it in two different directions.

The third chapter brings the post-1945 phase of integration to the focus. Here, how the discourse of integration was oscillating between the political and economic aspects of integration. When the federalist emphasized the necessity of erecting, at a single stroke, a federal organization for Europe, the economically driven scholars in turn emphasized the functionally characterized economic integration.

But the tendency towards the integration got transformed after the end of the cold war in 1990. The changed perception reflected in the signing of Maastricht Treaty in 1992. Here onwards the so far neglected cultural aspect of integration got its importance and the European Union starts focusing on the cultural angle of integration. The chapter four will exclusively deal with this cultural aspect of integration by focusing on the Union's cultural policies. The emphasis will be on how through the various policy proposals the Union tries to shift the loyalty of the people from the sedimented national sentiment to the broader European Community. Here the stress will be on how the language, education and media are being Europeanized so as to impute the much needed cultural legitimacy to the integration process.

After these explorations, in the final chapter, the study will take up the issue of visualizing the alternative theorizing of the integration. This chapter will emphasize the fact that it is not the fear of war or the nationality conflicts that had forced Europe to move in the direction of integration in the post-war era. On the contrary, the study will underline the contextual conditionality of decolonization that had made shrink the colonial markets available to Europe for over centuries. This shrinking of market forced the colonial masters to come close together to consolidate their own market so as to prevent the free movement of goods and persons from the underdeveloped countries, including their former colonies.

This book is the outcome of my doctoral research undertaken at the Centre for American and West European Studies, at Jawaharlal Nehru University, New Delhi. It is here that I have inherited a critical perspective that has not only guided my research but reshaped my personality over the years. I must be grateful to Prof. Christopher Sam Raj, my thesis supervisor, for his encouragement and valuable guidance. Indeed, the freedom and confidence he reposed upon me is memorable. This book would not have been possible without the encouragement and constant prodding of Prof. Rajendra K. Jain, Project Director, JNU European Union Studies Program. I must thank him on two accounts: for generously awarded a grant for publishing this book under JNU European Union Studies Program; and suggesting a catchy and comprehensible title for this book.

I am indebted to Prof. Bö Strath, Department of History and Civilization, European University Institute, Florence and Dr. Peo Hansen, Department of Thematic Studies, Linköpings

University, Sweden for their invigorating comments and generous suggestions.

I have immensely benefited from my friends - their provoking debates and demanding statements and above all their intellectual vigor that made me choose academic as my career; otherwise I would have landed up in some where else. I must thank them all.

R. Pavananthi Vembulu

Contents

	Preface	*vii*
	Introduction	1
1.	Europe: Towards A Definition	60
2.	The Meaning of Integration in the Cultural History of Europe	88
3.	European Integration and Institutional Historiography	120
4.	Culture and Community: European Union's Cultural Policy and the Dynamics of Europeanization	165
5.	Imperialism of European Integration: A Postcolonial Critique	207
	Bibliography	235
	Index	259

INTRODUCTION

UNDERSTANDING EUROPEAN INTEGRATION: THEORY AND DEBATE

Defining what European Union is about poses a serious theoretical challenge to the orthodox International Relations[1] scholarship. Any conventional International Relations textbooks contain a special chapter on International Organizations covering topics on United Nations Organization, International Labor Organization and World Health Organization etc. These are organizations of planetary scope and content intended to secure or promote a particular issue, say, security, labor and health on global level. At the same time, as a sub-division of this section, there will be a topic on regional organizations like NATO, ASEAN, OAU and SAARC. These are the organizations of a particular regional scope and specific issue content, mostly on security or economics.

This second trend has been identified and named as 'regionalism' in International Relations. Joseph Nye defined regionalism as 'a limited number of states linked by a geographical relationship and by a degree of mutual interdependence'.[2] It should be noted that Nye gives importance to geographically determined interdependence. On the surface level his definition would suite very well, since majority of the regional organizations were formed on the basis of some specific visible markers—sea or naturally bounded area. For example, the NATO and APEC were formed in the name of Atlantic and Pacific Sea markers respectively. Similarly, ASEAN, SAARC and OAU were organized around a specific area boundaries, say,

South East Asia, South Asia and Africa respectively.

But regionalism need not always signify a geographical aspect of interdependence. It sometimes crosscuts the known geographical boundaries and organizes itself on some other identification. The G-8 indicates an association of the most developed countries without any geographical coherency. That is why a new trend has emerged in International Relations recognizing regionalism as a part of globalization drive: 'regionalism is an *intermediate link in the chain* leading to the emergence of a new global structure'.[3] However, at the same time, regionalism has been identified as a reaction against globalization. In order to check the menacingly marauding globalization, it is said that the states of certain distinct cultural zones are organizing themselves around their common heritage to preserve and promote them. The controversial Huntington theory proposed this kind of analysis.

Anyway this regionalism versus globalism issue will be discussed in detail in the later part of this chapter it is enough here to note that there is no consensual agreement on the definition of regionalism. Hurrell[4] has classified five categories of regionalism that have been employed today in International Relations:

1. A process involving the growth of informal linkages and transactions derived primarily from economic activity.
2. A mixer of historical, cultural and social traditions lead to a shared perception of belonging to a particular community.
3. State or government sponsored agreements and co-ordinations to manage common problems and protect and enhance the role of the state and the power of the government.
4. State promoted regional economic integration where government and business interests pursue integration to promote the economic growth.
5. A process of regional cohesion intending to promote the global interconnectedness.

It is interesting to note that Hurrell's all these five categories are being applied to understand and define what the European Union is or to be.[5] The category 4 is the very common application to the Union where by it could be identified as mere an economic integration. This approach has been substantiated by the successful achievement of the Common Market in Western Europe. However the categories 1&3 have been brought into the field under the banner of functionalism and neo-functionalism respectively. Today these two streams are engaged in a major debate to give a holistic and universal explanation to the union formation any where in the world. Similarly, the categories 4&5 under the name of regionalism and globalism try to explain the Union albeit with different stress and strains.

Since Hurrell's categories are applicable to any kind of regional organizations floated in the international arena, one can ask, what is the special in the European Union? I think, Hurrell has missed one crucial point in his classification as far as the European Union is concerned. The European Union has been not only created to achieve some cooperation among the states in Western Europe but it goes even further and declares that its final goal would rest on achieving the political union in Europe, or at least in the western part of Europe by gradual integration of economic, political, social and finally cultural fields.

Therefore, for me, the very nature and intention of integration differentiates the European Union from the rest of other bunch of regional organizations. When these other organizations are content with the co-operation aimed through inter-governmental approach, the EU distinctly strives for achieving a 'supranational political formation' not only in economic but in political, social and cultural sectors. Preciously this issue of integration confounds our understanding of the EU whether it is merely an inter-governmental co-operative venture or a decisive move towards a supranational federal formation. Recently, one author has come forward to clear the doubt but finally landed in further mystifying the EU by giving a verdict on it: 'more than inter-governmentalism but less than supranationalism'.[6]

How then one can understand the European Union? For over two decades from the Second World War, the European integration has been the subject matter of International Relations. The other disciplines, particularly Sociology and

Political Science were showing a complete lack of interest in this phenomena. Their reluctant posture has given an undisputed legitimacy to International Relations having let it monopolize the subject matter. As a relatively new field as compared to other social sciences, and having been limited to the scope of studying exclusively the cause of war and its prevention, the International Relations reduced the European integration process as an novel attempt to achieve peace and overcoming the chronic problem of international anarchy. Through out the 1950s and early 1960s any theoretical understanding of the European integration had thus revolved around the axis of peace and stability.

However, in the early 1970s the tone and tenor of the theoretical understanding got changed. The issue of war and peace receded and instead the question about the retreat of state came to the foreground. The emergence of a new sub-field called 'International Political Economy' within the International Relations discipline helped understand European integration away from the predominant framework of war and peace. Structuring their argument on the question of interdependence and the emergence of transnational and multinational corporations, the new theorists argued that the role of state becoming obsolete in the condition of interdependence. To substantiate their stand they invariably would cite the example of European integration process. Thus, the European Union formation got a new theoretical foundation to explain.

But the last decade of the 20th century witnessed a flurry of theoretical adventures in the field of European integration studies. There are two obvious reasons for this enthusiasm: At first, the end of cold war made loose the rigid legitimacy given to the realist orthodoxy in International Relations. At second, the concept of globalization has brought the issue of integration into a broader theoretical spectrum. The collapsing of the realist orthodoxy along with the Berlin wall opened a vast space for undertaking different kind of theoretical adventure in world politics. The unprecedented boom of theories in International Relations as identified as 'Third Debate or Interparadigm Debate' helped situate the integration in different context away from the otherwise dominant cold war paradigm.

Similarly, the concept of globalization makes the hitherto rigid disciplinary divisions blurred. To understand the global situation properly, one has to comprehend its different and multitudinal dimensions. This compulsion has brought the different secluded disciplines onto the same plane. One of the immediate benefactors of the seemingly visible confluence of all social sciences is the European integration study. Almost all the disciplines including sociology and anthropology now show keen interest in the integration process and enrich the understanding of European integration. The questions about 'national' and 'post-national' identities and citizenship and multiculturalism are the issues of inquiry in post-Maastricht phase of European integration study.

In this chapter, I would first elaborate the various theoretical premises of the European integration. Here, my emphasis primarily rests on to highlight how different theories about the European integration that have been developed and improvised over the years have been determined by certain specific historical conditions. After this exposition, I would concentrate on the Indian academic's understanding of the European integration. In this section, the focus of the study will be on to show the Indian academic's uncritical importation and reliance of the western theories of integration. As a way out, the study would stress the necessity of evolving an alternative theory—a post-colonial critique of European integration by drawing inspiration from the works of 'Subaltern Studies' historians and postcolonial theorists.

I
EUROPEAN INTEGRATION IN INTERNATIONAL RELATIONS: THEORY AND DEBATE

Until after the First World War, one can hardly discern the International Relations as a separate and distinct subject field. On this point only, it is generally considered as a young branch of study in the group of Social Sciences. For most part, the International Relations was studied under a subcategory of history. Normally termed as diplomatic history, its main focus was either on some particular events or of particular decision of a state or to say more precisely the decisions of political personalities such as Napoleon and Bismarck. The zenith of the diplomatic history reached during and after the 1815 Vienna Congress. There was no theoretical underpinning for this diplomatic historiography except the concept of balance of power. It was this concept which actually shaped both the conduct of diplomacy and as well as writing of international history.

But a conceptual shift happened in the last two decades of the 19th century. It was during that time that a new and radical idea of internationalism taken root of. It is generally understood as a reaction against the German nationalism and its political unification in 1870. However, there are two tendencies in the 19th century internationalism: One stream exemplified by the British liberal school; and the other one propagated by the nascent Communist ideology. The first stream by bringing the concept of *laissez-faire* shifted the focus of international history from the monopoly of state centric view. Instead, it argued for lesser role for state in human affaires and stressed the free flow of goods and services through unrestricted trade. Distinctively shifting from state and focusing on market the liberal internationalists argued that the free trade would improve the state relationship and help prevent the recurrence of war.

On the contrary, the Communist better known as Marxist school, not only rejected the state centric traditional view but also the liberalist's market oriented internationalism. Instead of state and market, they emphasized on capitalism and class relations. By identifying capitalism as an international phenomenon (even though at the time of Marx, capitalism was more a European phenomenon, he believed that through its colonial expansion capitalism was bound to reach on world scale), Marxists called for overthrow of capitalism by consolidating the proletarian class across the given national or state boundaries. Marx in his manifesto clearly envisaged that the proletarians had no other identity except their class identity, which would cut across any earlier conceptual boundary:

> In the national struggle of the proletarians of the different countries, they point out and bring to the front the common interest of the entire proletariats, independently of all nationality. In the various stages of development, which the struggle of the working class against the bourgeoisie has to pass through, they always and everywhere represent the interests of the movement as a whole.[7]

Whatever may be the internal differences, these two streams - liberal and Marxists, shaped the theoretical understanding of International Relations. Even today every new theory propounded in this field has its umbilical connection with either of these two earlier versions: liberalism or Marxism.

The later history of International Relations has generally been written along the debates undergone over the years in this field: between idealist and realist; then traditionalist and behavioralist over the issue of methodology; and finally between all these classical theories and the new upcoming post-positivist theories.[8] Bordering on this line of classification, I would group the existing theories of International Relations under five headings: (1) Liberalism and neo-liberalism (2) Realism and neo-realism; (3) Behavioralism; (4) International Political Economy; (5) Critical International Relations theories. Though one cannot take for granted that these five categories are chronologically succeeding one another, I would consider the above-mentioned classification as a chronological sequence in that order. This chronological understanding is necessary to capture the ebb and flow of theoretical movement in the study of the European integration. Any theoretical shift in the history of International Relations has, in turn, created a new theoretical adventure in the integration study. It is exactly on this point, that is, the nexus between the theory of International Relations and the theory of the European integration, that the study will develop a critique in the last part of this chapter.

Liberal Internationalism

International Relations as a specific and separate subject field was indebted to liberal tradition and thinkers a lot. The liberalists were the first serious scholars who set international relations on firm theoretical foundations. Before those liberal scholars, the International Relations was content with in studying the nature and dynamics of balance of power systems. For them the power-balancing act of states was the crucial factor in International Relations. Where as the liberal thinkers would ask, what is the cause of war? Can war be prevented? And can a perpetual peace be attainable? The quest for attaining an ever-lasting peace, the liberalists would say, ought to be the sole purpose of International Relations. That is why, Jim George grouped these scholars under the banner of neo-Kantian and this phase of International Relations as neo-Kantianism.[9]

Under the shambles of the First World War, it was increasingly realized that the first objective should be to question the accepted Clautwitzian idea of war as an instrument of foreign policy. The liberals argued that the Allied Powers waged war with Germany in 1914 with the professed objective of 'a war to end war', that is, a war for peace. But could they end war after that? Indeed within 20 years, there was another war more destructible than the previous one. H.G. Wells called this vicious cycle of 'war for peace, peace for war' as 'drilling, trampling foolery in the heart of Europe'.[10] The First World War showed that war has become destructive on a scale unimaginable a couple of centuries ago. So the liberals campaigned for the ultimate end of war. Lord Bryce warned in a catchy word: 'unless we end war, war end us'.[11] In this context, for liberalists, the study of International Relations meant analyzing the causes of war and proposing concrete methods to overcome this evil and achieve an everlasting peace. Unlike the earlier diplomatic historians, the liberalists believed

> The study of International Relations is hardly just an academic exercise - it is an investigation of the chances for our physical survival or rather scholars' and intellectuals' attempt to determine what can be done to avoid a collective disaster initiated by the so-called political elite who act according to certain principles.[12]

This neo-Kantian longing for a perpetual peace was the sole motive force behind the setting up of institutions meant exclusively for studying the causes of war. For the first time a separate department for international politics was set up at Aberystwyth in 1919.[13] Subsequently, the British Royal Institute of International Affairs, American Council of Foreign Relations and Carnegie Endowment for International Peace were established in 1920. The main purpose of these institutions was said to be studying scientifically the causes of war and prevent its future occurrence. Thus, the study of war and peace had become the prime objective of International Relations in the inter-war period.

It was in this context, Brailsford published a book, 'A League of Nations' in 1916 in which he argued for setting up of a supranational body to regulate the relations of nations. Later drawing influence from this book, President Wilson supported the formation of the League of Nations in 1919. The Wilsonian vision of future world order revolved around two axis: one that had emphasized the formation of supranational body of the kind of League of Nation which would stress collective security instead of balance of power system; and the other one that had underlined the necessity of establishing the free trade which would promote peace and stability among the warring states. For over two decades, these two aspects had become pillars of liberal approach to International Relations. Jim George vividly captures this sentiment as "the League of Nations and the International Court of Justice were, in this sense, the institutional vanguard of the post-war liberal age in international affairs".[14]

However, the two subsequent historical events shattered the liberal institutionalist's dream of attaining perpetual peace through international institutions and rendered their idea of perpetual peace through supranational body evasive and useless. The collapse of the Weimer Republic with the rise of power of Hitler in Germany and the successive fascist wave that swept throughout out Europe had made the League of Nations dysfunctional. At the same time, the collapse of Czardom and the subsequent socialist revolution in Russia made the theoretical precinct of liberalism inadequate and ineffective. Under this challenging condition the liberals renewed their arguments by pressing for more closure union of the states. H.G. Wells reflected this liberal sentiment as 'the only way to organize world peace lies through a federation'.[15]

At that time there were two schools of thought on the causes of war: one asserting that war results from the rivalries of a competing groups of capitalists and the other asserting that war results from the anarchy of international system and the absence of effective international law. The first school known as, 'Critique of Imperialism', propagated by Lenin stressed the inherent war mongering nature of capitalism and the inevitable socialistic revolution of the world scale. Thus Lenin prescribed a radical break with the existing political, social and economic conditions in order to stop war in future. On the contrary the liberal bourgeoisie thought that the external anarchical conditions of international politics as the sole cause of war and therefore stressed the need for uniting all those states under one supranational 'Leviathan State' or at least place them under the purview of international law. When compared with the radical socialists, the liberals were very superfluous and contented with only in prescribing a federal set up as an alternative to the anarchical conditions of international politics.

However, both these schools stressed the obsolescence of nationalism and the importance of moving towards internationalism. Marx called for the workers of the world to unite. He even stressed that the proletarians had no nation and they themselves form as a nation in a world scale. Similarly the liberals too accused nationalism

> ..(Sic) as being held today with something like religious fervor... and the evils of nationalism result from the excessive tyranny which these states exercise over their members and the lack of legal restraint in their relations with each other.[16]

Hence, they stressed so long as international affairs are the battleground of the purely national politics of sovereign states, the larger issues concerning mankind as a whole will continue to be overlooked. One scholar even went to the extent of saying, 'we need both an extension and a moderation of the group consciousness at present associated with the nation'.[17]

If at all ready to extent our consciousness of nation, where have we to move? The liberals would answer towards federal union. Clarence Streit in his popular book, 'Union Now', written during inter-war period defined what a federal system is: "a logical application to the whole world of liberal democratic government already discovered by mankind to be the only way of combining liberty with order".[18] Streit's book has three main theses: one, the international government is necessary to create the world order and quarantine an everlasting peace. He in a Hobbsian tradition argued that unless there was an overarching supranational body, it was not possible to create a semblance of order in international arena. Two, the only form of international government, which is both workable and compatible with liberty and democracy, is federal union. He intended to create such a union through constitutional measures. That is why in his book, he included a model constitution based on the USA's in the annexure outlining the broader thematical issues of the futur federal union. Third, he argued this federal union should begin with a group of existing democracies instead of waiting until the whole world is ready. For him Europe was ripe enough to move towards such a federal union when compared to other continents. This Euro-centric approach still to date dominates the liberal understanding of the European integration process.

Realism

'The International Relations' story is in many respects a footnote to realism'[19] said Timothy Dunne. Such is the popularity and widespread acceptability of this theoretical legacy in current International Relations. Realists criticized vehemently the neo-Kantians as idealists sitting in the Tower of Babel. They accused liberal internationalism as a set of some *a priori* abstract principles which could not absolve the anarchical condition of the international system. Rather they argue, 'the world imperfect as it is from the rational point of view is the result of forces inherent in human nature'.[20] So it is through the empirical and pragmatic approach one should comprehend the objective conditions. For them, there is no room for any universal principles in international relations except a system of checks and balances as Dunne puts it 'realism concerns only three issues: statism, survival and self-help'.

The realists particularly Morgenthau pointed out despite

the flurry of activities and theories of these liberal thinkers and their brainchild of League of Nations, they could not have stopped the arrival of another war in European soil. Morgenthau emphatically asked: "if the evil of conflict and war springs from the divisions of the world into detached and competing political units, will it be exorcised simply by changing or reducing the lines of division?"[21] The liberal internationalists' longing for transcending the boundaries of both–nation and state, for Morgenthau, was like groping for heaven. Instead he argues,

> The supranational forces such as universal religions, humanitarianism, cosmopolitanism and all other personal ties, institutions and organizations that bind individuals together across national boundaries are infinitely weaker today than the forces that unite people within a particular national boundary and separate them from the rest of humanity. This weakening is the result of nationalism.[22]

Does the nation-state be simply overcome by the federalist will alone? This is a world whose moving force is the aspirations of sovereign nations for power. The objective law of International Relation is that the nation states aggrandize their power to promoting their national interests.

In this realist sense, he negates the entire move that is supposedly intended to go beyond the nation states. There is no place for such concept of internationalism of both liberal and socialists varieties. The liberal internationalism, with it stress on free market economy and liberal principles would always promote the national interest of the USA. On the other hand, the visible international force of communism in actual sense is a cloaked ideology for promoting the national interest of the Soviet Union. This is the case with the UNO. This is an organization where the super powers with their respective allies try to promote and preserve their interest.

In the same theoretical prism, Morgenthau was inclined to understand the process of European federal formation. He saw it in a traditional realist power sense: the EC is a revolutionary attempt at solving an age-old political problem – the problem of national superiority of Germany.[23] Europe witnessed two catastrophic wars within a short span of time because of the ambitious, power mongering nature of German state. So if it were to stop Germany's power and contain it, Europe should think beyond the mechanism of alliance forming; since alliance worked only to defeat Germany in war, not successful in arresting the growth of Germany in no-war period. For Morgenthau, the other West European states invented a novel idea of containing the monstrous Germany by not resorting to war. Hence, for Morgenthau, the community is

> A revolutionary departure from the traditional methods by which inferior powers have tried to counter a superior one. For instead of countering the potentially superior power by a system of alliances, the other nations of Western Europe are trying to draw, as it were, Germany into their arms in order to disarm it and to make to superior strength of Germany innocuous.[24]

This rendering of community process into a mould of diplomatic tactics draw plank from other writers. Milward castigates this approach for believing that the 20th century states could adjust their foreign policies on such purely pragmatic grounds and for explaining the process of European integration 'as a choice of tactics in a broad game and no more'.[25] For Milward, the European community has self evidently had other functions as well as embodying other aspirations and ideas. The purely diplomatic approach to the integration would miss both the present conditions of the states and compulsions around which they have to act and react.

However, Morgenthau changed his outlook as the European Community had successfully moved towards some semblance of supranationalism. Though he did not change his criticism on federalist, he accepted functionalist argument of binding the nation states into some broader institutional arrangements.

> Nothing in the realist position militates against the assumption that the present division of the political world into nation states will be replaced by larger units of a quite different characters, more in keeping with the technical potentialities and moral requirement of the contemporary world.[26]

Though he accepted the possibility of transforming nation states into broader units, he still believed that it would not be possible through federal idealist way of constitutional mode. Instead he stressed a 'workable manipulation'[27] of the perennial forces that have shaped the past, as they will in the future. He saw such a workable manipulation in the functional theory and supported it as 'a spreading web of international activities and agencies in which and through which the interests and life of all nations would be gradually integrated'.[28]

Functionalism

Functionalists, in a broader sense, are also liberalists; but unlike their federal counterparts, functionalists' central axiom is that of 'form should follow function'.[29] They do not see any merit or even possibility of achieving Union right through the political will of making a common constitution. For them, integration should be an informal and a gradual process. While the liberal federalists argued for setting up of a political institution through a committed work of men and human will, the liberal functionalists, such a supranational institutions could not be made at a single stroke but has to grow out of experience and learning.

David Mitrany, the founder of the functionalist school, like his fellow liberals in the interwar period, was preoccupied with the question: how to maintain peace? Where he differed from other liberals was his mode of achieving peace. He completely distanced himself from what he calls 'federal fallacy'[30] and exposed a different and radical approach to attain 'a working peace system'. In a true liberal spirit, Mitrany castigates the 'state centric' realist approach to international relations, more particularly, the balance of power concept to achieve peace and stability. He stressed, like federalists, the immediate transcendence of both 'nation' and 'state' so that these two concepts should not dictate and fix our mode of thinking and activities.

Rather these fixed boundaries should be opened up to facilitate the cross-border links and collaborations. To bring the people across the borders and within functional networks would invariably promote a community sense among them. Thus the functionalist approach would help the growth of such positive and constructive common work, common habits and interests, making frontier lines meaningless by overlaying them with a natural growth of common activities and common administrative agencies.[31]

Mitrany proposed a strategy of organizing multiple functional agencies and institutions to encourage such cross-frontier collaborations, instead of creating a formal overarching federal state. It was expected that the success of one functional linkage would lead to another and thus the spillover would continue until a true world community emerged. Thus Mitrany's theory was grounded in two premises: organizing multiple functional institutions and they will lead spill over into other areas. The 'sum of these functions' not any constitutional set-up of supranational state, must propel Europe towards an eventual integration.

Neo-Functionalism

Ernst Hass, who inaugurated the neo-functional phase in European integration theory, came into the field with the announcement of 'retreat of nation state in Europe'. While the previous liberal and realist traditions concentrated on 'war and peace', he was the one who brought the scientific theoretical base to the study of European integration. It is he who brought the very term 'integration' into the subject. He defined it as, "a tendency towards a voluntary creation of larger political units, each of which self-consciously eschews the use of force in the relations between the participating units and groups".[32]

Integration, for Hass, like functionalists, is a process by which the states would voluntarily give up certain sovereign powers and evolve new techniques for resolving conflicts between themselves. While functionalists of Mitrany variety emphasis of the role of cross-frontier functional institutions, the neo-functionalist of Hass and others stress the specific form of supranational organizations with its own power and jurisdictions. That is why Mitrany latter criticized Hass as an 'informal federalist'[33] whose objective was to create one supranational European State. In a sense, he was correct that the neo-functionalists in a distinct way combined those two streams of theories - federal and functional, successfully.

For Hass, it is both desirable and possible to construct a European State but not through federal constitutional methods or 'will to a United Europe'. Rather than relaying on these 'altruistic' or 'idealistic' conditions for integration, he focussed attention on 'interests' and 'values'. Integration, he says, "Is a process whereby political actors in several distinct national settings are persuaded to shift their loyalties, expectations and political activities towards a new and larger center, whose institutions pose or demand jurisdiction over the pre-existing national state".[34] Two forces would expedite the desirable transformation of loyalties and interests from national boundaries to a transnational setting: the elite of each nation and transnational technocrats.[35] The first one align themselves across the border to promote their presumed interests; the second one would help such aligning of interest through their expertise and build institutions to safeguard and promote them. It is in this combination of interests and institutions which Hass called supranational.[36]

Again for Hass, the pooling of interests across national borders should be initially restricted to economic matters only. Stretching in to political and cultural spheres would derail the very process of integration since these are highly sentimental and conflictual matters. However, at the same time, he did not limit integration in economic field alone. It was expected that once the economic integration was successfully achieved, through spillover effect the other fields would automatically come under the integrative phase without any frictions. Thus, Hass says 'supranationality symbolizes the victory of economics over politics'.[37] Exactly on this point Hass faced a lot of criticism.

Hoffman timely remained Hass the success in economic integration did not bring other matters, in his own words 'high politics', of foreign and defense policies into the integrative spring. On the other hand, as Hansen[38] showed, the very effectiveness of the economic integration in stimulating the economic growth in the member states of the EC has strengthened the capacity of those states to undertake independent actions in other areas of policy. Similarly Hass' reliance of the elite and technocrats to carry forward the integration was also got criticized. Hoffman[39] argued that the semblance of success of integration in 1960s was not due to the elite and technocrats' commitment to achieve supranational institutions but rather due to the support of the American leadership and the cold war conditions. The historical context not the elite agency that had brought economic integration successful in 1960s.

Despite these criticisms, the neo-functional theory reigned supreme in the field of European integration. Leaders like Jean Monnet and Henry Spaak overtly adopted the basic tenets of this theory and practiced it. However, the changes in 1970s compelled Hass to announce 'the obsolescence of regional integration theory'.

Transactionalism

The transactionalists' basic premise is that communication is the sole means of achieving the mutual relevance and responsiveness, which distinguish 'organized social group from the random aggregation of individuals'.[40] Deutsch, the important transactionalist theorist, brought cybernetics and general systems theory into the study of regional integration. Unlike Hass, he considered integration as a condition in which populations of a given region have attained a sense of community based on an agreement that common problems should be solved without resorting to physical coercion.[41] He also sets out to discover, in a scientific inductive methodology, those 'conditions' necessary to promote and sustain such a social consensus.

He studied in depth ten case studies such as the unity of American states, the unification of England with Wales and Scotland, and German and Italian unification. Similarly he also studied the failure of achieving integration, for example, the failure in uniting Ireland with England, the Austro-Hungarian monarchy etc. From these case studies, he proposed four background conditions for any successful integration: mutual relevance of the units to one another; compatibility of values and some actual joint rewards; mutual responsiveness; and some degree of generalized common identity and loyalty.

Deutsch argued if all these four conditions were satisfied, then an 'amalgamated security community' could be attained. On the other hand, anyone just concerned with peace and its maintenance a 'pluralist security community' is attained. He identified the European integration as a move to achieve an amalgamated security community where as NATO aiming a pluralist security community. Thus the transactionalism does not concern itself with any specific type of legal and institutional framework, but rather with the conditions necessary for a sense of community among the populations of a given region.

II
POLITICAL ECONOMY OF EUROPEAN INTEGRATION

At the fag-end of the 1960s, the world witnessed an all round crisis. The May 1968 student revolution was the good indicator of the mood of this period. With the beginning of 1970s the world entered into economic recession. Particularly for Western Europe, the previous two decades' unprecedented boom came to a grinding halt. The collapse of the Bretton Woods system and the consequent dollar convertibility crisis reminded one of the Great Depression years of 1930s. The situation further worsened by the Arab-Israeli war in 1973 and the subsequent OPEC induced oil crisis. Under the crippling debt crisis, the newly independent underdeveloping countries started organizing themselves and stressed the necessity of a 'New International Economic Order', which would redress their inequality in economic growth.

These pressing economic problems of the world and the easing of cold war tension after the American's Vietnam debacle made some scholars argue for a radical shift in the theoretical perspectives of International Relations. Criticizing the mainstream realist orthodoxy of International Relations for having given too much importance to the security related issues they emphasized the economic aspects of International Relations. In this context, Susan Strange by attacking what she called "the mutual neglect of economics and International Relations",[42] gave a call for "an end to the long separation of politics and economics in the theoretical precincts of International Relations".[43]

The American scholars were the first in undertaking such an assignment. The tone and tenor of the so-called International Political Economy was set by two American economists: Richard Cooper and Raymond Vernon. The former, in his book "The Economics of Interdependence: Economic Policy in the Atlantic Community" (1968) argued that the Atlantic alliance which was the pivotal, radial organization for checking the Soviet threat, would not be a solid, well-knitted one unless until the economic policies of the member states were better co-ordinated. By bringing the concept of interdependence, he emphasized the necessity of making members of western alliance not only dependent on each other over security related issues but also in the matters of economics which would further strengthen the alliance system.

Here, one can immediately sense the parallel between Cooper's argument with the earlier Deutsch's transactional approach to integration. What Cooper has done, it seems, just to replace Deutsch's terminology of 'amalgamated security community' with the new catechism 'interdependence'; however it did not open up any new theoretical avenues in the field of International Relations. That is why, Susan Strange laments, "it [i.e. International Political Economy] is narrowly constructed as a branch, almost, of foreign policy studies - but foreign economic policy as distinct from defense policy or bilateral or multilateral alliance building".[44] But contrary to Cooperian orientation towards International Political Economy, some scholars developed the concept of interdependence from mere precautionary policy proposal to picture the prevailing condition of 1970s international system.

Theory of Interdependence and European Integration

Robert Keohane and Joseph Nye of Harvard school, in their book published in 1971 "Transnational Relations and World Politics" opened up a new theoretical space for International Relations. They have transformed the Cooperian conception of interdependence from mere a policy proposal to an idea of 'complex interdependence'[45] for the first time to explain the current international scenario. "Interdependence in world politics", for them, "refers to situation characterized by reciprocal effects among countries or among actors in different counties".[46] Having thus understood interdependence, they further structured their argument on the Raymond Vernon's concept of erosion of sovereignty and brimming of multinational enterprises. The crux of their argument runs like this: "To understand international order in the 1970s was to understand a more complex matrix of power relations not reducible to the crude power machinations of sovereign states but influenced also by the activities of other [i.e. multinational and transnational] non-state actors and the politico- economic connections between them, at both micro and macro levels".[47] For Keohane and Nye, the international condition of 1970s was not 'anarchical situation' as argued by the Waltzian neo-realists at that time. Rather all states and their societies were drawn into the cobweb of interdependence - in trade, communication and other economic activities. In this condition, the nation-state cannot command the entire attention of International Relations. Instead as Puchala and Fagan suggested, "it is now clear that the international system is actually organized on at least four levels: subnational, national, transnational and supranational".[48]

Keohane and Nye took their argument further and suggested that integration was a defensive method available in the condition of interdependence. Interdependence, according to them, would always helpful to the powerful nations whereas it made weaker states vulnerable to the stronger. Thus the cost of interdependence to a weaker state could be theoretically reduced by the formalization of rules of interdependence, of which the best example they say, could be the process of European integration.[49] By saying that, the states are pursuing integration with the objective of regulating and even limiting the consequences of interdependence, both Keohane and Nye seemed to propose a theory of integration which is explicitly a policy choice designed to limit the cost of interdependence.

On somewhat improvising Keohane and Nye's argument, Puchala and Fagan duo differentiate integration from integrative process. According to them, there is a qualitative difference in

International Relations of 1970s, where integration means "*peaceful transnational problem solving*"; whereas integrative process means "*the fashioning and use of instruments for such transnational problem solving*".[50] As far as they are concerned, the supranational integration is one among the different instruments of the integrative process. Hence, for them,

> Regional integration economic, political, or more narrowly functional, circa 1970 is not simply a return or revised version of more familiar traditional phenomena such as federalism or nation building. Nor is it imperialism.... Regionalism today is rather a collection of procedures and techniques, set in particular attitudinal environments, by which governments and peoples maximize mutual positive payoffs by exploiting their interdependence.[51]

Thus, the theorists of interdependence have transformed the integration debate from the federalist and functionalist approach to procedural techniques of overcoming the specific condition, which they identified as complex interdependence. However, in due years the interdependence had become a debatable one and brought issues of hegemony and its relation to interdependence and integration.

Hegemony, Regimes and European Integration

On a sequel to the debate on 'interdependence', new terms have found place in International Relations discipline: hegemony and regime. Robert Gilpin developed the concept of hegemony in International Relations by criticizing the interdependence theory on two points: he accuses it of subordinating politics to economics. Instead, he argues "Politics determines the framework of economic activity and channels it in directions, which tend to serve the political objectives of dominant political groups and organizations".[52] He identifies such a dominating political frame work as hegemony, which actually determined all the economic activities, not only the present historical juncture as interdependence theorists argued, but even in the past histories. So, for him, interdependence is not a new phenomenon happened to arise in 1970s but much older one. Also he sees a link between hegemony and interdependence where the hegemony has created the condition of interdependence. Secondly, he turns his ire towards the argument of multinational corporations replacing the states in International Relations. He refutes this argument by showing that actually the MNCs are the instruments of a hegemonic power to spread its tentacle world over.

Once he laid the foundation for the theory of hegemony in International Relations, he visualizes a short of history of International relations: with the beginning of *Pax-Britanica*, that is the first hegemon, the world interdependence had actually begun. But the British hegemonic power started eroding in the last decades of 19th century and was replaced by United States after the First World War. His history runs like this:

> That the pattern of international economic relations is dependent upon the structure of the international political system is to review the origins of the Pax-Britanica, its demise in the First World War and the eventual rise of Pax-Americana after the Second World War. What this history clearly reveals is that transnational economic processes are not unique to our own age and that the pattern of international economic activity refers to global balance of economic and military power.[53]

Where is to one place the relatively recent regional integration within the Gilpin's history of International Relations? Though his idea about the European integration is not clear and focused, his writings indicate two directions of understanding: one which revolves around the concept of the decline of the US hegemony which would have helped create multipolar world of which the European integration is a symptom; second, which is the most visible part of his argument emphasizes that the European integration is itself the handy work of the US to strengthen its position in cold war situation.

However, his first line of argument becomes the predominating source of explanation to the European integration. Based on Gilpin's theory of hegemonic stability and the cyclical raise and fall of hegemony, both Payne and Gamble[54] proceed to explain the emergence of regionalism in international field. Their narrative of world history put regionalism after the two successive hegemonical systems, which they identify like

Gilpin as *Pax-Britanica* and *Pax-Americana.* From the late 18th century to 1870, the world system was like Pax-Britanica, where Britain reigned supreme and set the terms and regulations for international relations. But the raise of Germany and the two successive destructive world wars finally brought down the British hegemony by around 1920s. After that the world witnessed the emergence of the US hegemony – *Pax-Americana.* When compared to the British, it was a short period and had collapsed in mid 1970s. From now onwards the world has not come under the spell of any single hegemony. Instead the world has proceeded towards a multipolar system with different centers of activity - including Japan and Western European countries. In the absence of any overarching hegemon, they argue, the regional actors may emerge and play a crucial role in international arena. What is interesting in their argument is that the successful linking of the 'decline of hegemony' with the 'emergence of regionalism'.

However, critics point out the excessive US centric worldview and relating each and every thing with the USA. Their criticism had been substantiated by the mind-boggling controversy of whether actually the USA's hegemonic power has declined in the post-Vietnam period or not. To come out of this controversy, one stream of scholars known as 'Grotians' sought to replace the concept 'hegemony' with another one 'regime'. The regime theorists questioned the earlier hegemonic theory's assumption that the hegemony is a necessary condition for any mode of interdependence and co-operation in world politics. As Keohane polemicized "there is little reason to believe that hegemony is either a necessary or a sufficient condition for the emergence of co-operative relationships".[55] On the contrary, he stressed "post-hegemonic co-operation is also possible".[56]

If then, how could co-operation be achieved without any hegemony? Here comes the question about regimes. Krasner defined the term regime as ' principles, norms, rules and decision making procedures around which actor expectations converge in a given area of international relations'.[57] Based on this concept, Krasner explains integration as a 'bundle of regimes', purportedly aimed to reach certain goals, say peace, economic growth and development. The popularity of this regime theory could be gauged from the fact that even the guru of neo-functionalism, Ernest Hass proclaimed in 1975 the obsolescence of regional integration theory and turned his attention to this new theory.

This regime theory is almost the offshoot of the earlier interdependence theory but replaced its stress on integration to co-operation. The co-operation is an outcome of the regime arrangement, a set of creation of common rules and regulations constraining all the states in pursuing their interests. The regime has thus made world politics "neither hierarchy nor anarchy... [where] states rarely practice self-help".[58] In this sense, the European integration process was understood as regime production and the various institutions of the European Union as protectors or guardians of these regime arrangements.

World-System Analysis and European Integration

The interdependence phase of International Relations theory though helped regional integration come out of the federal idealist dream and the crude realist power tactics, it finally led it to the point very close to the realist paradigm against which it started its criticism. One can see this shift in the works of Robert Keohane. In 1971 along with Joseph Nye, he stressed the importance of concentrating on the non-state actors and non-political aspects of international system. But in 1982, he reached the point of bringing again the state into International Relations theory. Now for him, "*intergovernmental co-operation takes place when the policies actually followed by one government are regarded by its partners as facilitating realization of their own objectives, as the result of a process of policy coordination*".[59] Thus, for once an outright critic of realist orthodoxy, he has now reduced the regional cooperation as a policy choice of the governments to achieve their desired goals. The reduction of everything in international system to politics and giving primacy to state provoked Susan Strange — the first theorist of the kind who argued for an interdisciplinary approach to international economic relations, to accuse the interdependence school as: 'economic processes are conceived as taking place within the political structure. It does not admit of the reverse process - of political process taking place within the existing economic structure".[60]

But the reverse process was not completely neglected. Indeed, for many years, even before the emergence of interdependence concept, the Marxist scholars through their base and superstructure argument stressed the economic determination of politics. This reverse process had been brought into international relations by Lenin in his trend-setting book "Imperialism, the Highest Stage of Capitalism" and given economic explanation to international politics. He saw the anarchical condition of international politics and the frequent wars among the leading European states as the contenders over the imperial monopoly. That is why, he underlined the need for socialist revolution not only to create internal transformation within a single country but also to bring world peace. He even believed that the internal contradiction and the war among the imperial powers would finally lead to crumbling of the capitalist system which would in turn pave the pay for perpetual peace.

But his fellow comrade Kautsky differed from Lenin over the issue of contradiction among the capitalist powers. Kautsky envisioned that instead of contradiction there was a concerted effort for cooperation among the imperial powers to collectively exploit the world resources. However, the Leninist line of thinking got legitimized when the capitalist states waged a bitter war among themselves in 1939-45. But after the Second World War there was not only no war among the capitalist states but there was a move on the part of them to establish some sort of cooperation among them. The best example was the European integration. This has vindicated Kautsky's 'ultra imperialism' of collective exploitation of world by all the capitalist states. But Lenin was not insensitive to the rhetoric of European unity. Even in 1915 when the discourse on European integration was at its rudimentary stage, he caught the issue and analyzed its historical necessity. In his article "On the Slogan for a United States of Europe", brought the issue to the fore and explained it as,

Of course, temporary agreements are possible between capitalists

> and between states. In this sense a United States of Europe is possible as an agreement between the European capitalists.. but to what end? Only for the purpose of jointly suppressing socialism in Europe, of jointly protecting colonial booty against Japan and America.[61]

Thus Lenin saw two pronged strategy of the creation of European federation: on the one hand, the bourgeois strategy to quell the burgeoning voice of socialism that had been raising in Europe; on the other hand to pool their energies collectively to enhance the unimpeded colonial exploitation in Africa and Asia and to outpour the American and Japanese challenge in this exploitation.

Hence, what was assumed as a cooperation among the imperial powers by Kautsky, seemed to be a strategic maneuver on the part of the European powers to outwit their American and Japanese rivals, for Lenin. This Leninist understanding of European integration process is still the domineering theoretical foundation of most of the recent works.[62] What is interesting more is that whether Marxist - Leninist approach, which gives primacy to economics over politics, or the neo-realist of Gilpin variety, which gives importance to politics over economics, both have understood European integration as a deliberate move on the part of the European states to strengthen their position vis-à-vis the American hegemony and the impounding Japanese threat. Whatever may be the differences in theoretical and methodological outlooks, both these approaches arrived to the same conclusion about the European integration process.

Apart from these two approaches, in 1960s there was another one, which was called as theory of modernization. Though it has not helped directly evolving any understanding of regional integration, in a subtle and indirect manner developed an understanding. Reposing their faith in 'progress', the theorists of modernization emphasized the stages of development. Based on this, the western countries were presumed as reaching the highest stage of development whereas the Asian, African and Latin American countries were at the lowest stage. To contrast these two groups, they have showed the transnational cooperation of the western countries as a result of their highest stage of development, while the third world countries' underdevelopment symbolized in their failure to even construct a coherent, solid nation-state without any primordial divisions. Oran Young expressed this sentiment as "in the contemporary system, the level of interdependence among the industrialized states of North Atlantic area is considerably higher than that among the states of third world".[63] In a sense, the regional cooperation was assumed as an indicator of the developmental stage and maturity of political culture.

In opposition to the modernization theory, a group of Latin American economists associated with United Nations Commission for Latin America (ECLA) under the aegis of Paul Prebisch developed the theory of dependency. They had challenged the modernization theorists' arrogance in linking the underdevelopment of the third world countries to their primordial and feudal political and economic conditions. Instead, the theorists of dependency school blamed the division of world into core and periphery for their countries' underdevelopment. The core industrialized countries, they argued, acquired wealth and prosperity only through their unequal exchange with the peripheral countries. The price of manufactured goods exported by the core increased more rapidly than the raw materials they imported from the periphery. This 'declining terms of trade', to put it in Paul Probisch's words, has made the periphery always dependent upon the core countries. Thus, the international economic relation is not interdependence as the western scholars expounded; rather a one way dependence of periphery on the core. Here, one should note that though the theorists of dependency were successful in introducing a radical shift in the theoretical perspective of international economic relations, their theory has failed to comprehend the political aspect of the international system. It is well exposed in the case of their discrete silence over the question of European integration despite its visible presence in the international arena at that time.

This lop-sidedness has been rectified by Immanual Wallerstein. He introduced the concept of world-system as a unit of analysis. Before him, all the attempted theories have brought forth the economic issues within the framework of politics, or more correctly within the state boundary. Even the Marxist-Leninist who insisted capitalism as an autonomous world phenomenon, had to accept the state as a unit of analysis when came to study the internal contradictions of imperialism. On the other hand for Wallerstein "world-system is an economic but not a political entity... It is a world-system, not because it encompasses the whole world, but because it is larger than any juridically defined political units".[64] The setting up of this world-system, as far as Wallerstein is concerned, was made possible by two historical phenomena happened at the late 15th century Europe: One, Europe's transition from feudalism to capitalism; the other one, Europe's expansion into other continents.

However, with the arrival of world-system, the international relations was structured in two but contradictory modes of organization: On the one hand, the capitalist world economy with its planetary reach produced world as a single discernible unit. On the other hand, by organizing on the principle of nation-state, the world was divided into numerous political units. Thus, according to Wallerstein, the world-system was structured by two contrary forces: universal, internationalist outlook of economics and the particularistic, nationalist sentiment of politics. However, he does not see any contradiction in the world-system in the form of nationalism versus internationalism. Rather, he understands this as fragmentary tendencies:

> At some point in time the major economic and political institutions are geared to operating in the international arena and felt that local interests are tied in some immediate way to developments elsewhere in the world. At other point of time, the social actors tend to engage their efforts locally, tend to see the reinforcement of state boundaries as primary, and move towards a relative indifference about events beyond them.[65]

The political organization of the modern world-system is not a fixed and bounded one. According to Wallerstein, it is bound to change and acquire any of the political forms such as empire, city-state, nation-sate or confederal one. One can choose from the political choice of any of these organizational options, which suits and supports his interest.

If so, then immediately a question would arise: why this flexibility and fluidity in the political organization of the world-system? To explain this, Wallerstein introduces two more categories of explanation along with the earlier core and periphery division: cyclical phases of world-system and hegemony- rivalry. Gunther Franck and Gills call these three categories of Wallerstein as his 'descriptive trinity".[66] For Wallerstein, the world economy is not a stable one; instead it has to have a long or short economic cycle of alternating ascending and descending phases. This cyclical fluidity in world economy must have influenced indirectly the formation of the political organization of that period. He further explains that each ascending cycle of world economy will witness the corresponding rise of a hegemon who will control competitiveness in other core markets, subsequent commercial competitiveness and financial competitiveness. When a power attains all of these three competitiveness, it will automatically become a hegemon. But the descending phase of the economy would threaten the hegemonic position of a power by eroding its competitive edge over the other core countries.

This decline of the hegemonic power in turn gives way to a situation where other core countries would challenge the hegemon by staking claim in economic, political and military superiority. Thus Wallerstein visualized a sequential model of hegemonic political organization in tune with the cyclical rhythm of world economic phases. With this theoretical foundation, Wallerstein proceeds to explain the recent phenomenon of the European integration process. He understands it as a consequence of three structural chances happened at the world-systemic level at the end of 1960s. First, the last decade of 1960s witnessed the shift of world economy from the ascending phase to descending one; the unprecedented economic boom of the period 1945-67 in the West reached its limit and began to trickle down. Second, the American hegemony in world-system started decreasing correspondingly. "With the ending of the expansionary phase and the frittering of the US monopolistic advantages",[67] Wallerstein argues that the American hegemony was ceased to be true eventhough it has not been replaced by any other contending power visibly or decisively.

Along with these two factors of structural change, he emphasizes a third one: the chance in the ideological structure. Here, he introduces a fourth category of explanation in addition to his descriptive trinity. In the 19th century the modern world-system had undergone an ideological rivalry in the line of 'Liberalism versus Marxism' and the rivalry reached its culmination in the post 1945 cold war condition. But the 1968 revolution delegitimaized both these ideological premises. The loosening of these ideological grip as well as the descending phase of world economy and the decline of the US hegemony all encompass the background for Wallerstein's explanation of the European integration process. It is in this context, he argues "Europe will take significant initiatives in the process of economic, political and ideological reorganization"[68] in the form of moving towards the direction of European unity.

Despite his grand effort in formulating a theoretical base and explaining European integration in tandem with it, there remains a nebulous area in his argument: whether he visualizes the move towards European unity as a symptom of a total change or break with the world-system (since Europe constructed the existing world-system, any systemic change in Europe would invariably create a change in world-system) or mere a structural change within the world-system. Some of his writings may indicate his inclination towards the second line of thought. That is why, he gives much importance to the question of the decline of the US hegemony and its accompanying effect upon international system.

This point of approach, however, is not unknown to International Relations scholarship. Robert Gilpin's works have already created such an outlook in International Relations years before. So, irrespective of the grandeur and nitty-gritty of his theoretical construction, Wallerstein fails to shed any new light on the understanding of the European integration process.

III
SOCIOLOGY OF EUROPEAN INTEGRATION

From 1945 onwards, each decade witnessed the development of distinct theories regarding regional integration. The reason cited for this trend was the deterministic conditions of those individual periods over the act of theorizing. In 1950s, the immediate post-war period, the most pressing problem was to have a peaceful and warless world. The federalists and functionalists through their respective theories of integration outlined each specific way of attaining such a peaceful world. The 1960s, a decade of unprecedented economic boom and decolonization, created an ambience that drove scholars to find out a true scientific law of integration that could be employed to avert any conflictual situations. Both Hass and Deutsch claimed to have deciphered such a scientific law of integration through their empirical case studies. But history did not freeze itself there. The 1970s witnessed the decline of the supremacy and legitimacy of both the superpowers and the raise of Japan and Germany in international arena warranted a fresh theorizing about regional integration. The scholars in turn responded with theories of interdependence and decline of hegemonic stability and the subsequent emergence of multipolarity.

The 1990s witnessed a mushrooming of theories in International Relations, which has provoked one scholar to admonish it as a divided discipline. The so called 'Third Debate' or the interparadigm debate that is currently going on in International Relations gives an opportunity to problematize the positivistic epistemology of realism, which has so far successfully compartmentalized International Relations and prevent it having any sorts of interaction and interchange with the other disciplines of the social science. The emerging Critical International Relations theory of various kinds – neo-Kantian[69], neo-Gramscian[70], post-structuralist[71] and feminist[72] have questioned the realist foundation and widened the scope of debate in International Relations. What Krippendorff years before longed,

> I found it important…to go beyond the boundaries of my own discipline, to dig deeper, to ask questions and to look for answers in other disciplines if this proved necessary. I think, we ignore such territorial boundaries of specialization (or intrude into other scholars' territory), the better it is both for our at this point rather overly scientific discipline as well as for its results,[73]

has come true and transgressing one's own boundary and prodding into other's territory is an established practice in recent times. Nowadays International Relations is borrowing not only terminologies but also the theories propounded in other fields. In turn, other social science disciplines started showing interest on the issues so far relegated exclusively to International Relations.

For example, on a stark contrast to their earlier position where they have taken for granted the nation-state as a unit of analysis, the theorists of International Relations are now in a mood of bringing the historical contexts of the emergence of nation-state into their boundaries. In this sense, Fred Halliday announced in a rather compulsive tone "it is time for (*Sic*) to engage in greater dialogue with sociology".[74] Similarly, sociologists have now turned to international relations and started considering the anarchical and conflictual situation among states as a category of explanation in the development and change in the evolution of state. Theda Skocpol, the historical sociologist has brought the external relations of state in explaining the social revolution within the state. So far, sociologists concentrated only on the internal conditions of a state in order to explain the sudden eruption of the revolution. But, Skocpol was the first to link international relations and sociological phenomena.[75] In the same vein, Anthony Giddens, the sociologist of structuration, brings war and its impact (which has been so far the domain of International Relations) on society into the perimeter of sociology. "My main point", he proclaimed, "is to emphasize that the impact of war in the twentieth century upon generalized patterns of change has been so profound that it is little short of absurd to interpret such patterns without systematic reference to it".[76]

The traffic between International Relations and Sociology

has thus been carried forward around the issue of historical emergence of the nation-states system. However, in recent times there is a yet another commonality evolved between them: the question about the crisis of nation state. The emerging condition of globalization is presumed as creating a situation where the nation-state could have only limited value and utility. This has compelled both International Relations and Sociology to wind off their old theories based on the nation-state. That is why Martin Shaw argued "the future of world politics depends a great deal, however, on the growth of global civil society, and this must be starting point for a new politics of the international".[77] Thus the study of globalization has brought these two subject fields into the same conceptual terrain. In this era of confluence of disciplinary outlook, the theoretical understanding of regional integration gets changed and opens up hitherto uncharted space. In this section, the study would thematically classify these new trends in understanding the European integration.

Globalization and New Regionalism: Issues of World Order

The 1990s brought with it the concept of 'globalization'[78] into the realm of regional integration theory. There are two opposing schools of thought over the issue of globalization in International Relations. One stream argued that it was not new to the subject field since it had been already discussed and theorized in the early 1970s under the concept of interdependence. Both Keohane and Nye expressed this sentiment as, "Globalization emerged as a buzzword in the 1990s, just as 'interdependence' did in the 1970s, but the phenomena it refers to are not entirely new. Our characterization of interdependence more than twenty years ago now applies to globalization at the turn of the millennium".[79] The other stream stresses that globalization is a much broader concept, which cannot be reduced to the terminology of interdependence alone. In addition they have pointed out that the interdependence school excessively focused on the economic side of the issue and neglected totally the political and cultural aspects. Then what actually do they mean by globalization? They would reply:

"By globalization we simply mean the process of increasing interconnectedness between societies such that events in one part of the world more and more have effects on peoples and societies".[80] It is the focus on the societies, not on states as the previous interdependence school did, differentiate the new globalist school from the others.

How then this globalist school of 1990s understands and interprets the issue of regional integration? First, they want to differentiate the regionalism of 1990s from the regionalism of the previous decades. Then the question would arise: what this *new regionalism*[81] is about? The 'new' in the regionalism of 1990s is that it has emerged after the collapse of East-West division based on socialist and capitalist worldview. The another distinction that has been highlighted is that the regionalism of old variety was actually a state project where as the new one is not state led project. Rather it is seen as a "combination of historical emergent structures - a complex articulation of established institutions and rules and distinctive *new patterns of social interactions between non-state actors*".[82]

Bringing the globalization concept into the study of regional integration, however, has not produced any consensual point of view in International Relations. On the contrary, there emerged a set of approaches diametrically opposing each other: on the one side, regionalism is considered as a part of globalization where boundaries and frontiers would disappear under a cosmopolitan worldview. This new regionalism is being contrasted with the age old, fragmentary ethnic and religious worldview. In this 'globalization Vs fragmentation' paradigm, some scholars placed regionalism comfortably at the side of globalism. In fact they consider regional integration as a first and initial stage in the direction of globalization. To substantiate this point, particularly in Western European context, one scholar tried to prove through his empirical data analysis, how the European community and the building of Common Market actually helped downsize and overcome the sedimented sentiments of nationalism in that part.[83]

Contrary to this, some others place regionalism in opposition to globalization. They set to see regionalism as a face saving 'fortress' construction in the period of reckless globalization drive. For them, regionalism like nationalism is a boundary creating effort and not an opposition to nationalism as some think to be. This understanding has encouraged viewing regional organizations as in opposition to the principles of globalization: "globalization can be contrasted with localization, nationalization or regionalization".[84] The point has well made in the economic sphere. Albert has argued that the globalism stands for free trade while regionalism means strategic trade. Since both of them are part and parcel of capitalism, he dramatizes the situation in a catchy word: 'Capitalism against Capitalism'.[85] Nevertheless in contrast to Albert, one economic historian compared regionalism with the medieval mercantilist practices. He drew parallels between the 'new regionalism' and 'old mercantilism' of Europe and came to a conclusion that the European Community is nothing but an aggressive mercantilist strategy towards market aggrandizement. The fortress creating aggressive aspect of regionalism has provoked one scholar to predict " the emergence of competing regional blocs could lead to increase global conflict.... Paradoxically globalization engenders the regionalization of conflict".[86]

Recently Richard Falk[87] has attempted to reconcile the two opposing discourses on regionalism and globalism. For him, globalism has two faces: a negative globalism associated with the adverse impact of global market forces; the other, a positive phase of globalism associated with the capacity to achieve desirable world order goals. Then he set to explain how regionalism would favor the growth of positive globalism while at the same time to check the adverse effects of negative globalism. The role of regionalism, he exhorts, "is to help create a new equilibrium in politics that balances the protection of the vulnerable and the interests of humanity as a whole against the integrative, technological dynamic associated with globalism".[88] Despite his intellectual compromise of these concepts - regionalism and globalism, still in International Relations they have been employed in opposing way to explain the European integration process.

European Union: A Post-modern Political Space?

Like the term globalization, 'post-modernism' is a new entrant into the vocabulary of International Relations. Indeed, the idea of post-modernism is emerged as a result of a distinct philosophical tradition that had emerged in the early years of the 20th century. It is a philosophy of negation - a negation of the fundamental principles of the Enlightenment project, erected in the 17th century Europe. Since writing the of history of post-modernism[89] is beyond the scope of this chapter, I would content to focus on two schools of thought: one school of scholars consider post-modernism as a distinct way of 'theorizing'; an agenda of 'reflecting' on the ossified terrain of previous theories. To say it in a post-modern jargon it is to 'reject the hitherto promulgated meta-narratives' of all sorts. On the other hand some scholars relate post-modernism with a specific kind of 'existing conditions'. For them, the arrival of post-modernism represents a historical disjuncture where a profound shifts and transformations happened in the fields of economics, political, social as well as cultural. This school of scholars may have some resemblance and resonance with the globalization theorists, since both these two streams concentrate and theorize the 'involution' of the present time.

Both these connotations, post-modernism as a reflective theory and as well as a peculiar historical condition found their place in International Relations scholarship.[90] Richard Ashley, Shapiro, Der Derian and David Campbell et.al, through their relentless crusade against the neo-realist and neo-liberal orthodoxy in International Relations, eventually have opened up some space for post-modern theorizing. Similarly, scholars like John Ruggie brought the 'post-modern condition' problematic into International Relations. As far as regional integration is concerned, the latter school is active and visible, but as far as the first school is concerned still there is a conspicuous silence over the post-modern theorizing of regional integration.

What are the post-modern conditions that have been identified by the second school in International Relations? Norgaard[91] answers that 'the state system and global capitalism are the two dominant institutional pillars of modernity in the international realm' and since both of them have reached an end, 'different organizational principles could evolve in response to the relative decline of states and global capitalism'. If it is true, then the next question would arise: what are those emerging new political and economic configurations? Ruggie when acknowledging the break with the modernity, nonetheless laments

> We are not very good as a discipline at studying the possibility of fundamental discontinuity in the international system; that is, at addressing the question of whether the modern system of states may be yielding in some instances to post-modern forms of configuring political space.[92]

Yet, recently there is an attempt to draw the European Union as one such post-modern political space. Nogaard argues that "Westphalia has become obsolete as *the state will cease to be sovereign*". [93] In place of the sovereign state, he would say with confidence new institutions would be invented and let coexist with the states. He identifies the European Union as one such an institution in a post-modern global landscape. This has been repeated and re-emphasized by the current sociological understanding of the European integration as we witnessed in the writings of Featherstone:

> Post-modernism ...(Sic) is undermining the cultural integration project of the nation-state. At the same time, and an important part of this process, we have both the '*incorporation of states into larger units*' and the transformative effects of global economic and cultural flows. Both point to larger and necessarily more abstract units: the unity within which diversity can take place. *An example of the former is the current efforts to create a European identity sponsored by the European Community.*[94]

Therefore, for Featherstone, the European integration is meant for an attempt to create 'a larger unit of states' necessitated by the global post-modern conditions. In this sense, it is a decisive move towards a supranational political set up. Still there is a difference cropped up within the post-modern approach over this point. Some understand the integration process as a defensive mechanism of the nation-state to keep intact some of its powers in the post-sovereign global interdependence. One author expresses this point as "the EU is an organization not for pursuing a European interest, but for pursuing national interests more effectively, in post-modern sense, without being obliged to resort to military means".[95] Whatever may be the dissenting voice, the European Union is increasingly being perceived as an institution meant for the emerging post-modern political space.

European Union as a Civilizational Zone

The debate on globalization has brought yet another new concept, this time civilization, into International Relations thinking. However, as happened with the concept of globalization, the term civilization created different opinions and divided perceptions among International Relations scholarship. For convenience's sake, I have grouped them over the issue of whether the world has one civilization or many civilizations.

The scholars of single, universal civilizational approach have argued that the world is moving progressively towards a higher civilizational stage. The supposedly this long process did indeed start actually before five centuries with the expedition and expansion of Europe into the other continents. "For five hundred years that followed", Modelski proclaimed "it was they [i.e. the Europeans] who determined the speed and the character of globalization; they also thereby shaped the structure of world politics".[96] In this sense, it is said that Europe made all continents known to each other by integrating them through the web of capitalism and nation-state system. At the same time it has consistently been highlighted that both the capitalism and nation-state were the creation of the European civilization. By the sheer burden of its civilizing mission, Europe has finally implanted the fruits of civilization into the other dark continents. In this sense, European civilization is *the* civilization *par excellence* and deserves to be hailed as the civilization of the world.

However, the progressive march of European civilization

as a universal one had been challenged by the emergence and spread of Communism in the early years of the twentieth century. Even then Communism was identified as a by-product of European history, there was a keen tussle going on between the capitalist, free market, liberal democracy and the socialist, authoritarian form of government. With the final collapse of the Soviet Union, the serious contender to the universal position has finally disappeared. From now onwards, it is said that, the liberal European civilization is the sole universal civilization. This has been interpreted as "end of history" by Fukuyama.[97] Within this theoretical understanding, the European integration is being visualized as the one more forward movement of Europe towards its five-century-old agenda of integrating the world as a single unit.

Contrary to this universalistic posture, there are some scholars who in a mood of generosity accepted that there are other civilizations in the world along with the European one. The best example of this line of thinking is Arnold Toynbee. He has identified and classified some twenty-seven civilizations that the world witnessed past and present. However, his notion of civilization was not a rigid, static and compartmentalized one. Rather he envisioned a state of fluidity and a lot of give and take among the civilizations, both ideas and materials. As a scholar associated with the Royal Institute of International Affairs, one of the first major institutions of the kind to study international relations in Britain, Toynbee had given a new outlook to the study of international relations as inter-civilizational relations.[98] But his idea was successfully marginalized in the realist-dominated discipline of International Relations.

Nevertheless, in the post-cold war context, Toynbee's idea of discrete civilizations has been employed in International Relations albeit for different purpose. Samuel Huntington, like Toynbee, has pictured out the current world as a composition of nine different civilizational zones. For him, "Civilizations are the biggest 'we' within which we feel at home as distinguished from all other 'thems' out there".[99] He thus has replaced the nation-state with civilizational zone as a unit of analysis in

International Relations. At the same stretch, he visualized a change in the nature of international relations. From then onwards, he says, "in the post-cold war world the most important distinctions among peoples are not ideological, political or economics. They are cultural".[100] What Huntington means by culture here is the commonality of perception and worldview shared by the people of a particular civilizational zone despite of having some internal differentiation. Though he not listed any such essential common cultural features or traits of a civilization, overtly he has given much stress upon the category of religion. His idea of civilization is thus in actuality geographically bounded religious zone. Once classified the world according to geo-religious category, Huntington proceeds to propose a theory, which is based on two principles. As a first principle, he put forward a thesis whereby it has been emphasized that within a civilizational zone people are moving beyond their respective national boundaries and aligning themselves along the civilizational line. Next, as a second principle, he expects that international relations in the post-cold war era has become a site of renewed conflict among the different civilizational zones. International relations, from here onwards he declared, is a 'Clash of Civilizations' where

> Culture and cultural identities, which at the broadest level are civilizational identities, are shaping patterns of cohesion, disintegration, and conflict in the post-cold war world. The inter play of power and culture will decisively mold patterns of alliance and antagonism among states in the coming years.[101]

Having thus sorted out the course of international relations in the coming years, Huntington, in his later part of the book, emphasized the need for a political action designed to defend his own Western Civilization from the expected assault from the other civilizations. Here comes the importance and new meaning to the European integration process. Scholars, who out and right reject Huntington's theory of clash of civilizations are at the same time seem to have adopted his thesis of replacing nation-state with civilizational zone as an unit of explanation in International Relations. The European integration has given empirical support to such a move. Any way, after Huntington's theory, the European integration has acquired a new but controversial meaning, color and content.

European Union and Policy Studies: Issues on Citizenship, Identity and Race Relations

The European integration does not evince interest either in sociology or in anthropology just because of its empirical validity in the theoretical debate about the concept of globalization or of nation-state. Apart from these two broader theoretical interests in recent years, the European Union has installed a sense of curiosity among other social scientists on the micro level issue-based policy programs. So far, the nation-state was the sole agent of proposing, making and implementing a set of policies meant for the welfare of its people residing within its boundary. But "in the era of postmodernity, the nation-state is no longer at the center of social policy making and delivery".[102] The non-governmental and supranational organizations have started encroaching upon the terrain of policy making. This has posed a serious challenge to the classical theory of citizenship. According to this theory, citizenship was defined in terms of membership of a nation-state, which not only assure some inalienable fundamental rights but also assumes the paternalistic role in providing welfare measures to the well being of its members. With the arrival of non-state actors and supranational organizations, the blending of citizenship - nation-sate - welfare policy measures has been ripped off. In this context, it is argued that "it will be important to monitor the European Union, as a working model of a new transnational level of societal organization in modernity... in terms of new forms of transnational and societal citizenship, which came to be constructed within it".[103]

After the signing up of the Maastricht Treaty, there are quite large numbers of sociologists who have turn their attention towards European citizenship. They highlight the radical shift happened in the domain of the concept of citizenship, where the nationality and citizenship, state membership and citizenship need not be a concurrent and concordant one. This aspect has encouraged Brubacker to lay out the European Union as "a model of dual citizenship organized as concentric circles: an inner circle of citizenship, based on nationality and an outer circle of denizenship, based on residency".[104] On the other hand, Yasemin Soysal understands it as a wider "postnational model of political community, whose legal and normative base are located in the wider community, and whose actual implementation is assigned to the member states".[105]

While sociology has concentrated on issues such as citizenship and postnational form of political community, its sister subject field anthropology has until unto some recent years, did not develop any interest in the European Union affairs. As one anthropologist later lamented, "While political and economic unification in Europe have become major issues for a range of practitioners and academics, anthropologists have contributed relatively little to the analysis of these processes - either at a theoretical level, or in terms of ethnographic study".[106] But the situation gets fast changing. Once the presence of Europe felt strongly in the post-Maastricht period and the European Union's increased role in making policy proposals covering the much sensible areas such as culture, persuaded more and more anthropologists to show interest in the European Union.

Cris Shore's works represent the anthropologically enlightened approach to the European Union's institutional framework and policies. His intention in bridging anthropology and the European integration study has two fold agenda. As he himself declared in one of his articles, he is more concerned about "the extent to which the anthropological models of identity-construction inform our understanding of European integration, and whether studies of the dynamics of integration in Europe might lead us to re-think those models".[107] To carry forward this mutually influenced and informed research, he concentrates more on the cultural policy of the Union. What attracts Cris Shore toward this cultural policy is the Union's attempts to construct a cohesive European identity thereby inculcate a sense of commonality among the people of different nationality. He, thus, concentrates more on the constructive aspect of the Union's policy initiatives irrespective of his skepticism about the success of these initiatives.

On the contrary, another anthropologist, June Nash highlighted the negative side of the integration. He is highly doubtful about any positive outcome of integration in the cultural field. Focusing his research exclusively on multinational corporations, he comes to the conclusion that though they might have been successful in integrating the nation-states in politico-economic level, they have however failed so far in creating any logico-meaningful integration in cultural fields. Rather, they have played a negative role, in a sense, by helping collapse the existing cultural foundation of the nation. To put it simply, he argues that the multinational integration drive, with its political, economic integration could only be able to create a consumer community but not the culturally integrated collective community of the kind nation-state produced earlier. This has prompted Nash to say that

> The expansion of multinational corporations at the expense of existing cultural enclave destroys the regenerative base of those sectors that are caught up in the consumer economy. The kind of integration achieved at the international level by multinational corporations undermines the logico-meaningful integration in culture that provides motivation and purpose for the individual.[108]

The failure or what Nash would have preferred to say, the impossibility of the multinational corporations in producing a more inclusive and integrated community has developed a disjuncture and division between politico-economic and cultural domains.

Though there may be an increased skepticism developed over the ability and possibility of constructing a European wide community based on some shared common culture, still the European Union's cultural initiatives attract and draw fascination for many scholars. Philip Schlesinger, like Cris Shore, concentrates much on the cultural aspect of the European Union's policy and its adventure in constructing common collective identities in Europe. His area of interest revolves around the European Union's communication policy and how through media it is striving to promote and circulate such identities. As he himself proclaimed,

> I take contemporary Europe as my starting point for some reflections on the relevance of communication for analyzing the formation of a collective identity. Europe exemplified in acute form the problem of constructing a collective identity for diverse people among whom nationhood and statehood remain key principles of sociocultural and political economic cohesion.[109]

Thus the question of the European Union has invited a host of scholars from different disciplinary denominations to ground test the validity of their theoretical foundations. Or to put it in different words, the European Union becomes an empirical minefield. While these scholars by their focus on policy studies illuminated only that aspect of the question - how far the European Union has succeeded in achieving a collective identity and culture, some others started criticizing even the very intention of having such a common culture and identity.

In the era of multiculturalism and consciousness about the cultural diversities, a group of scholars have brought the European Union, more particularly its cultural liaisons under a critical dissection.[110] Their point of contest is whether the European Union promotes a multicultural environment in which different shades of identities can find their place or a more authoritarian, closed one, in which all other identities would be neglected and finally suppressed under one overarching identity, say Europe. As far as these scholars are concerned, Europe is not and cannot be a homogenous entity either in history or at present. Apart from its national and linguistic diversities, they pointed out that for over a century, Europe has been a place for other peoples of different ethnic, religious and racial backgrounds. These complexities are further complicated over the years by the increased momentum in migration experienced in recent times. In this context, any move on the part of the European Union promoting a common cultural identity for the entire Europe should invariably bring suspicion in the minds of non-white population residing in this region. In fact, in the post-Maastricht phase of European integration these non-white peoples of Europe stared asking "is it not high time then to open up the imperial façade of European culture to place it under an x-ray and ask, what here is really Europe and what is not".[111]

The raise of neo-Nazi right wing political parties in almost all of the EU member countries and even in some countries the coming into power of these political parties have helped renew xenophobic tendency and raise the frequent attack on minorities. These tendencies have vitiated a fearful atmosphere where the European Union has just helped Europe move from an ethnocentric racism to Euro-centric racism. Their fear is further aggravated by the cultural orientation of the European Union, which has given importance only to the Hellenistic- Latin-Christian aspects of Europe. What the European Union signifies for Europeans, as opening up of Europe in all frontiers would actually mean closing it of to non-Europeans. When the European Union dismantles the border control and allows its native citizens to move freely throughout the Union territory, at the same time it placed more harder and harsher restriction on the immigrants.

Thus the European Union is presumed by others as a collective mechanism of the Europeans to prevent and suppress not only the visible presence of non-Europeans but their culture also. This understanding has prompted one scholar to write: "The problem for an open Europe was 'how to close it' - against immigrants and refugees from the third world - how to erect a common policy, a common set of rules, a common administrative apparatus, informed by a 'common market racism' to keep them out".[112]

From the above survey of works, one can become aware of the fact that the sociological, anthropological and other critical engagements with the European Union have shed new light upon the question about European integration unlike the International Relations which has so far monopolized the issue. However, these critical engagements have failed to evolve a holistic, theoretical foundation of European integration. Instead, they are satisfied in studying this and that policy aspect of the Union; and their only concern about the Union is its empirical relevance to the debates going on in their respective subject fields. Although their contribution in inculcating a critical vision and polemical tone in European integration study is highly commendable, when comes to the question of evolving an alternative theory building, they are so far fragmentary and fractured. And it is this feeling that has prompted me to bring and introduce the postcolonial theoretical ventures into the field of European integration study.

IV
TOWARDS A POST-COLONIAL CRITIQUE OF EUROPEAN INTEGRATION

The International Relations as a distinct subject field was an offspring of Anglo-American tradition. The legitimacy of this tradition is so deep to the magnitude that there has been no space for theorizing international relations independent of this tradition up to this day. Groom rightly identified this trend as parochialism in International Relations.[113] However, in the same article, he singles out 'non-alignment movement' as a different and original thinking on the part of some leaders of the newly independent countries as a new venture in International Relations independent of the influence of the Anglo-American tradition.

India was the staunch supporter and promoter of non-alignment. Its first Prime Minister Jawaharlal Nehru was indeed the theoretician of the idea of the concept of non-alignment in the cold war ravaged situation. The development of International Relations in India was diametrically opposite to the Anglo-American one. When International Relations as a new subject field was developed both in USA and Britain, the main concern was about how to conduct the foreign policy of a country in order to avoid a war situation. In this sense, International Relations was primarily conceived as a *status quo* maintaining program. But in India, International Relations was perceived on different grounds: for major part of the centuries, the colonial state controlled the affairs of external relations, that too in tandem with the colonial masters in the parent country. The colonial country's priorities had actually shaped India's approach towards other counties. This mentality was amply displayed during the two world wars when without the Indian people's consent Britain dragged them into what were primarily the European wars.

The Indian national liberation movement questioned this authoritarian way of formulating and conducting the relations of external affairs. The Indian National Congress, the party that had mobilized people against the colonial rule took initiatives in external affairs after the First World War. It gave prim importance to the other similarly colonized countries. It was the consequence of the realization of the fact that unless until the resurgence of national movement in the entire Asian and African countries, the fight against the imperial powers would be futile and fruitless. On this basis, they visualized the Asian solidarity. This solidarity against the imperial powers was the bedrock of the Indian leaders' perspective of the International Relations.[114]

This understanding had structured India's external relations even after the independence. Nehru, years before independence declared: "A free India would inevitably play a growing part in international affairs, and that part is likely to be on the side of world peace and against imperialism and its offshoot".[115] The non-alignment was thus a continuation of anti-colonial struggle in the cold war crippled condition of world politics. The spirit of Bandug conference had created a space for the newly independent countries and their problems in world politics. For over two decades the non-alignment was the theoretical premise of India's external affairs. Its main concerns were to preserve the national sovereignty and promoting solidarity among the third world countries. But the Indo-China war in 1962 shattered the dream of having achieved the Asian solidarity. The humiliating defeat in the hands of Chinese collapsed the consensus secured around the concept of non-alignment in India.

The post-1962 period had witnessed the emergence of realist criticism of non-alignment. The Indian realists attacked it as too idealist and insensitive to the power and strategic aspect of International Relations. Thus in India, the so-called idealist and realist debate was structured around the desirability and possibility of professing the concept of non-alignment. Gradually, the overarching idea of non-alignment was disappeared from the theoretical premise of India's international relations. Instead, realism occupied its place. This has been well demonstrated from the fact that from 1970s onward the conduct of external affairs of the Indian state revolved around the axis of realist paradigm. The explosion of atomic bomb and the concentration on military might exposed the presumed shift in the Indian perspective of international relations. In this circumstance, the non-alignment was given realist cloak. Theorists like A.R. Rana even gave realist color to non-alignment: "as a subtle instance in a essentially balance of power politics, one particularly suited to the needs of a weak state navigating a rough waters of a polarizing world".[116]

In this context, the issue of regional integration hardly drew any attention of International Relations theorists in India. They saw the integration theories especially of Hass and his neo-functionalist school, as a direct opposition to the principles of non-alignment. The most important principles of non-alignment were to preserve the national sovereignty and avoid getting into the cold war condition. On both these points, they envisaged that the neo-functional integration theory professed and promoted the squarely opposite tendencies. This has been well reflected by one Indian scholar as

> India had just become independent and sovereign, and, to the extent that integration connoted an abridgement of independence and sovereignty, Indians were suspicious. It did not help that integration, especially regional integration, seemed to be sponsored by the west in the service of cold war goals.[117]

That is why, South Asia was the only region which did not create any sort of regional co-operation until 1980s despite the fact that in all the regions of the world, there were regional co-operation of the kind ASEAN and OAU formed well before in the late 1960s. But only in 1985, the SAARC was formed. Even then in its charter, it was clearly stated that it would be content with an association of sovereign states and respect the mutual independence of its member states.

However, the 1990s witnessed a sharp shift in the Indian approach towards the regional co-operation. It may be influenced from the dramatic changes happened at the beginning of the last decade of the twentieth century. With the evaporation of the cold war condition, India's suspicion about regional organization as an instrument of cold war machination did also disappear. Instead, there is a perceptible change in their outlook: "The spirit of SAARC needs to be sustained by a vibrant civil society throughout South Asia, which is actively engaged in forging link across national boundaries".[118] Thus from the notion of mere "a vital instrument of co-operation to establish the positive sum gains",[119] the Indian scholars begin to acknowledge the regional organizations as an inevitable mechanism of moving towards some kind of integration cutting across national boundaries. This shift in the perspective has created a new interest in the European integration process. Indian scholars have now started treating the European Union as a successful model to be emulated in the South Asian region too. This modular approach to the European Union is dominating the Indian academics currently.

The thematical fountainhead of this approach is to understand regional organizations as a historical necessity, not as a strategic maneuver of cold war politics. This sentiment has been clearly expressed by one Indian scholar as

> The emergence of constructive regional entities... is a natural development dictated by the forces of history. Regional co-operation is a demand of our times, and one that will play an increasingly important role in building a better and more secure future for mankind.[120]

Another scholar who was once India's External Affairs Minister and later ambassador to the US went one step forward and declared that

> Regional groupings are essential intermediate stage between the nation-state and the United Nations. Ultimately, global society will develop as a result of the growth of these regional organizations and unions which would then form what Tennyson once called 'the parliament of the man - the federation of the world'.[121]

Thus by echoing the European federalist argument, these scholars have jumped from one extreme polarity of considering regional groupings as a strategic tool in the superpower conflict to the another polarity of legitimizing it in the name of a forward march of history towards World State.

Once this cognitive shift happened within the Indian scholars, the European Union has become a model for the South Asian countries. It is believed that if France and Germany could be able to come out of their historical hostility by promoting a regional organization, it is being argued that why not India and Pakistan could not be able to achieve this? If conflict over Alsace-Lorain had not prevented France and Germany coming into a single regional structure and pooling of their sovereignty, then can the problem of Kashmir conflict be allowed to stumble down any co-operation between the two important countries of South Asia? This modular approach to the European Union has been well expressed by one author as

> The EU is surely one of the great miracles of history. The fact that nations that were on each other's throats for centuries, whose conflict kept the whole world in turmoil, have now been able to transcend their differences and are moving towards an economic union with a significant political input. Surely, we in South Asia also have sooner or latter to move towards some such regional arrangements.[122]

Indeed, thinkers of this line of thinking staunchly argue for the creation of a South Asian Community to promote and preserve peace and stability in the region. Lamenting that South Asia was being left out in the historical necessity of organizing regional institution, these scholars felt that "there were strong compulsions for the member states of the region to move faster towards co-operation and that it requires recapturing and reiterating the vision of a South Asian community".[123]

On the contrary to the world-federal approach, some scholars envisage the formation of the European Union as political restructuring of a civilizational zone. Treading on the path laid down by Huntington, these scholars in turn staunchly stressed the need for organizing South Asia around such a civilizational mould. They believe that "it [i.e. South Asia] has an unity in geography and civilization which rivals that of Europe".[124]

Apart from these two approaches, in recent times the

scholars from other social science disciplines particularly from sociology have turned their attention to the European union. Apparently their interest revolves around the issues of pluralism and multiculturalism. So far their methodology is to compare India with the European Union to highlight some social conditions. The best example of the comparative approach adopted is the recent article by the sociologist T.K. Oommen. What attracts Oommen most is the gradual metamorphosis of Europe from nation-state to post-national phase:

> Started as the European Economic Community in 1956, graduating into the European Community, now in the incarnation of EU, I see the gradual formation of a multi-national state. That is, the cradle of nation-states, West Europe, is also becoming the graveyard of nation-states.[125]

Having thus dramatized the European integration process, he like his counterparts in the West concentrates much on the concept of dual citizenship. Understood it as "a de-coupling of citizenship and nationality",[126] he further demonstrates that the European Union is a post-national state where pluralism and group identities are assured and protected. Exactly on this point, that is, drawing pluralism as a comparative category he compares and contrasts Europe with South Asia: "If, starting with individual equality graduating on to group rights is the story of West Europe, the trajectory of South Asia is exactly the opposite".[127]

One overarching notion that has structured the Indian scholars' (irrespective of their subject field, whether International Relations or Sociology) understanding of the European Union is its ideational, progressive model that should have to be emulated and adopted through out the world. Unknowingly, these scholars have internalized and re-circulated Europe's old colonial discourse - Europe as a vanguard of historical march and the people without history has no other choice but to follow it forever. By universalizing what is exclusively a European experience, the Indian scholars have given legitimacy to those western scholars who see American and European experiences "were now everywhere modularly imagined".[128] Is the European Union, a newly imagined political community in the era of digital capitalism, as Anderson would have put it, a modular one to be copied in the third world countries? Are not we, the third world scholars producing a "derivative discourse" and letting "our imagination must remain forever colonized"?[129]

The very purpose of this work is to problematize the uncritical acceptance and application of the western theories in our side, more particularly in Indian academia. Drawing inspiration and insight from the recent theoretical ventures such as subaltern studies historiography and post-colonial theory, the book intends to open up a new space for re-theorizing the European integration process by bringing the issue of colonial discourse into the question.

REFERENCES

1. International Relations with capital letters signifies the separate discipline while with small letters indicates the actual subject matter.
2. Joseph S. Nye, ed., *International Regionalism: Readings* (Boston, 1968), p. vii.
3. Maciej Perczynski, "Comment on the Mayall's Paper", in *The End of the Century: The Future in the Past* (Tokyo, 1995), p. 461. Emphasis added.
4. A. Hurrell, "Explaining the Resurgence of Regionalism in World Politics", *Review of International Studies*, vol.21, no.4, 1995, pp. 16-17.
5. By the term European Union I mean to signify all the institutions created under the various treaties - from Rome to Amsterdam Treaties.
6. S. Joseim, "More Than Intergovernmentalism and Less Than Supranationalism", *Millenium: Journal of International Studies*, vol.13, no. 3, Summer 1994, p.132.
7. Prakash Karat, ed., *A World to Win: Essays On The Communist Manifesto* (New Delhi, 1999), p. 102.
8. For a comprehensive study of all these theoretical debates in International Relations see, Steve Smith, "The Self-Images of a Discipline: A Genealogy of International Relations Theory", in Ken Booth and Steve Smith, ed., *International Relations Theory Today* (Cambridge, UK, 1995), pp. 1-37. And, Ray Maghroori, "Introduction: Major Debates in International Relations", in Ray

Maghroori and Bennett Ramberg, ed., *Globalism versus Realism: International Relations' Third Debate* (Boulder, Colorado, 1982), pp. 9-22.

9. Jim George, *Discourses of Global Politics: A Critical (Re) Introduction to International Relations* (Boulder, Colorado, 1994), p. 74.
10. H.G. Wells, quoted in W.B. Curry, *The Case for Federal Union* (Hardmondsworth, 1939), p.5.
11. Ibid., p. 22.
12. E. Krippendorff, *International Relations as a Social Science* (New Delhi, 1982), p. vii.
13. For a comprehensive history of International Relations as a separate subject field, see, Ibid., p.23.
14. Jim George, no.9, p. 75.
15. Quoted in, no.10, p. 20.
16. W.B. Curry, no.10, p. 65.
17. Ibid., p. 65.
18. Ibid., p. 113.
19. Timothy Dunne, "Realism", in John Baylis and Steve Smith, ed., *The Globalization of World Politics: An Introduction to International Relations* (New York, 1997), p.110.
20. H.J. Morgenthau, *Politics among Nations: The Struggle for Power and Peace* (New York, 1961), edn.3, p.14.
21. Ibid., p. 504.
22. Ibid., p. 322.
23. Ibid., p. 512.
24. Ibid., p. 512.
25. A. Milward, *The European Rescue of the Nation State* (London, 1992), p. xi.
26. Morgenthau, no.20, p.10.
27. Ibid., p.18.
28. Ibid., p. 30.
29. Paul Taylor and A.J. Groom, "Introduction: Functionalism and International Relations", in Taylor and Groom, ed., *Functionalism: Theory and Practice in International Relations* (London, 1975), p.1.
30. David Mitrany, "The Prospect of Integration: Federal or Functional?", in Taylor and Groom, ed., no.29, p.59.
31. David Mitrany, *A Working Peace System*, quoted in Morgenthau, no.20, p. 506.
32. E. Hass, *Web of Interdependence: The United States and International Organization* (Englewood Cliffs, 1970), p.608.
33. Mitrany, no. 30, p. 63.
34. E. Hass, "International Integration: The European and Universal

Process", in Michael Hodges, ed., *European Integration: Selected Readings* (Harmondsworth, 1972), p.92.

35. E. Hass, "Technocracy, Pluralism and the New Europe", in Stephen Graubard, ed., *A New Europe?* (Boston, 1964), pp. 62-88.
36. E. Hass, no.34, p. 96.
37. Ibid., p. 98.
38. Roger Hansen, "Regional Integration: Reflection on a Decade of Theoretical Efforts", in Michael Hodges, ed., no. 34, pp.184-198.
39. A good example is Stanley Hoffman, "Obstinate or Obsolete? The Fact of the Nation State and the Case of Western Europe", *Daedalus*, no. 95, 1964, p. 867.
40. Karl W. Deutsch, "Attaining and Maintaining Integration", in Michael Hodges, ed., no. 34, p. 108.
41. Ibid., p.113.
42. Susan Strange, "International Economics and International Relation: A Case of Mutual Neglect", *International Affairs*, April 1970, pp. 304-15.
43. Susan Strange, "Political Economy of International Relations", in Ken Booth and Steve Smith, ed., no.8, p. 154.
44. Ibid., p.164.
45. Robert O. Keohane and Joseph S. Nye, ed., *Power and Interdependence: World Politics in Transition* (Boston, 1977).
46. Ibid., p.8.
47. Robert O. Keohane and Joseph S. Nye, *Transnational Relations and World Politics* (Cambridge, 1971).
48. Donald Puchala and Stuart Fagan, "International Politics in the 1970s: The Search for a Perspective", in Ray Maghroori and Bennett Ramberg, ed., no.8, p. 40.
49. Keohane and Nye, no.45, pp. 32-33.
50. Puchala and Fagan, no.48, p. 46.
51. Ibid., pp. 46-47.
52. Robert Gilpin, "The Politics of Transnational Economic Relations", in Ray Maghroori and Bennett Ramberg, ed., no. 8, p. 176.
53. Ibid., p. 178.
54. Anthony Payne and Andrew Gamble, "Introduction: The Political Economy of Regionalism and World Order", in Gamble and Payne, ed., *Regionalism and World Order* (London, 1996), pp.1-20.
55. Robert O. Keohane, *After Hegemony: Cooperation and Discord in*

the World Political Economy (Princeton, N.J., 1984) p. 31.

56. Ibid., p. 32.
57. S.D. Krasner, "Structural Causes and Regime as Intervening Variables", in Stephen D.Krasner, ed., *International Regime* (Ithaca, 1983), p.2.
58. Ernst Hass, "Words Can Hurt You; Or, Who Said What to Whom about Regimes", in Stephen Krasner, ed., *International Regime* (Ithaca, 1982), p. 27.
59. Robert O. Keohane, no. 55, pp.51-52. Emphasis original.
60. Susan Strange, no.42, p. 165. Also refer, Susan Strange, "International Economic Relations: The Need for an Interdisciplinary Approach", in R. Morgan, ed., *The Study of International Affairs* (Oxford, 1972).
61. Quoted in Walter Hallstein and Hans Barker, "European Economic Community" in C.D. Kering, ed., *Marxism, Communism and Western Society: A Comparative Encyclopedia* (New York, 1972), Vol.3, p. 341.
62. Refer the works, Michel Albert, *Capitalism Against Capitalism* (London, 1993). In this book Albert outlines the contemporary two models of capitalism: Anglo-American model and Rhine-Alpine model. Also refer, Ernest Mandel, *Europe Vs America: Contradictions of Imperialism* (New York, 1970).
63. Oran R. Young, "Interdependence in World Politics", in Ray Magroori and Bennett Ramberg, ed., no. 8, p. 68. For an elaborate discussion on this point refer, Edward L. Morse, "The Politics of World Politics", *International Organization*, vol. 33, Spring 1969, pp. 53-68.
64. Immanual Wallerstein, *The Modern World System I, Capitalist Agriculture and the Origins of European World Economy in the Sixteenth Century* (London, N.Y., 1974), p. 15.
65. Ibid., p. 225.
66. Andre Gunther Franck and Barry K. Gills, ed., *The World System: Five Hundred Years or Five Thousand?* (London, N.Y., 1993), p.7.
67. I. Wallerstein, *Geopolitics and Geoculture: Essays on the Changing World-System* (Cambridge, N.Y., 1991), p. 53. Most of his arguments regarding European unity have been traced from the Chapter 4 titled "European Unity and Its Implication for the International System" in the above-mentioned book, pp. 49-64.
68. Ibid., p.53.
69. Andrew Linklater, *Beyond Realism and Marxism: Critical Theory and International Relations* (Macmillan, 1990).
70. Robert Cox, "Gramsci, Hegemony and International Relations:

An Essay in Method", *Millenium: Journal of International Studies*, vol.12, no.2, 1983, pp.269-291; Mark Neufeld, *The Restructuring of International Relations Theory* (Cambridge, 1995); and Stephen Gill, "Two Concepts of International Political Economy', *Review of International Studies*, vol.16, 1990, pp.369-81.

71. Richard Ashley, "The Geo-political Space: Towards a Critical Social Theory of International Politics", *Alternative*, vol.12, 1987, pp.403-34; Der Derian and Michael Shapiro, ed., *International / Intertextual Relations: Postmodern Readings of World Politics* (Lexington, 1989).
72. Spike K. Peterson, ed., *Gendered States: Feminist (Re)vision of International Relations Theory* (Boulder, 1992); Christine Sylvester, *Feminist Theory and International Relations in a Postmodern Era* (Cambridge, 1993).
73. E. Krippendorff, no 12. p. ix.
74. Fred Halliday, "A 'Crisis' of International Relations", *International Relations*, vol. 8, Nov 1985, p. 412. For sociologically endowed international relations approach see, Fred Halliday, "State and Society in International Relations: A Second Agenda", *Millenium: Journal of Internatioal Studies*, vol. 12, no. 2, 1987, pp.215-29. Also, Faruk Yalvac, "The Sociology of the State and the Sociology of International Relations", in Michael Banks and Martin Shaw, ed., *State and Society in International Relations* (Hamel Hempstead, 1991).
75. For an elaborate argument refer, Theda Skocpol, *States and Social Revolution* (Cambridge, 1979).
76. Anthony Giddens, *The Nation-State and Violence* (Cambridge, 1985) p.244.
77. Martin Shaw, *Global Society and International Relations: Sociological Concepts and Political Perspectives* (Cambridge, 1994).
78. For globalization concept in International Relations Theory, see, J.A. Scholte, "The Globalization of World Politics', in John Baylis and Steve Smith, ed., n. 19, pp.14-29.
79. Robert O. Keohane and Joseph S. Nye Jr., "Globalization: What is New? What is Not? (And So What?)", *Foreign Policy*, no.118, Spring 2000, p. 104.
80. Baylis and Smith, "Introduction", in Baylis and Smith, ed., no.19, p.7.
81. For a comprehensive discussion on New Regionalism, see, Gamble and Payne, "Conclusion: The New Regionalism", in Gamble and Payne, ed., no. 54, pp. 247-64.
82. Ibid., p.248. Emphasis added.

83. Mattei Dogan, "Comparing the Decline of Nationalism in Western Europe: The Generational Dynamic", *International Social Science Journal*, May 1993, pp.177-98.
84. Keohane and Nye, no 79. p. 105.
85. M. Albert, quoted in Gamble and Payne, ed., no. 54, p. 250.
86. J.H. Mittleman, "The Dynamics of Globalization", in James H. Mittleman, ed., *Globalization: Critical Reflections* (Boulder, London, 1996), p. 17.
87. Richard Falk, "Regionalism and World Order After the Cold War", *Australian Journal of International Affairs*, vol. 49, May 1995, pp. 1-15.
88. Ibid., p.14.
89. For a comprehensive historical outline of the development of 'Postmodernism', see, Gurpreet Mahajan, "Reconsidering Postmodernism: What is New in the Old Lamp", *Economic and Political Weekly*, January 28, 1995, pp.45-52.
90. The detailed discussion on postmodernistic explorations in International Relations could be found in, Nick Rengger and Mark Hoffman, "Modernity, Postmodernism and International Relations", in Joe Doherty, Elspeth Graham and Mo Malek, ed., *Postmodernism and the Social Sciences* (London, 1992), pp. 127-47.
91. Asbjorn Sonne Norgaard, "Institutions and Postmodernity in IR: The 'New EC'", *Cooperation and Conflict*, vol. 29, no. 3, p. 245.
92. John Ruggie, "Territoriality and Beyond: Problematizing Modernity in International Relations", *International Organization*, vol.47, no.1, pp.143-44.
93. Norgaard, no.91, p.246. Emphasis added.
94. Mike Featherstone, *Consumer Culture & Postmodernism* (London, 1991), p.145. Emphasis added.
95. Robert Cooper, *The Post-Modern State and the World order* (London, 1996), p.30.
96. George Modelski, "Globalization", in David Held and Anthony McGrew, ed., *The Global Transformations Reader: An Introduction to the Globalization Debate* (Cambridge, 2000), p.50.
97. For an elaborate argument refer, Francis Fukuyama, *The End of History and the Last Man* (New York, 1992).
98. Though Toynbee has not developed his idea of international relations as inter-civilizational relations in any of his books, this idea found its rudimentary exposition in one of his dialogue made with Daisaku Ikeda, a Japanese scholar. Refer the book, *Choose Life: A Dialogue*, ed., Richard L. Gage (Delhi, 1987).
99. Samuel Huntington, *The Clash of Civilizations and Remaking of*

World Order (New York, 1996), p. 43.

100. Ibid., p. 21.
101. Samuel Huntington, "The Lonely Superpower: The New Dimension of Power", *Foreign Affairs*, vol. 78, no. 2, p.46.
102. Norman Ginsburg, "Postmodernity and Social Europe", in John Carter, ed., *Postmodernity and the Fragmentation of Welfare* (London, 1998), p.269.
103. Maurice Roche, "Rethinking Citizenship and Social Movements: Themes in Contemporary Sociology and Non-Conservative Ideology", in Kate Nash, ed., *Readings in Contemporary Political Sociology* (Oxford, 2000), p. 234.
104. Brubacker quoted in, Yasemin Nuhoglu Soysal, "Towards a Postnational Model of Membership in Europe", in Kate Nash, ed., *Readings in Contemporary Political Sociology* (Oxford, 2000), p. 265.
105. Ibid., p. 272.
106. Cris Shore, "Inventing the 'People's Europe': Critical Approaches to European Community 'Cultural Policy'", *Man*, vol. 28, no. 4, December 1993, p. 779.
107. Ibid., p. 779.
108. June Nash, " Anthropology of the Multinational Corporation", in Gerrit Huizer and Bruce Mannheim, ed., *The Politics of Anthropology: From Colonialism and Sexism, Towards a View from Below* (The Hague, Paris, 1979), p.424.
109. Philip Schlesinger, "Wishful Thinking: Cultural Politics, Media, and Collective Identities in Europe", *Journal of Communication*, vol.43, no.2, Spring 1993, pp.6-7.
110. On this aspect refer the two special issues brought up by the journal, *Race & Class* under the titles, "Europe: The Wages of Racism", vol. 39, no.1, July-Sep 1997, pp.1-75. And, "Europe: Variation on the Theme of Racism", vol. 32, no. 3, Jan-March 1991, pp. 1-63.
111. Jan Nederveen Pieterse, "Fictions of Europe", *Race & Class*, vol. 32, no. 3, Jan-March 1991, p. 5.
112. Frances Webber, "From Ethnocentrism to Euro-racism", *Race & Class*, vol. 32, no. 3, Jan-March 1991, p. 15.
113. A.J.R. Groom, "International Relations: Anglo-American Aspects-A Study in Parochialism", in Kanti P. Bajpai and Harish C. Shukul, ed., *Interpreting World Politics* (New Delhi, 1995), pp. 45-89.
114. For a comprehensive narration on this point see, A.K. Damodaran, "Before Non-Alignment", in Bajpai and Shukul,

ed., no. 113, pp. 190-205.

115. Nehru quoted in, ibid., p.193.
116. A.R. Rana quoted in , Kanti P. Bajpai, "Introduction: International Theory, International Society, Regional Politics, and Foreign Policy", in Bajpai and Shukul, ed., no. 113, p. 14.
117. Ibid., p. 16.
118. SAARC Vision Beyond the Year 2000 - Report of the SAARC Group of Eminent Persons Established by the Ninth SAARC Summit (Delhi, 1999), p. 21.
119. Ibid., p.13.
120. L.L. Mehrotra, "Why Regional Cooperation?", in L.L. Mehrotra, H.S. Chopra and Gert W. Kueck, ed., *SAARC 2000 and Beyond* (New Delhi, 1995), p. 13.
121. Karan Singh's forward written to the above book, p.viii.
122. Ibid., p.viii.
123. L.L. Mehrotra and others, no.120, p.x.
124. Eric Gonsalves, "South Asian Cooperation: An Agenda and a Vision for the Future", in L.L. Mehrotra and others, ed., no.120, p.34.
125. T.K. Oommen, "Reconciling Equality and Pluralism", *The Hindu*, April 28, 2001, p.10.
126. Ibid., p. 10.
127. Ibid., p. 10
128. Benedict Anderson is the most acclaimed theoretician of this line of argument. For further reference see his book, *Imagined Communities: Reflection on the Origin and Spread of Nationalism* (London, 1995), Revised ed.
129. Partha Chaterjee, *Nation and Its Fragments: Colonial and Postcolonial Histories* (Delhi, 1994), p. 4.

Chapter 1

EUROPE: TOWARDS A DEFINITION

In Tyros, on the Asian shore of the Mediterranean (in modern Lebanon), there lived a Princess named Europa. She was the daughter of the king Agenor. One night she had a following dream: Two countries in female form were fighting over her. One of them, who embodied the 'land of Asia', wished to keep her while the other – taking the form of the 'land of elsewhere'- wanted to bear her out to sea at the behest of the god Zeus. When she awoke the next morning, the Princess went to the seashore to gather flowers. A bull, mighty yet peaceable, rose from the waves and persuaded the Princess to get on his back. He then flew away, revealing to her that he was Zeus himself, having transformed himself in to a bull. On the Greek Island of Crete he coupled with her, and she became - as legend has it – "the mother of noble sons".[1]

I
EUROPE: A CONTINENT, OR CIVILIZATION, OR CONSCIOUSNESS?

Like all origins, the origin of Europe is a myth. However, in everyday common usage, 'Europe' signifies two specific meanings: First, the more prevalent and pervasive one, as a concrete manifestation of a geographical entity; and the second one as an idea, deduced from the historical and cultural terms. In the geographical sense, Europe denotes a landmass of irregular shape with islands circumferenced by Atlantic, Artic and Mediterranean seas on the west, north and southern sides respectively and the Ural Mountains on the eastern side. On the other hand, in a historical sense, it connotes a civilizational zone, originated from Greeks and expanded and extended successively by Roman Empire and Latin Christendom. Normally these two images, both geographical and historical, are superimposed on one another thereby imputing a clear-cut meaning to the word Europe.

But etymologically the word Europe is devoid of any such loaded meanings. If we take cognizance of the Phoenician root-word of Europe, *ereb*, it merely signifies the westward direction where the sun sets in. Or otherwise, if we relay on the Greek root-word, it literally means just to identify any huge landmass differentiated from the islands. Anyhow, it should be noted here that the word Europe was used by the ancient people simply to identify with or differentiate from either a direction or a landmass. Thus, it had been employed in a broader yet in vague sense without any fixed geographical mappings or cultural moorings.

Nevertheless, in the modern period the word has been employed to frame a certainly demarcated geographical area where a series of civilizations presumed to have originated and flourished. However, the juxtaposition of these two categories of definition, that is, geographical and civilizational is not without problematical. When one proceeds to define Europe exactly within some etched geographical outlines, then the category of civilization becomes questionable. For example, say if one considers Europe stretching between Atlantic to Urals (prevalent and widely accepted boundaries), the Russians will be left out despite their common sharing of Christian civilization. There is no convincing justification to substantiate the exclusion of the Russians while their fellow Slavic brethren like Ukrainians and others were admitted in to the European boundaries. As a way out, if we take civilization as a legitimate category, then there would arise an even more incongruity. It is well known that the Hellenic, Roman and Christian civilizations, all did have Asia Minor within their boundaries. If that were the case, it is hard to find any justifying arguments to exclude the present day Turkey from the geography of Europe except by citing its distant Islamic conversion. Here one might have to face squarely a delicate dilemma over treating the Nordics as legitimate inheritors of Hellenic legacy while at the same time denying that legacy for the Turks.

Despite these problems, today Europe is being defined either in geographical or in civilizational terms as if there were no discrepancy crept in this endeavor.

Europe as a Geographical Entity

Mythology usually lends its name to geography; or geography makes itself meaningful only when it is married to some mythologies. The good example is the Greek mythical figure *Europa* who lends her name to a particular geographical area. This tendency is almost common to all Indo-European languages.[2] But bridging mythology with the actual historical geography is always a conflictual one. From medieval crusade to modern Indian politics the dangerous coalition of mythology with geography breeds into war and conflicts.

It is easy to exhort "Europe can be thought in several ways; the simplest way is to think it in geographical term".[3] If geography as a subject field concerned with the description and explanation of the areal differentiation of the earth's surface, will it be possible to differentiate Europe as a set of landed area with natural differences, separating it from the rest of the landmass? In actuality, it is a part of one single landmass called 'Eurasia'. On this point only, Gottmann admits, "Europe scarcely deserves to be called a continent".[4]

Europe as a geographical entity does not exist from time immemorial. It was a historical construction and emerged only through historicity. In the time of Herodotus, the earth was conceived of divided into three continents: Asia, Europa and Libya. This division, one might easily understand, covered only the core area of the Mediterranean Sea-based landmass. Greeks had no idea of west or northwest landmass of today's Europe. The later day Roman conquest of these areas gradually brought them into contact with the Mediterranean sea and unified culturally under Roman Catholic Church. However, here the idea was Christendom not Europe, with Jerusalem as its central point. That is why it waged successive crusades to liberate

Jerusalem and other holy places from the heathen hands. Therborn captures this historicity of the idea of Europe vividly as,

> The territory of Europe itself is a historical construct. From the Hellenistic period till the rise and challenge of Islam, what later became 'Europe' was the Mediterranean region, including Alexandria and other centers of south shore civilization. The European space acquired its current extension only gradually, with the Christianizing of the north, completed only in the 14th century.[5]

Europe thus historically evolved but with continuously changing boundaries. That is why the journal, *International Affairs* has had to bring out a special issue to deal with the question "Europe, where does it begin or end?"[6] Further, this historical geography of Europe had a definite link with war and conflicts. The Greek conception of Europe was shaped by their Persian wars. Similarly, the Roman imperial expedition to the west and northwest expanded Europe geographically in those directions.

The historicity of European geography brings forth a peculiar and an interesting situation: Even the countries, which have been traditionally recognized as European, did not claim it as such. Once the British Foreign Secretary, George Cannig said "Europe's domain extends to the shore of the Atlantic, England's begins there".[7] On the contrary, Russia, which had turned its face toward west only during the reign of Peter the Great, claimed itself as a legitimate European nation. Britain, though claimed as not a part of Europe behaved in its colonial territories as if a vanguard of the European legacy. Similarly the erstwhile Soviet Union had meticulously built its 'Asian image' over the years to differentiate itself from the 'imperial Europe' and make it legitimate and natural friend of the newly independent Asian nations. However, the reverse occurred after the cold war. Nowadays, it tries hell-bent to procure a European image for itself. Ironically, most of the East European nations claimed their 1989 revolutions as a 'return to Europe'.

These examples are enough to convince one that the bare interest of the country will determine its willingness to be a part of Europe or not. Martin walker[8] explicates this point with reference to American view of 'Greater Europe'. He exposes how the different and diversified American interests mask the European image accordingly: While its security interest compels America to invite Turkey into the folds of Europe (through NATO alliance), its self conscious Christian image prevents Turkey to be brought into the cultural orbit of Europe. On the contrary, America is ready to acknowledge Russia's Christian heritage but that will not quarantine its inclusion into the European security arrangement. The interests and against whom you are align with will determine the boundaries of Europe. That is why, Michel Foucher says, "It is as if Europe cannot create boundaries without an adversary. It used to be the Barbarians, then the Turks. Only yesterday it was the Soviet Union. What about tomorrow...?"[9]

Europe as a Civilizational Unit

If Europe could not be defined geographically, then there was an attempt to define it historically. The quintessential example of this line of definition is Arnold Toynbee. Taking 'civilization' as an 'intelligible field of study', he starts defining Europe by adapting certain 'mental operations on a large scale',[10] by which he means looking for a civilizational unit that has an existence and extension both in space and time. His argument revolves around two axes: one, the synchronic assessment, where he extracts two essential fundamental characteristics-industrial system of economy and democratic system of politics that would define Europe as a civilizational unit in space; second, the diachronic engagement, where he traces some sort of continuity of affiliation with the Graco-Roman civilization to prove the extension of Europe in time.

But on both these accounts Toynbee is bereft with problems. Under the compulsion of the historical events such as the World War I and the rise of Fascism in Europe, Toynbee longed to transcend the national division of Europe and as a way out, he imagined Europe as a single civilizational unit. On this move Toynbee was blind to the internal differences of Europe. The one glaring example was the German experience. The entire

Sonderweg thesis highlighted how different the German experience was from the rest of the European countries. The debate, at least in one respect, shed new light on how European countries were different among themselves and mediated the modern industrialism and nationalism differently. In this context, Toynbee's comfortable, cool claim of 'Europe as a comprehensible civilizational unit' is nothing but a forced uniformity on the part of the historical experience of Europe.

Similarly his claim to diachronic unity or affiliation with the Graco-Roman civilization is not without problems. The classical Greek civilization was the result of the confluence of different streams of influences coming from neighbouring civilizational zones such as Egyptian and Persian bordering around the rim of the Mediterranean Sea. The decades of Hellenic studies have clearly documented how the ancient Greeks developed their geometrical ideas from the rudimentary Egyptian mathematics, their Orphic, Dionysian cult from Thrace and the sea-faring and commerce from the Phoenicians. Recently it has been demonstrated that how the Black Africa contributed to the flourishing of Greek civilization. If that were the case, how could Europe claim in wholesale the legacy of the ancient Greece and boast of as the sole legitimate inheritor of the Greek experiences? Spengler, sensing this problem years before Toynbee, declared 'it is sheer delusion to speak of the Hellens as 'European Antiquity' and to enlarge upon their 'mission' as such".[11]

The third important problem that Toynbee faced is the relationship of the 'New World' (America and Australia) with the European civilization. If one accepts his parameter of European civilization- industrial economy and democratic politics, then these two continents would automatically come under the boundary of European civilization. This not only made the geographical idea of Europe senseless but also made the very idea of Europe too small to be replaced by the term 'West'. That is why, without any hesitation Spengler declared:

> The word Europe ought to be struck out of history. There is historically no European type... 'East' and 'West' are notions that contain the real history, where Europe is an empty sound.[12]

What else if not irony, that in an attempt to seek an answer to the question what is Europe, the very word Europe itself evaporated and becomes meaningless empty sound? Europe as a continent is too big to imagine whereas Europe as a civilization is too small to comprehend. In this situation, there are only two possibilities before us: either to get rid of the idea of Europe and embrace wholeheartedly the term west; or instead of imagining Europe in terms of some concrete manifestations like geographical or civilizational, we have to look for some abstract categories of expression like European consciousness or spirit.

Since the aim of the study is to critically understand the on-going European integration process, treading on the path opened by the first possibility would not help us theoretically except to pass judgement of the impossibility of achieving any political unity for such a broad civilizational unit covering at least three continents. But for over half a century the European integration process is visible and in recent times more accelerated. So it would be more useful to explore the second possibility to comprehend the current process.

Europe as Consciousness

If there are problems in defining Europe geographically or culturally, then how is to conceptualize it? I wonder, have not the geographic and civilizational perceptions agreed that there exists already a separate entity called Europe, but they differed only in describing or explaining what it is? These two streams begin *post festum* and understand Europe in the meaning of its conscious existence in history. They have simply taken for granted the existence of Europe in history (as geographical or civilizational) and all their subsequent arguments are put in the service of defending that notion. Their apologia runs like this: The consciousness of Europe has never lost trace of its origin in history. The Europeans always have the feeling that they are the children of Hellas. Nevertheless, it is hard to find any concrete, convincing representation to express this consciousness. Thus, the history of Europe is to be understood as a process in search of finding an adequate expressive form to European consciousness.

On the other hand, some argue, citing the continuous war and conflicts in the history of Europe, that there is no European consciousness at all. They claim that if at all any such European consciousness exists, the people of Europe should have claimed as 'I am a European'. But we hear all sorts of identifying, say Christian, French or German except the one 'European'. So they believe that the European consciousness has yet to be constructed in history.

These diametrically opposing traditions lead to different interpretations of the European integration. For the first stream, the European Union is a legacy of those statesmen who constantly strove to achieve some sort of unity in Europe; that is to find an adequate representative form for the already existing consciousness. But for the second stream of thought, the EU is the vehicle to induce a consciousness of Europe among the different nations of Europe.

Can we infer it as a failure on the part of these thinkers to find out an adequate 'categories of expression' to represent Europe? If history fails to eliminate the mystery of Europe and elucidate what it is, then the philosophy enters to define it in terms of either spirit or consciousness. In 1947, immediately after the Second World War, a conference was arranged in Paris in that all the important philosophers of the day participated to stake stock of the future of Europe. In that conference, it was pointed out that the lack of European consciousness had actually led Europe into two successive wars within the short period and the subsequent horrific experiences. It should be noted that this stream of argument has been employed to stress the importance of European political unity and gives legitimacy to the functions of the European Union even today.

However, the celebrated philosopher Merleau-Ponty opposed this kind of dogma and explained in clear terms that there has already been a completely different type of European unity existing. Criticizing his fellow friends for having given much importance to the representational form of Europe, he said

> It seems to me that a European spirit should be defined less by an idea of representation,...than by certain kind of relation

> between humans and nature or between an individual and others.[13]

Thus for him, the European spirit or consciousness could only be explained through the acts of Europe or what it has achieved over the years and not by some essential representational characters. He identified three such important acts or inventions of Europe: Humanism, Universalism and State as realization of freedom. On similar line, Paul Valery argues that 'Europe is above all the creator of science. There have been arts in all countries; there have been true science only in Europe'.[14]

These three inventions in turn structured the acts and behavior of the Europeans. Thus according to Merleau-Ponty, the Europeans or those who have European consciousness are those people who have invented the three cardinal principles and behave according to these principles. The one who has the social science background would immediately recognize what the philosopher of phenomenology of perception explains as European spirit or consciousness is broadly known as 'Modernity'. Based on the theoretical premise of Merleau-Ponty, one could define European consciousness as distinctively a modern one and a result of the transformation – both mental and material, that the Western European countries experienced in the 17th and 18th centuries.

While these thinkers well defined the European consciousness and its nature, they have failed to answer the question what is the purpose or practical use of this consciousness. The European consciousness is more visible and its effects tangible in Europe's colonial encounters. It was during the colonization of the other people that the European consciousness came into full dimension. It gave them the notion of superior race and inculcated a sense of 'mission civilization' to educate the barbaric people.

Thus any definition of Europe should be based on two categorical imperatives- modernity and colonialism. In this chapter an attempt would be made to construct a theoretical sketch based on this understanding.

II
EUROPE AND MODERNITY: A PARADOX

At 19th century there emerged a distinct way of defining Europe. The rise of Social Sciences as a separate branch of knowledge witnessed yet another definition of Europe. The founding fathers of these new subject-fields laid down groundwork for understanding Europe from the 'Great Transformation' happened in the 18th century. Saint Simon and his disciple August Comte defined Europe as an industrial society; Weber saw it as a rational bureaucratic one; for Marx it was industrial capitalism. They in a single stroke cleared the mystery of Europe and explained it in the 'miracle of Europe' which later came to be known as 'Modernity'. The categories of modernity in turn become the categories of expression of the idea of Europe. To put it in Merleau-Ponty's words 'Europe is in act not in representation'.[15] That is, what Europe achieved historically should become the defining characteristic of Europe. Action not representation is signification. Thus, modernity is the sole biographer of Europe.

Why modernity has chosen to write the biography of Europe alone? Or to put it simply, why the so-called miracle of modernity happened in Europe but not somewhere else say, in China or India? By reflecting upon the pre-modern period of Europe, Weber explained it in terms of Protestant ethics and asceticism; Marx in terms of change in mode of production; Wallerstein in terms of ceaseless accumulation of capital. A sort of solipsism developed here: What is Europe? It is a modern one – a rational, bureaucratic, industrial-capitalistic society. And why modernity emerged only in Europe? It is because of the internal peculiarities of the medieval Europe. By their circular arguments, the scholars were able to prove the existence of Europe both in time and space. That is why, Agness Heller has to say, "Modernity, the creation of Europe, *itself created Europe* and this is more than a paradox".[16]

Europe in an Epic Narration

It may seem that Heller's statement sounds like Kaffkasque

puzzle or Marques magic. For me, it sounds rather like an epic plot. Could it be possible for a writer of a story be created by the story itself? How could the storyteller and the story be the one and the same? Heller simply understands this as a paradox. I wonder would not a paradox develop in the narration of a story rather than the story itself. So it would be more useful in concentrating on her epic narration of the story of Europe rather than the story itself.

Her story starts from the 18th century. Before that there was no entity called Europe. Only Christendom was there. Its *urbs* was Jerusalem; *lingua franca* was Latin. The Papacy and the Holy Roman Empire were the two institutional pillars on which the medieval Christendom was erected. The Roman Catholic Church was the nerve center of the Christendom. With its clerical hierarchy of priests, bishops, archbishops and finally the Pope, it had brought almost all the western and middle parts of Europe under its control. The most crucial aspect of the Church was to bring the people irrespective of their regional and linguistic differences under one institutional setup and ruled their minds and hearts, persuading them that they lived under divine guidance in divinely ordered universe. The Holy Roman Empire on its part was intended to bring these people under one political unit and manage the affairs of temporal matters. But in reality, the feudalism- that is, the manorial system with its locally autonomous Vassal- Lord relationships and the independent city-states governed by the commercial guilds did not allow the Empire to wield its power completely. That is why, Mann considers the Christendom was 'an acephalous federation'.[17]

However, his judgement is one sided. The Church and the idea of Kingdom of God indeed played a major role in unifying the people and impute a sense of community. Or otherwise, it would not have been possible in such a headless, porous political setting, a series of crusades that the Christendom waged on the eastern infidels. But the two historical events- the Protestant Reformation and the Enlightenment challenged the durability and stability of this Christendom. The reformation by its attack on the 'universal Church' delegitimized its claim to authority of salvation. The Enlightenment by its stress on rationalism even questioned the place of religion in man's life. The secularization of mind and life finally made the Christendom collapsed.

By the time of beginning of 17th century, there emerged a unique and distinctive *Weltanschauung* broadly termed as 'Universal Humanism'. In this Copernican revolution, Man and his subjectivity replaced cosmos and cosmic order. However, this made the stability and unity of Christendom collapsed. Instead of one single Christianity many Christian sects emerged; instead of one Holy Roman Empire, numerous small states were evolved. Thus, the single unified Christendom was transformed into modern but fragmented pieces. Luther and Calvin, Louis XIV and Henry VIII and Galileo and Newton transformed Christendom into modern but fragmented one. Despite this fragmented plurality, this was the moment Heller identifies as when Europe was born:

> The new world of modernity, the one which came about through the combination of diverse and distinctive experiences, discoveries and visions, has been termed 'Europe or the west' only from the eighteen century.[18]

Europe, thus became a common terminology to denote the diverse and distinctive modern experiences of the 18th century.

Then, what is modernity?

To answer this question, different classical theories of modernity- with Marxian, Weberian and Durkheimian varieties were propounded in the 19th century. However, there are two broad tendencies in explaining modernity: philosophical and pragmatic. For the first stream, modernity means the arrival of a specific *historical moment* (as in Hegelian term) where the traditional foundations crumbled down and instead a new critical worldview emerged. The second approach is a sociological one; for it modernity is a peculiar *social condition* and concentrate more on the existing social, political and economic situations in the everyday spheres of life. Heller names these two tendencies as dynamics of modernity and modern social arrangement respectively. The combination of these two forms the essence of modernity.

She identifies the dynamics of modernity as positing a series of infinite questioning without allowing any foundational ground to be erected. Simply it is *nihilism*; nihilism to the root. It is more comfortable and satisfied in criticizing and finally destroying the rigid traditional edifices. Its most famous call is 'Dare to think' and not accepting any given values. Once this was achieved then comes the constructive part- building a modern, ideal social structure compatible with its philosophical visions. This constructive part of modernity tangible in everyday life situations is known as modern social arrangements.

Though the dynamics of modernity first appeared in Athens, through Socrates and Plato, however, the Greeks failed in their endeavor in constructing a new social arrangement over the debris of tradition. All that could Plato do was to theorize an ideal society yet but miserably failed to realize it. When this dynamics of modernity revealed once again in 18th century Europe, the 'philosophers of Enlightenment' like their counterparts in Athens, started demolishing the foundations of tradition. But unlike the Greeks, they in turn strived to erect a new modern social arrangement where they could embellish their philosophical visions. This stride from enlightenment to enlivement was not without contradictions.

Two sets of contradiction peeled off: between their philosophical vision and practical reality; and discrepancies among the modern social arrangements. While industrial capitalism had its reach and scope in universal level, in politics nationalism brought in particularism. What would be the reason for this pragmatic contradiction? Heller outlines the reason on two axes of arguments: The most glaring and perplexing one is between the supposed ideality and actual reality. Generally known as pragmatic contradiction, like all the philosophical vision the modern enlightened one also faced the dilemma over the 'translatability' of its visions into lived experience. Sensing this dilemma, Hegel the quintessential modern philosopher resolved this contradiction by aesthetizing the philosophy. Philosophy for him is not a bunch of prescriptions of 'ought to be', but 'its time comprehended in thought' and 'the rose within the cross of present'.[19] That is, philosophy sets its flight only after the ideality translated into the reality. Despite the Hegelian endeavor of aesthetization of modern philosophy, it was remained crippled with the schizophrenic tendency caught between the wedge of what Heller names it as rational enlightenment and romantic enlightenment. The first one stressed the universal, individual, nihilistic approach; while the second one emphasized the communal, particularistic one.

The same had happened in the modern social arrangement too. The modern political arrangement – nation-state is not compatible with the development of modern economic arrangement. Thus, the development of modern social arrangement is not uniform and free of contradiction. Rather Wallerstein highlights the tension existing between the economic and political arrangements:

> Although the continuous drive towards the accumulation of capital, which is the main characteristics of the (modern world) system, has proceeded on the basis of a single global division of labor, political activities within the system have largely been oriented around the nation-state.[20]

And he understands the tension as antinomy creeped into the modern world system. For Heller, the discrepancies are the result of the employment of three different developmental logics of modernity. This in turn created modernity in plural: "Modernity is not to be seen as a homogenized or totalized whole, but as a fragmented world of some open but not unlimited possibilities".[21] If modernity was a plural and phenomenon one then she should have known that it could have created Europe heterogeneously. Her earlier paradoxical statement should be appended as: The manifold modernity, the creation of Europe, created Europe fragmentedly. When she feels this inevitability, her narrative tone becomes more and more melancholic.

Accepting this logic, Heller proceeds to explain the fragmented nature of Europe. Modernity has not established Europe as a single political unity; instead numerous independent nation-states were emerged. These nation-states were not ruled by any common set of paradigms; instead they were governed by monarchical to republican and democratic to totalitarian forms of government. Similarly in religious domain, the post-Enlightenment period witnessed the multiplicity of Christian sects. Thus, from the beginning of the modern period, Europe was to be polymorphous and polyphonic. In this sense only, Heller laments 'Europe is rootless'[22] and requires a cultural backing, a brand new cultural mythology.

For Heller here lies the heroic adventure of Europe. If it was not possible to create any single European identity within its boundaries, Europe tried to construct one such an identity universally. By assuming that it had a historical destiny to carry forward the 'Universal Truth' on the planetary scale, the European spirit or genius imagined, projected and thus created a human kind as well as other universal notions such as art and culture. Since this universalism is inclusive of all races and continents, Heller said 'European identity has been brought into focus by non-identity'.

It is exactly at this point that her epic narration reaches its climax. Like the Ulysses of the *Odyssey*, (whose return to home was to be achieved only through having conquered the other territories), Europe has arrived to its own identity by having created an identity for whole of the universe. An arrival by conquest; an identity by non-identity!

But the others of the Europe, unlike the sirens of Homeric myth, did not let Europe create its identity through non-identity. They were well aware of the fact that indeed the 'Universal Humanism' of Europe was a cloak of racial humanism. That is why they rejected the universal posturing of Europe and endeavored to create and preserve their own identity independent of it. Realizing the difference of ancient Greece and modern Europe, Heller laments "the world which embraced one or another aspect of the European vision, did not behave in the manner of Hellenistic city-states".[23]

The implied accusation of Heller is that in spite of manifold differences (of Athenian and Spartan political systems and life style), wherever the Greeks gone the Hellenism had followed. However, this was not true of Europe. Wherever Europe gone, indeed modernism followed; but with a tinge of irony, the idea of Europe was rejected while the modernism was accepted. Heller thus concludes her narration: "Together with modernity, Europe created history a kind, which does not allow its self-created cultural tradition to be disseminated together with its real identity- modernity".[24]

To sum up her story: Once upon a time, there was an entity called Christendom, which got transformed into a modern one in the early 18th century. However, this transformation had destroyed the unity and instead created fragmented, manifold identities. But the modern Europe tried to construct one such a unified identity through its 'Universalistic Humanism'. Unfortunately this move was brought down by the other people who have embraced modernity but rejected Europe. Thus, Europe is still a dream.

Whatever controversial or questionable may be her narration of the story of Europe, there are two points that are interested to us more. First, unlike the other theorists of modernity, she clearly differentiates the idea of modernity from the idea of Europe. These two ideas, as far as she is concerned, are not co-terminus or coeval even though the idea of Europe was a modern one. Further her narration amply captures the inherent tensions that exist between these two ideas. Second, the link that she makes between the idea of Europe and Universalism. This is the most gifted of her argument that would illuminate the complexities, which lie behind the idea of Europe. But she failed to see the interconnectedness of universalim with colonialism. What she celebrates as heroic (the achievement of European identity by universalism) is indeed sweeping away of the identities of the other people. The making of the European identity was possible only at the cost of making the other as beast and savage.

Exactly where Heller stops, from there I develop my narration of Europe. My storyline would exclusively focus on the colonial adventure of Europe. If modernity failed to create a united, single European identity, it was colonialism that had achieved this unity. This is not a paradox but an irony. What else if not irony, when Europe had to construct its identity and find its unity outside the Europe- that is in the colonized space?

III
A PORTRAIT OF EUROPE ON THE COLONIAL WALL

When Paul Valery cared to define who are Europeans, he thought of "A true European (is) a man in whom the European mind can come to its full realization".[25] How could this specifically distinguished European mind come to its realization? When and where?

Merleau-Ponty sought to answer these questions by bringing the notion of the distinct acts or behavior of Europe, carried out at some specific historical juncture; these acts in turn produced the European mind or consciousness. Treading on the same path, but in a different lane, Heller narrates a story in which, if Europe can be said at all to have aspired to an identity for itself, it would have been that of the only true purveyor of the Universal Humanism. We have, then two models of narration about the European mind: One that which suggests European mind as a consequence of some inner transformation on the part of Europe. For convenience' sake, we can call this as *interior monologue*. The other one argues that European consciousness as a product of what it has achieved outside of Europe or inclusive of the entire universe. Again for convenience, I can name this model as *exterior monologue*.

The identity or consciousness of oneself cannot be realized by some internal revelations of a monologue. Even Hegel, who first philosophized the concept of consciousness, declared 'self-consciousness exists in itself and for itself'. But he had to say immediately in the next line ' it is only by being acknowledged or recognized'. Recognized by whom? While Hegel was uncertain about the answer to this question and further complicated this by his idea of "double self-consciousness",[26] the relatively recent post-foundational philosophical ventures ably demonstrated that the self or subjectivity is being constructed against and through the 'significant others'. Charles Taylor, the reputed Hegelian scholar, without mincing words declared

> My discovering of my own identity does not mean that I work it out in isolation but I negotiate it through dialogue, partly overt,

> partly internal, with others...*My own identity crucially depends on my dialogical relations with others.*[27]

If identity could be produced only through dialogue with others, then what was 'the other' by whom Europe made a dialogue to produce its own identity?

V.G. Kiernan, the acknowledged historian of imperialism would help us approach this question (but only to some distance); unlike both Merleau-Ponty and Heller, he accepts and acknowledges the role of other in the production of European identity:

> With its (Europe's) divided soul, as well as its shallower national divisions, it may have been moving toward some kind of unity under the logic of its own inner development, but it was the contrast between itself and the outer world that enabled it most fully to recognize itself and what it had in common.[28]

It should be noted that while he accepts 'the logic of Europe's own inner development' (like Merleau-Ponty and Heller), he at the same time acknowledges the role of the other world in the production of a European identity.

What was the 'other' of Europe? What was the role of this other in the production of European identity? What was its mechanism? In order to answer these questions, Kiernan brings colonialism as a category of explanation. By doing so, he is able to shed new light on the production and circulation of the European identity. He argues that only in the backdrop of the historical colonial situation or the encounter of Europe with the other, the Europeans developed their sense of European consciousness. As far as he is concerned, there were two sources of production of this consciousness: First, the perception of the Europeans about the colonized people. Though the Europeans were divided among themselves along different categories, they encountered their 'commoness' only through realizing how different was of these other people from theirs. In this sense, Kiernan identifies colonialism as an amplifier, which magnifies the hitherto existing commoness of Europeans. He says "Europeans were primarily interested in themselves and much more as Italians and Yorkshiremen than as Europeans: as a rule the outer world was only an amplifier, or a long shadow, making their own sensations more audible or visible to them".[29] The other one was the perception of the colonized people about their colonizers. Through their contorted perception of grouping the entire colonial Europeans as 'white people' (more technically as Frengis), the other played an active role in the production of European identity. Kiernan says "the Malays and Chinese saw not so much difference between one European and another, and this had an effect of reminding them of their kinship".[30]

Thus, for Kiernan, the other had played two roles: on the one hand, it was employed as a passive mirror, where the Europeans themselves realized their commoness. On the other side, they played a more active role by grouping all the Europeans as common stock of people, there by helped Europeans in creating their common identity.

Colonialism and European Consciousness

Kiernan, though sets his arguments differently from both Merleau-Ponty and Heller, surprisingly he too arrives at the same destination, or more accurately an alley where the other two had already reached. This is because of his treating colonialism merely as an identity securing system; as a site, where the Europeans produced the image of themselves and the colonized people in turn help them in this endeavor. These two images were, Kiernan taken for granted, identical and superimposeable. There was no contradiction between them; and that is why for him, colonialism seems to be a mirror or an amplifier, just a mere reflecting or magnifying device of something 'real Europe' that exists both for self and the other.

Mirror or amplifier is a trite metaphor. And Kiernan's use of it does not capture either the complexities or the contradictions inherent in colonialism. On a close dissection, we would find that despite of his bringing the concept of other into the question of European identity, his was not the method that has been propounded by Taylor, that is, a dialogical mode of production of an identity. Rather, his method is also a monologue; a monologue albeit different from the kinds discussed above. Whether in the interior monologue of Merleau-

Ponty or in the exterior monologue of Heller, the agent of monologue is always being Europe. But in the case of Kiernan, it is not one but two monologues; of both the self and other. What is more interesting in the case of Kiernan is his understanding of these two monologues as complementary and complicit with one another in the production of a European identity.

Then what would Taylor say to Kiernan? To be fair to Kiernan, one could not criticize him for having rejected the idea of dialogical production of identity. Taylor's model of the production of identity is an ideal one. For any kind of dialogue needs two equal partners; it is only between the equals and more accurately between the equal friends that a dialogue is possible. But colonial situation was a different one; it was not a partnership but a partisanship on the line of colonizer and colonized. In this circumstance, there could not have been any possibility of having a dialogue. If then, can we have any option except to have to presume that European identity was a product of either a monologue (both the varieties of interior and exterior) on the part of Europe or the monologues of both Europe and its other?

Though one accepts the impossibility of a dialogue between the Europeans and the others, at the same time, one should be critical of the monological methods as exemplified in the works of Merleau-Ponty, or Heller or Kiernan. These scholars made the other either as invisible or non-existent entity or given an imputed voice with secondary fiddling. Is there any other way of imagining the relationship of Europe and its other? I have tried one such an attempt. For me, European consciousness or identity is neither the product of a monologue nor of a dialogue; rather, I would identify it as a product of *ser-monologue*.

The Concise Oxford Dictionary explains the word sermon: (i) discourse on religious or moral subject delivered elsewhere or published; (ii) a piece of admonition or reproof, lecture. In the first case, sermon means a discourse delivered by someone to others. The delivering of the sermon is always meant for the others; and not for the one, he who delivers. So we cannot consider it as a monologue. On the other hand, the listener has no active participation or voice in the discourse; he is a silent spectator. Then the sermon is not a dialogue. Thus, the sermon is neither a monologue nor a dialogue.

In the second case, this word exposes a power relations that exists between the deliverer and the listener of a sermon. He who admonishes the other should be naturally a superior one-like the Yogi to his disciples; a teacher to his student; a father to his son. Therefore, I mean by *ser-monologue* two but interrelated ideas: (i) a moral monologue intended not for the self; but for the others; (ii) a power relationship of the kind superior / inferior, known / unknown and speech / silence. The *ser-monologue* is neither a monologue nor a dialogue; rather a monologue for others - the inferior others; a speech depended on silence; or more accurately a speech which produces silence.

The another aspect of the *ser-monologue* is its nature of 'being addressed'. In one sense, it conveys a performance; a performance of addressing to others of some morals. In another sense, it gives address (or identity) to the one who speaks as superior and the one who listen as inferior. Combined, these two characters make *ser-monologue* as 'addressed'. In both these senses colonialism is a *ser-monologue;* a monologue addressed to the other by the Europeans; and which has given address to both of them as colonized and colonizer, superior and inferior races and civilization and barbarism respectively. Once we understand the nature of this colonial *ser-monologue,* then the remaining question will be what was its content.

The content of the colonial discourse has been thoroughly analyzed and exposed over the years by the so-called condemned "Third world' scholars. From Amilcar Chabral to Fanon, and Edward Said to Indian 'Subaltern Studies' historians all helped us see deep into the interior caves of the colonial horrors. All of them have exposed how the colonial Europeans through their ser-monological discourse had erased the identity of the colonized people. Fanon laments "Because it is a systematic negation of the other person and a furious determination to deny the other person all attributes of humanity, colonialism forces the people it dominates to ask themselves the question: In reality who am I?"[31]

The colonial ser-monologue was not only produced the silence of the others but branded them as savages and inferiors just because of this silence. Edward Said ably demonstrated in his study on orientalism how the so-called civilized Europe through their oriental discourse not only swept away their histories but conveniently enframed them according to their own fancies. One of the most prevalent and worst cruel forms of enframing the other was to consider them as the left-out in the process of history. Blaut termed this tendency as "theory of our ancestors".[32] Even the extreme radical personality of Marx and the later Marxists were not immune to this syndrome. Marx, in a mood of utter callousness and indifference, exonerated the imperialist England from its colonial atrocities just because of his belief of "whatever may have been the crimes of England, she was the unconscious tool of history in bringing about the revolution in India".[33] This Marxist mentality does not change even after the passing of a century and many historical events. Frederick Jameson, the much acclaimed Marxist literary critic, exhorted

> The third world novel will not offer the satisfaction of Proust or Joyce; what is more damaging than that, perhaps, is its tendency to remain of outmoded stages of our own first- world cultural development and to cause to conclude that they are still writing novels like Drieser or Sherwood Anderson. [34]

The Marxists accusation of 'the outmoded stages of third world' is not much different from the highly racial connotation of Saul Bellow's supposed statement quoted in Taylor's: "When the Zulus produce a Tolstoy we would read him".[35] Thus, the *ser-monological* tendency was so prevalent and seeped into all sorts of European thinking, of both radical and racial varieties. With this *ser-monologue* the Europeans were successful in making "the orient receded inexorably into a kind of paradigmatic fossilization" and by this enframing, fossilizing discourse of orientalism, as Said unearthed, the Europeans produced "the imaginary geography"[36] of third-world as orient- a land of snake charmers and heart of darkness.

Both Fanon and Said have demonstrated clearly how Europeans had painted the other with their own colors. Yet, the other side of their argument how the Europeans succeeded in producing an identity for themselves in the very process of the coloring of the other has not been much explored. The Fanonian question 'in reality, who am I?' or the Saidian category of the 'imaginary geography' is *applicable* to Europeans also. As explained above, the *ser-monologue* is always addressed. It not only produces silent listeners but also active speakers. In this sense, the Europeans not only produced the subjugated others but their own superior self identity. While creating a sense of inferiority in the minds of colonized people by inculcating a sense of doubt about 'who am I?', in turn the colonial Europeans found irrefutable answer to the question 'who they are?'.

The *ser-monologue* of Europeans not only created the imaginary geography of the orient; but also of their own, the Europe - a rational and civilized one. Thus, *Europe is an imaginary geography created through and by colonial ser-monologue.* If then, Europe is neither a real geographical entity, nor a civilizational unit, nor even an intuitive consciousness. But, to put it in E.P. Thomson's words used in different context, *Europe is not a thing in itself; but a relationship.*

Europe: A Sign of Power Relationship

What was the purpose of the imagining of Europe? Why they would have to create one such Europe? Exploring these questions will be must before one proceeds to theorize the on-going European integration process. If Europe was a relationship, then what kind of relationship was that? One might easily say, by taking cognition of oppressed condition of the colonialism, it was a power relationship; a relationship which produced one side more powerful over the other; and most importantly, a relationship which sustained and perpetuated this power for ever.

Europe was thus a sign of power relationship. Then what sort of power relationship that it signified? It was not merely a direct military oppression; but rather more persuasive and as well as more pervasive one. Indeed, the Europeans, irrespective of their nationalities, landed in the shores of India to do commerce and business. But gradually they defeated the local dynasties and transformed themselves as the rulers of 'Hindoostan'. Instead of wondering how they had achieved this, it is useful to ask how they were able to rule such vast territories and persuaded the people to be ruled under their suzerainty. The imperial historians of both past and present have used this phenomenon as a supporting and substantiating example for their attempt to project the Europeans as a superior race. But to understand this phenomenon clearly, we have to understand the manifold faces of the power. Foucault explains "power is neither given, nor exchanged, nor recovered, but rather exercised".[37] It is through a particular form of exercise of power that the colonial masters were able to pacify the colonized people and perpetuate their hold over them.

What sort of exercise was that? Again, Foucault would say an exercise designed to "perpetually reinscribe (the power relations) in social institutions, in economic inequalities, in languages, in the bodies themselves of each and every one of us".[38] The magnitude and multitude of this exercise could be seen when almost in all these centuries, from Rammohan Roy to Tagore to Gandhi, all of them once had the strong belief in the inherent progressive nature of the British empire and its destiny in civilizing the people of India. How could the Europeans be able to pacify to that extent? It was through the sermon; by the *ser-monologue* they projected them as morally superior and entitled to admonish the left-out, degenerate, people without history. It was to this purpose, irrespective of the division and plurality, they conceived themselves as superior white race and to contrast the colonial degraded space, they invented the imaginary geography of Europe despite the fact that no such thing existed before or later.

In order to explain this clearly, I would cite an issue that had worried very much the British government in the late 1920s. During this period the Hollywood silent films flooded into India and were being screened almost in all the important cities and by the touring cinema they were even screened in the remote parts of India. These films were immediate success and popular among the masses. But these films had created a peculiar problem for the colonial masters in India. They thought "the lower class of American films does misrepresent western civilization, and lower it in the eyes of Indian".[39] The cautiousness on the part of the British demonstrates how desperate they were in projecting them as morally superior creed than the natives. So they seriously weighed the option of banning such films. Further they contemplated of allowing only the British films under special quotas.

Sensing the government's intention to ban or curtail the screening of the American films, Charles B. Spoffod Jr., the then American Trade Commissioner in India submitted a written statement before the Cinematograph Committee which had been set up to look into these matters. In it, he categorically refuted the British argument by declaring "there is no intention on the part of American film producers to fill their pictures with propaganda of a nature to subvert certain institutions in other countries". The American response clearly demonstrates how the British were worried about their image and the impact of lowering of this image on the institution of colonialism. Interestingly, the American not only gave assurance of not subverting the Europe's colonial institution but it claimed itself the legacy of Europe:

> Even three hundred years is not enough to clear racial tradition and folkways out of a man's consciousness and consciously there is not an American family of educated and semi-educated classes which does not bear in mind knowledge of its particular European decent, near or distant. America is Anglo-Saxon by tradition, custom, speech and law.[40]

These examples demonstrate clearly how the white race of west irrespective of their national difference invented the imaginary landscape of Europe in order to perpetuate their interests and hold over the colonized people.

If Europe was an imaginary geography or the official address of corporate colonial business, how to understand the much harped up and adulated European integration process? An integration of some imaginary geography! The understanding of this irony would be the prerequisite of any understanding of the current integration process.

REFERENCES

1. The story narrated in Hermann Schafer, "Is Europe Ready for Museum?", *German Comments*, no. 50, April 1998, pp. 76-87.
2. It should be noted that a Sanskrit mythic character, Bharatha lends his name to the geography, which later came to be known as Bharath.
3. George Licheim, *The New Europe: Today and Tomorrow* (London, 1964), 2nd ed., p. 3.
4. Jean Gottmann, *A Geography of Europe* (New York, 1954), p.1.
5. Goran Therborn, *European Modernity and Beyond: The Trajectory of European Societies, 1945 – 2000* (New Delhi, London, 1995), p. 34.
6. *International Affairs*, special Issue on "Europe: Where Does It Begin and End?", vol. 76, no. 3, July 2000.
7. Quoted in George W. Hoffman, ed., *A Geography of Europe, Including Asiatic USSR* (London, 1965), 2nd ed., reprint, pp.7-8.
8. Martin Walker, "Variable Geography: America's Mental Maps of a Greater Europe", *International Affairs*, vol. 76, no. 3, July 2000, pp.459 –74.
9. Michel Foucher, "The New Maps of Europe: Fresh or Old Perspectives?", in Carl Grundy-Warr, ed., *Eurasia, World Boundaries, Vol.3* (London, 1994), p.63.
10. Arnold J. Toynbee, *A Study of History*, Abridged Vols. I-IV (London, 1954), 5th Impression, p. 15.
11. Oswald Spengler, *The Decline of the West: Form and Actuality*, trans. Charles F. Atkinson (London), p. 16.
12. Ibid., p.16.
13. J. Merleau-Ponty, "Crisis in Europeans Consciousness", in *Texts and Dialogues*, Hugh J. Silverman and James Barry Jr., ed., (London, 1992), p.14.
14. Paul Valery, "But Who, After All, is European?", in *History and Politics*, trans. Denis Polliot and Jackson Mathews (Princeton, 1978), p. 17.
15. Merleau-Ponty, no.13, p. 14.
16. Her narration of the story of Europe has been traced from chapter 11 "Europe - An Epilogue?", of her book, Agnes Heller and Ferenc Feher, *The Postmodern Political Condition* (Oxford: Polity Press, 1988), p. 146. Original emphasis.
17. Michael Mann, "European Development: Approaching a Historical Explanation", in Jean Baecheler, John A. Hall and M. Mann , ed., *Europe and the Rise of Capitalism* (Oxford: Basil

Blackwell, 1988), p. 12.
18. Agnes Heller, no.16, p. 147.
19. All these quotations are taken from Hegel's "Philosophy of Right and Law", in *The Philosophy of Hegel*, trans and ed., Carl J. Friedrich (New York, 1954), pp. 226-228.
20. Immanuel Wallerstein, *Geopolitics and Geoculture* (Cambridge, 1991), p. 91.
21. Agnes Heller, *Theory of Modernity* (Oxford, 2000), p. 65.
22. Agnes Heller, no. 16, p. 147.
23. Ibid., p. 150.
24. Ibid., p. 150.
25. Paul Valery, no.14, p.5.
26. All these quotes have been taken from Hegel's, "The Phenomenology of Spirit", in *The Philosophy of Hegel*, trans and ed., Carl J. Friedrich (New York, 1954), p. 399.
27. Charles Taylor, " The Politics of Recognition", in David Theo Goldberg, ed., *Multiculturalism: A Critical Reader* (Oxford, 1994), p. 80.
28. Most of my arguments have been developed from chapter 6 "Europe in the Colonial Mirror" in V.G. Kiernan, *Essays on Imperialism* (Boulder, 1993).
29. Ibid., p. 146.
30. Ibid., p. 151.
31. Frantz Fanon, *The Wretched of the Earth* (New York), p. 250.
32. His argument is developed fully in J.M. Blaut, *The Colonizer's Model of the World: Geographical Diffusionism and Eurocentric History* (New York, 1993), p. 16.
33. Karl Marx, "The British Rule in India", in *On Colonialism* (Moscow, 1978), 7th ed., p. 41.
34. Frederic Jameson, "Third World Literature in the Era of Multinational Capitalism", *Social Tex*, vol. 15, Fall 1986, p.65.
35. Quoted in Charles Taylor, no. 27, p. 84.
36. Quotes taken from E. Said, "Orientalism Reconsidered", in Francis Barker, et al., ed., *Literature, Politics and Theory: Papers from the Essex Conference, 1976-84*, (London, 1986), pp. 211, 215.
37. Michel Foucault, "Two Lectures", in Nicholas B. Dirks, Geoff Eley and Sherry B. Ortner, ed., *Culture/ Power/ History: A Reader in Contemporary Social Theory* (Princeton, New Jersey, 1994), p. 208.
38. Ibid., p.209.
39. A British official's oral evidence given before the Indian Cinematograph Committee set up by the Central Legislative

Assembly in 1927. See for more information, *Report of the Indian Cinematograph Committee 1927-28* (Calcutta: Government of India Central Publication Branch, 1928), p. 129.

40. Written statement of American Trade Representative submitted to the Cinematograph Committee, Ibid., p. 298.

Chapter II

The Meaning of Integration in the Cultural History of Europe

In the previous chapter we have seen the problem in defining what Europe is. The various attempts by different scholars ranging from philosophers to historians to sociologists did not provide any convincing definition of Europe. It is still elusive to the philosophical mind and evasive even to the braving assiduous hands of the historians. How could we then surmount this mysterious fugitive nature of Europe? It seems to be that the problem does not lie with the inherent nature of Europe; rather than with the inadequate and inefficient methodologies that these scholars employed in this endeavor. They have heavily relied on and taken for granted one specific *a priori* category, say continent or civilization or consciousness, enough to capturing the essence of Europe. This has inevitably made them land on the swamp replete with surfeit of paradoxes.

To avoid the pitfalls of the earlier studies it is necessary to be cautious over the methodology that should not have given much emphasis either on some concrete manifestations or abstract ramblings. One should be aware that Europe could neither be captured by geographer's charcoal nor the Gothic towers and baroque buildings nor by encompassing on the so-called distinct spirit of Europe. On the contrary, it needs a different method and treatment. One such methodology proposed here is to understand the meaning of the word 'Europe' not through some observable singular empirical fact or by means of abstract, abstruse impersonation. The meaning of Europe lies in the other words, which have been projected on the image of Europe.

The apparent whimsicality and the altogether frivolous nature of the word 'Europe' could only be captured by making montage of some words, which have lend meaning and color to it. It is by identifying such key words that one could solve the methodological problem of the definition of Europe. One can filter out two such words - culture and civilization, which would illustrate the meaning of Europe. The choosing of these words was determined by two reasons: first, the time of the birth of these two words coincided with the imagination of Europe as a distinct landscape; second and most importantly, the change in the meanings of these words in turn produced a corresponding change in the meaning of Europe. That is why no other words except these two could be able to demonstrate both the origin as well as the flux in the meaning of Europe over the centuries. To put it simple, it is by tracing the genealogy of these words that one could write the biography, or even perhaps the biology of Europe.

To be fair, this supposed methodology is not a new one. Indeed, the Annales school historians in France pioneered it in 1930s itself. Broadly known as history of mentality, those historians focused on the history of some words, which they thought, that had amply reflected the social change France witnessed from the Enlightenment period onwards. Lucien Febvre, one of the early pioneers of the Annales school historiography, in his trend setting article "Civilization: Evolution of a Word and a Group of Ideas"(1930) traced the modern history of France along the gradient of the origin and the successive shifts and twists of a single word "civilization'. For him,

> Constructing the history of the French word *civilization* would in fact mean reconstituting the stages in the most profound of all the revolutions which the French spirit has achieved and undergone in the period starting with the second half of the eighteenth century and taking us up to the present day. And so it will mean embracing in its totality, but from one particular point of view, a history whose origins and influence have not been confined with in the frontiers of a single state.[1]

Thus, the very word civilization has become the personification of the modern French spirit. Further, the birth of the word civilization had not only coincided with the birth of the Enlightenment but also became an indices of the successive historical events - the French Revolution to the civilizing mission of France in colonial territories.

Similarly, the British cultural historian Raymond Williams traces the modern British history along the birth and evolution of a single word 'culture'. Having captured the moment of the origin of the word culture in Scottish Enlightenment and the succeeding industrial revolution in the early seventeenth century he conflated the study of the history of modern Britain with study of the history of a word 'culture': "The discovery that the idea of culture and the word itself in its general modern uses, came into English thinking in the period which we commonly describe as that of industrial revolution".[2] What specifically attracts us towards the work of Williams is that of his methodology employed in understanding the industrial revolution by capturing the dynamics of meaning making with the word culture in that period. Culture has thus become a reflective mirror of "our response in thought and feeling to the changes in English society since the late eighteenth century".[3]

Both Fevbre and Williams make a miniature model where the words - civilization and culture become prefecture synonyms of the French and British history respectively. However, the case with Germany differs from these two countries. The German scholars trace their nation's modern history not specifically with either of these words. On the contrary, the German modern history was portrayed along with the development of a one specific German word *Bildung*. The blossoming of the meaning of this word could only be understood in the context of the socio-historical conditions of Germany in the late eighteenth century, when the rhyme of the waves of the Enlightenment of both British and French streams started sweeping the entire Europe.

Germany too caught hold of this new wave and its intelligentsia welcomed it wholeheartedly. Kant's much acclaimed essay "What is Enlightenment?" had not only the best example of the German's acquiescence of the concept but also made it familiarize among the intellectual class of the Germans.[4] Thus the Enlightenment had not only become the domineering philosophical world view but legitimized the French language and the customs and manners of the French court, particularly the court of Louis XIV as the true embodiments of the Enlightenment spirit. So, the French language and manners pervaded all the princely states of Germany and by over some years it had been assumed that being to be an enlightened one was meant to behave like a French.

It was in this context of the French cultural hegemony, the word *Bildung* had become the conceptual currency in Germany. The word owed its origin to the German bourgeois intellectuals. Although the word originated in the lexicon of the German Enlightenment thinkers, it eventually came to be associated with the very idea of opposing the Enlightenment, which was known in Germany as *Aflarung*. Thus the word *Bildung* has assumed its meaning as an oppositional counter-concept of French Enlightenment. The German specific *Bildung* / *Aflarung* dichotomy could only be understood by making sense of the peculiar position of the German bourgeoisie in that period.

Unlike the bourgeoisie of the France and Britain, the German bourgeoisie were relatively kept outside the royal courts and there was a large division existed between the aristocratic and bourgeois sections of the Germany. The German bourgeoisie's invention of the word had two prong strategy: On the one hand, they had opposed the foreign cultural influence over their thought and feelings; on the other hand, they used this concept to accuse their aristocratic counterparts of having imitated the external behaviors of the French.[5] The concept of *Bildung* thus acquired a meaning of cultivation of internal self rather than imitating certain alien influences and shallow exterior sophistication. This artistic notion of self-creation first found its expression in the German literary movement popularly known as 'Strum and Drang' in 1770. The early works of both Goethe and Schiller represented the spirit of *Blidung*.

With French Revolution and the subsequent Napoleon's rise

to power in France and his victory over Prussia (1806-1807) and the struggle for liberation in Germany (1813-15) all had added new vigor and vitality to the seemingly simple dichotomy of *Bildung / Aflarung*. As a consequence, the concept of *Bildung* came out of its literary and educational connotations and acquired the philosophical predilection and political disposition. The German Romantic Movement (1790-1830) both in literature and philosophy further transformed the dichotomy of *Bildung / Aflarung* into a more complex and oppositional polarities - *Kultur and Zivilization*. Unlike the thinkers of France and Britain, the German romantic scholars did not presume culture and civilization as synonymous and interchangeable concepts. On the contrary, they saw them as squarely opposing mutual poles. While civilization represented a mere external transformation of material existence, individuality and capacity of reasoning of the human beings, culture was considered to be a more personal and even perhaps the spiritual aspect of existence with emphasis on the community and fellow feelings.

Kroeber and Kluckhohn in their classic study have identified two different but complementary German approaches towards culture.[6] The first stream known as *volk* notion of culture evolved from the writings of Herder. His was an ethnographic conception where culture was presumed as an inherited and still inheritable permanent resource that could be employed against any foreign influences. This shared cultural consciousness could be perceptible only when there was a reflective activity of self - understanding, that is, *Bildung*. His simple proposition was that the Germanic people could preserve them against the onslaught of the French cultural imperialism by making conscious of and preserve their historically distinct cultural tradition. The second stream known as *geistlich* notion of culture found its origin in the later writings of Schiller. In his version of culture, he emphasized the collective creative potential of the Germans. For him, the Germanic culture was not a 'it-is-there-to be- inheritable category' as Herder visualized; rather the Germanic culture, he argued, was to be created in fullness - philosophic and creative, sensitive and energetic by the German peoples.

Whatever may be the internal difference over defining what is German culture, the one commonality that they shared with was its supposed opposition to the French notion of civilization. Silvia Federici has well captured this opposition as "the civilization/culture dichotomy originated in post-Napoleonic Germany, when in the aftermath of the nation's defeat, German culture (defined as a spiritual entity) was opposed to the external exteriorized French civilization".[7] The same critical outlook was echoed by John Rundell and Stephen Mennell with even more in depth analysis:

> In their hands [i.e. Germans], *zivilisation* came to mean 'something which is indeed useful, but nevertheless only a value of the second rank, comprising only the outer appearance of human beings, the surface of human existence'. In contrast, it was through the word *kultur* that German intellectuals expressed their own pride, achievements and identity, and it came to be associated, in contrast to the *zivilisation* of the court - the superficiality, ceremony, polite conversation - with inwardness, depth of feeling, immersion in books, development of the individual personality, with all that was natural, real and genuine... So, at first, the antithesis of *zivilisation* and *kultur* expressed exclusion and exclusivity.[8]

Thus, for Federici and John Rundell and Stephen Mennell, the idea of the antithesis of *kultur* and *zivilisation* was the ideological apparatus in the hands of German scholars to make the German nation independent in the milieu of threatening French subjugation both politically and culturally.

However, Lionel Gossman has imputed a hermanutical problem into the supposed idea of *kultur* and *zivilisation*. Though he shares the idea of spiritual revival of the German nation and its existential antagonism with the enlightened France, he sees a historical precedent of the antithetical position in the Greek and Latin tradition of the European history. His logic of reasoning runs like this:

> The opposition of *zivilisation* and *kultur* - a cliché of German kulturkritik or culture criticism, *zivilisation* being a kind of artificial culture, an external polishing, an accumulated treasury of knowledge and techniques, *kultur* an *inner*, 'organic'

> development, a creative potential, a 'natural' culture, so to speak - conveys very well the term in which a greatness of patriotic and idealist Germans rejected the 'artificial' Latin tradition, both in the form of the aristocratic French culture that had imposed itself on the courts and ruling classes of Germany in the 17th and 18th centuries ...[9]

It should be noted that Gossman moves beyond the other scholars' interpretation of the antithesis and sees in it not only the French and German national rivalry but in addition to that he stresses the conflict over reviving and bringing of either Latin or Greek tradition in to the modern Europe alive. That is, in his hands the antithesis has got an added meaning where it not only represents the French - German rivalry but also the modern predicament of Europe and its meaning.

'Antithesis of Culture and Civilization' as a Methodology

The theory of the antithesis of culture and civilization has thus assumed the role of explanatory device to demonstrate the rise of German nationalism in the early years of the nineteenth century. However, in the late nineteenth and early twentieth centuries the specific German national orientation of the concept of the antithesis of culture and civilization had come out of the German experience and got transported as a universal category of explanation of modernity. This was the moment of birth of the different branches of the Social Sciences. From then on, the idea of the antithesis has acquired methodological significance in the domains of Social Sciences to explain the new phenomenon of modernity both within Europe and where ever modernity spreads.[10]

A comprehensive exposition of the methodological appropriation and utilization of the concept of this antithesis of culture and civilization is necessary here because I intend to bring this methodology into the study of the European integration. Sigmund Freud is the best example to start with. He brought the idea of antithesis to explain the psychological trap in which the Modern Man destined to fall. For him, civilization is a process by which man reaches the specific modern condition, whereby his natural life instinct has been suppressed and disciplined by the reasoned intellect. This self-suppressing unnatural condition of civilization is the fountainhead of all the psychological problems of the pathetic modern man. Further, he argues the civilization has killed the creative instinct in the man and instead moulds him in to the repetitive mechanical life.[11] It should be noted that in the hands of Freud the supposed German idea of antithesis has elevated as an explanatory category of the modern universal man.

Similarly, following closely on the heels of Freud, Oswald Spengler has further developed the idea of antithesis and effectively woven around this idea a methodology to write the history of what he considered as the rise and fall of Western Civilization.[12] Culture, for Spengler, means a natural organism. Like any other organism culture too is bound to have an evolutionary growth. He further stretched his argument that the civilization is the highest stage and the culminating or in more accurate sense terminating point where the natural growth of a culture comes to stop. Thus for him, civilization means a spent out, barren stage from then on the only possible course of movement could be towards decadence and finally death of a civilization. The world history, he would say, is the burial ground witnessed the cyclical rise and death of so many civilizations. What is interesting to us here is Spengler's extraordinary transposition of the idea of German antithesis into a philosophy of world history.

Again, it was in the field of sociology that the idea of antithesis of culture and civilization found its ultimate expression and utilization as an effective methodology.[13] The early pioneers of German sociology like Max Weber, Simmel, Max Scheler et.al improvised the idea of antithesis into the paradigm of tradition / modernity dichotomy. Particularly Weber understood modernity as a civilizational process where individualism, bureaucratization and impersonalization of everyday relationships were the defining characteristics. On the contrary, he brought culture as a domain of tradition where organic communal relationship conditioned the day to day life process. In this paradigmatic schema, his sociological works reflected the same sentiments of the earlier German romantic thinkers.

The sociologist Alfred Weber, the younger brother of Max Weber was even more categorical in utilizing the idea of antithesis for the purpose of sociological analysis. He distinguished both the terms, culture and civilization as,

> Civilization represents the human effort to conquer the world of nature and culture by means of intelligence in the spheres of science, technology and planning... Culture, as distinct from civilization, is based on the realization of the mind, of the philosophical and emotional self.[14]

Thus, the younger Weber unlike his brother perceived the antithesis as a division of external and internal domains of modern man and set to synthesize the two domains through his theory of culture-sociology.[15]

While the first generation German sociologists developed the idea of antithesis of culture and civilization into a well drawn out methodology to depict the binary polarities of tradition / modernity or external / internal dimensions of the modern man, the second generation sociologists, particularly Norbert Elias transformed it as a methodology to explain the origin of nation-state in Europe. For him, the moment of birth of nationalism in Europe could be gauged from capturing the moment of shift from the universalistic notion of civilization to discreet national cultures.[16] Similarly, the French anthropologist Louis Dumont has effectively used the antithesis idea to extricate what he calls the phenomenon of "global acculturation to modernity".[17] Like Max Weber, he too understands civilization as modernity and culture as traditional non-modern category. But for him every traditional culture has to modernize itself; that is to accept the modern civilization. However, he demonstrates that the civilizing of every cultures is not identical and linear. Rather, each culture accommodates modern civilization selectively and in its own terms and conditions. Thus for Dumont the idea of antithesis signifies the different patterns of acculturation of modernity.

So far we have comprehensively posited the specific historical origin of the idea of antithesis of culture and civilization and its conceptual elaboration and methodological utilization in the successive periods. This idea has been effectively used as a method to explain the psychological condition of modern man, ontological cycle of world history, and sociological process of global modernity. If it has been so effective in the fields of psychology, history and sociology, then would it not also be useful in the study of European integration? In fact, understanding the integration process in the framework of some binary opposition is not new to the integration study. The binary framework of war and peace and nationalism and post-nationalism are the two major theoretical premises which have been employed to explain the integration process over the years.

However, these two frameworks treated the process of integration as a universal one and neglected the internal dissention and division of Europe. In this context, by bringing the yet another binary of culture and civilization and its mutually opposing tendencies visible within the history of Europe, the remaing of this chapter would interpret the European integration as an attempt to reconcile the antithesis of culture and civilization. Thus the idea of antithesis has two fold purpose in the study of integration: first, to prove that Europe was and is never a single identifiable unit; exactly this point has been elaborated in the previous chapter. Second to interpret that European integration process is nothing but an attempt to synthesis the antithesis that has been plaguing the entire course of European history or at least from the medieval period onwards. This point will be taken up in this chapter.

I

Norman Hampson was absolutely right and justified when he commented "Historians, in their search for origins, always tend to push back the beginning of what they are studying".[18] When the mainstream International Relations pinned down the origin of European integration to the subsequent two World Wars, the historians tend to push it back to the possible extent. One writer went to the extent of saying,

> A united Europe is not a new idea. By 14th century BC, Augustus Caesar had consolidated a vast Roman Empire with a single

> currency. Others like Charlamagne, Napoleon and Hitler have since tried to create great European empires albeit by force rather than by mutual agreement.[19]

This discursive practice makes Europe an idea immortal across time and space. The essentialised reading of history promotes an idea of 'perpetual presence of Europe' right from the *ancient regime* of Hellenic metaphysics, Roman jurisprudence, Medieval Latin Christendom to the Modern Enlightenment. Douglas Johnson identified this trend as "a school of history which emphasises the existence of Europe as an entity over many centuries...(Sic) thereby the creation of some sort of federation in present-day Western Europe can be seen as a return to source rather than as a sudden invention".[20]

There is no consensus among the historians about the source of emergence of the European idea. As we have seen, some have attributed it to the ancient Romans who consolidated the entire west and north-western Europe under their suzerainty. Some have identified the medieval Latin Christendom which had created an "Holly Roman Empire' under the rule of Charlemagne. The historian Lord Gladwyn[21] gives credit to King Charlemagne having established a united political unit roughly covering the present day European Union territory. Whereas Braudel[22] attributes to King Charles V, the idea of creating a European entity, which was abandonee by his son Philip II who was more Ibero-Atlantic.

However, the other school of historians dismiss these claims of European idea. They have pointed out the alleged European unity of both Charlemagne and Charles V were of empire building, not of an outcome of a genuine European idea. As far as they are concern, the genuine non-hegemonic idea of Europe emerged only during the Enlightenment. It was visible, they say, in the writing of French *philosephs*, English empiricists and German idealists. They trace some kind of history of idea of Europe from the writings of Erasmus of 16th century through Abbe de Saint-Pierre (1658-1743), Rousseau, Kant, Saint-Simon (1760-1825). Particularly, the specific work of Kant's 'Perpetual Peace'[23] influenced the latter thinkers to have to achieve a federal Europe. Kant in that work with a rational argument emphasised the confederal cooperation would be the final progressive step towards attaining a perpetual peace in Europe.

But it was during the inter war period (1919-39), there were mushrooming of works arguing persuasively to achieve the federal goal. Identified as 'liberal idealists'[24], these scholars stressed that to prevent any future war in Europe it had to federate. Particularly the works of Norman Angell, H.G. Wells, W.B. Curry and C.E.M. Joad et.al. Emphasised the need to unite Europe.

II

The ancient Greece is a subconscious, surrealistic phantasm that haunts Europe even today. It is still considered as a mystery pregnant with solutions for the present day puzzles of Europe. It is being said that a systematic decoding of that mystery would help unravel the nature and the historical course of Europe. In this sense, Greece means origin; the origin of politics and philosophy, arts and science. Tracing the continuity from the archaic Greece to present or at least comparing the present with the past of Greece is the normal and prevalent methodological premise in social sciences research. Whether on the question of totalitarianism (Popper, 1966), democracy (Josiah Ober et.al., 1994) or philosophy (Russel, 1961), the ancient Greece is presumed as the proper starting point.[25]

One striking common feature that all these studies share is that the existing historical moment determined their understanding of the ancient Greece. Under the thick clouds of Stalin's Russia and Hitler's Germany, Popper started tracing a genealogy of totalitarianism and found it in the figure of Plato. At the same time Athenian democracy has been cited as a predecessor of American one. Similarly, Kissinger compared the cold war with the Peloponeasian war. Thus, the ancient Greece is considered to be an originating point or a counter signature to whatever Europe experienced and still experiencing in the modern phase. If that were the case, then how could the ancient Greece illuminate the seemingly specific post-cold war phenomenon of the European integration? Or otherwise, what is the presumed thematical chain that might have linked the archaic Greece with the explicitly modern phenomenon of European integration?

One who follows the discourse of the current European integration process would not have missed the frequent circulation of the image of ancient Greece as a legitimizing technique. Those who support the integration move invariably emphasize the legacy of the ancient Greece to subordinate their claim to perennial, unbroken cultural unity of Europe. One historian, in his unconcealed zeal to see European political unity declared emphatically,

> We Europeans are the children of Hellas. Our civilization, which has its roots in the brilliant city life of the eastern Aegean, has never lost traces of its origin, and stamps us with a character by which we are distinguished from the other great civilizations of the human family, from the Chinese, the Hindus, the Persians, and the Semites.[26]

Even the official European Union documents and speeches claim these days the legitimacy of the hoary, classical Greek culture to imparting a sense of legitimization to their integration drive.

Here it must be stated in clear terms that the intention of bringing the ancient Greece into the question of European integration is not based on any conviction of believing in the cultural continuity that exists between the archaic Greece and the present day Europe. Rather, its purpose rests somewhere else: To reflect on an irony that was inherent in the nature of the ancient Greece; and by unfolding of this irony try to comprehend the present on going integration process. It might be asked, why despite the common Olympic Gods and festivals and even more glaringly, the experience of facing a common Persian enemy, the Greeks never tried to construct a single unified political structure replacing the numerous, quarrelsome warring city-states. Thucydides, the celebrated historian of the Peloponeasian war, amply demonstrated in his work how the ancient Greece was ruptured and devastated by the internal wars and conflicts.

In their overwhelming enthusiasm for having to achieve their desired goal of European unity, the protagonists of European integration resorted to uncritical reflection on ancient

Greece. Their arguments, hence, have only propagandist value. On the contrary, any sensible understanding of European integration should start with the paradox of the Greek antiquity. Even though the Greeks had shared a common cultural space and enviable collective civilizational achievements, they never minded or even desired to have a single overarching political set up covering the entire Hellas.

The only modern European thinker who touched upon this paradox, although for different purpose and in different context was Hegel. For him,

> Greek ethics made Hellas unfit to form one common state. For the necessary condition of that degree of freedom which the Greek achieved was the existence of many small states separate from one another, and the concentration of life in the cities where the interest and spiritual culture pervading the whole could be the same for all.[27]

Hegel known for his love and longing for synthesizing every oppositional antitheses, employed the same strategy to explain the supposed Greek antithesis of cultural unity and political diversity. His line of reasoning runs like this: for Greek the ultimate objective goal was to reach the pinnacle of spiritual personality where their imaginative potential and creative instinct could excel and transcend the material constraints of the abject existence. This transcendental longing could be translated into a reality only when the state must be small. Hegel once again reemphasized what Plato and Aristotle envisioned and encouraged through their philosophical presuppositions. It was only within the small states that they were able to have achieved their creative spiritual excellence.

Thus, in Hegel's argument, the division of Hellas into a numerous city-states (*polis*) was the essential precondition for their achievement in other fields. Further the division of Hellas into a number of political ensembles which might have breeded acrimonious wars among themselves did not jeopardize the spiritually endowed cultural unity. To put it simply, the ancient Greece was an enticing ensample where cultural unity could not and need not promote the corresponding political unity.

The same line of argument can be traced from the writings

of Nietzsche also. He considered *polis*, philosophy and tragedy were the three peaks of Greek culture. Disclosing an abject apathy towards the division of city-states, Nietzsche explained how the distinct invention of Greek tragedy played a unifying force uniting the Greeks spiritually as well as aesthetically.[28] It was neither the rhetorics of Pericles nor the crafty philosophical musings of the Sophists that had united Greece spiritually; rather, Nietzsche would argue, the creative instinct of the tragedians - Aescylus and Sophocles and their theatrical spectacles in the majestic ampitheaters that had actually united them forever.

Thus for both Hegel and Neitsche, in spite of the political divisions of ancient Greece, the Hellas behaved as if it were a single organic unit - for Hegel philosophically and for Nietzsche aesthetically. To stretch their arguments further, integration in the archaic Greek lexicon meant philosophic and aesthetic meanings and not of smacking any slightest tinge of political connotation of entrusting centralized political unification. In a sense, one can say that the ancient Greek was a philosophic idea, rather than a political one that had reflected in its reluctance in having formed any sort of unified political set up. In this context only one can understand Deleuze and Guattari's delaration "Philosophers are strangers; but philosophy is Greek".[29]

Then one cannot resist asking the question: If the ancient Greek resisted the temptation of having political integration, then had Europe, which claims to be the sole inheritor of the Hellanic legacy not violated the Greek spirit and ethos by deliberately moving towards a solution of having to establish a common overarching political organization for the entire Europe through its integration drive? The only possible way that the ancient Greece can at all have an influence over the on going European integration debate is to provide a modular form of unification that would not encourage any eventual political integration but for some spiritual cultural unity.

On the contrary, the succeeding emergence of Roman Empire however offered a different model to be emulated. It should be remember that under the Roman *imperium* Europe came under single centralized political control with its center in Rome. That is why, the European integration process has been interpreted as a wishful longing for reviving the glory of the distant Roman Empire. However, it should be noted that the Roman Empire though had brought the entire Europe under one political organization, it was not a one coherent cultural unit as in the case of ancient Greece. In a stark contrast it was a multicultural and polyethnic cosmopolitan composition, where the reign of sword of Caesar made the people come under one roof rather than the shared and treasured common spiritual outlook.[30]

Europe, thus, has before its hands two modular forms of integration where the Greeks emphasized the philosophical unity while the Latin Romans developed a political union in the form of empire. However, the Greeks failed to translate their philosophical unity into a political one. To put it in the words of Hannah Arendt, Greeks were constrained by the "problem of translating from philosophical to political idiom".[31] On the contrary, the Romans brought political unification in the guise of empire but without any cultural unity or philosophical vision. That the word integration assumed two different meanings in the ancient period: philosophical and political. With the arrival of Christianity, Europe witnessed one more shift in the meaning of the word integration: this time, an act of synthesis of the antithesis of philosophy and politics.

Christianity and European Integration

At the Asiatic corner of the Roman Empire, there emerged a distinctively radical religion - the Christianity. Though blossomed in the ancient land of Israel, it had gradually traveled to the European part of the empire. Initially, it had to have faced the oppressive subjugation in the hands of the Roman Emperors. But in 313 AD the emperor Constantine removed all the suppressive legislatures and in 380 AD Christianity had become almost the official and lawful religion of the empire.

The interesting aspect of the coming of Christianity in Europe was its unification of the different ethnic and racial groups under the Holy Grail and the Universal Church. What the brute and carnal march of the Roman legionaries failed to achieve over the centuries, the simple and simplistic religion of the distant land achieved in the name of Jesus Christ. Thus, Christianity had inculcated a sense of philosophical unity to the internally divided empire. But, the greatest irony was that while the empire, for a first time was being united under one catholic philosophy, the political edifice of the very Roman Empire started crumbling. When the Alaric the Goth captured the Rome in 410 AD, he began to destroy the entire structure of the empire without any pinch of hesitation, but nevertheless accepted the supposed official religion of the empire and kept it intact. Philosophical unity of Europe was dawned on the debris of the Roman Empire. Once again Europe reverted to condition of the antiquity of the Greece where the philosophical unity was preserved at the cost of political unity.

With the arrival of Christianity in Europe, the centuries old antithesis of philosophy and politics got transported into new idioms. This has been well captured by Russel, the historian of the western philosophy:

> The medieval world, as contrasted with the world of antiquity, is characterized by various forms of dualism. There is the dualism of clergy and laity, the dualism of Latin and Teuton, the dualism of kingdom of God and kingdom of this world, the dualism of the spirit and the flesh. All these are exemplified in the dualism of Pope and Emperor.[32]

Out of these lists of dualism, the one which directly concerns us very much and relevant to the question of integration is the dualism of Pope and Emperor. While Pope symbolizes the philosophically endowed cultural unity, the Emperor was identified with the political unity of Europe. Almost the entire Middle Ages (400 AD to 1400 AD) Christianity strove to overcome this pressing antithesis of Pope and Emperor. Through out these periods, intellectual energy was directed towards what Russel called 'Catholic synthesis"[33] of sacred and temporal matters.

When we historicize the discourse of the integration of Europe, its genealogy could at least extend over to the late medieval period. With the decline and fall of the Roman Empire

Europe lost the one overarching political set-up that had so far united it. Even the establishment of the Universal Roman Catholic Church failed to unite Europe politically, though it had succeeded in uniting the people along one single religious belief. Here Europe landed in a delicate pathological schizophrenia where it had united as a sacred space under the Holy Grail but nevertheless remained divided in a temporal plane. To overcome this division of sacred and temporal space, one stream of the medieval scholars emphasized the necessity of Pope himself assuming the responsibility of temporal aspect of living. This line of argument could be found in St. Augustine's book "The City of God".

St. Augustine (354-430 AD) was the first Christian scholar who had undertaken the project of uniting the Europe or what was generally known at that time as Christendom. His was the conscious attempt to reconcile the emerging institutional structure of Catholic Church and the already existing empire. However, his attempt was purely based on his theological underpinnings. His book divided the universe into two realms: earthly commonwealth and heavenly commonwealth. Due to the original sin, man condemned to suffer in the realm of earthly domain. In order to redeem oneself from this sin, one has to pray for his salvation and peace with the heavenly commonwealth. The authority of Pope and the church was considered to be the agency helping man to reach the heavenly abode.

On the contrary, the emperor was given the authority over the mundane matter, who in actuality prevents one from committing further sin in the world. Or other wise, according to the saint, the emperor help people approach the pope and the church for the final salvation. In this sense, the saint had given a subordinate role to the emperor to carry on his avowed duty in the world. The Pope is a Prime Mover, something like God. He is the source of the cosmic order, of all movement, and of the legal rights of princes and nations. The Emperor receives his temporal power from him, just as the moon receives the light it reflects from the sun. All authority derives from the Pope. Thus, by clearly demarcating the realm of human existence and again by envisioning the role of Emperor in the service of the Pope, the saint successfully synthesized the institutions of papacy and empireship; or a successful integration of Europe both philosophically and politically.

His theory or more accurately his theology had indeed encouraged the emergence of Carolingian Empire in Europe. In a longing for the revival of the antique Roman Empire, the Pope had delegated the governance of temporal matters to the one Frankish ruler known as Charlemagne in 800 AD. Charlemagne's Europe was a sacerdotal empire.[34] The conflicts over 'Investiture claims' put an end to its spiritual unity. What mattered now, what was the subject of passionate interest, was the struggle for primacy between Empire and Papacy. The two parties based their claims on the one and common idea of Christendom. Then the idea of Europe staged a dim re-emergence, as the new symbol of a unity that so far had been taken for granted. But the nascent empire did not withstand the course of history despite the blessing and support of the Pope.

In spite of this failure, the attempt to revive the edifice of empire did not altogether vanished. Once again, in 962 AD, the empire was resurrected in the new tag of Holy Roman Empire. From then onwards, Europe caught trapped in a web of controversy over the question of who is the supreme controller and around whose insignia that the entire Christendom should be united and revolved. Now, however, the Pope is opposed by the Emperor. According to Marcilius of Padua, the true repository of all authority is the Pope, who delegates it to the Emperor. The Emperor thus represents the fullness of jurisdiction. Apart from him, there is no authority. The Church can admonish, enlighten the souls; the Emperor rules the earth. On the contrary, St. Thomas Aquinas (1225-1274) emphasized the overarching suzerainty of Pope over the rule of Emperor.[35] However, at the same time, he underlined the necessity of having one temporal ruler for the entire Christian world.

The same sentiment and support for the Emperor echoed more convincingly and categorically in the works of Dante. He was the towering personality who had almost overshadowed the entire horizon of the late 13th and early 14th centuries mental landscape of Europe. His political philosophy was impersonated with his poetical imagination. Though he accepts the medieval concept of *corpus Christianum,* he differs with his contemporaries in entrusting the Emperor as the epicenter of the corpus not the Pope as used to be. The Pope had only the authority over the otherworldly matters. He and his church as far as Dante was concerned, might have been the holders of the key to the heavenly abode but they had nothing to do with this worldly affairs, which was the legitimate and divinely ordained domain of the Emperor. For him, "the temporal monarchy, which men call 'empire', is a single sovereign authority set over all others in time, that is to say over all authorities which operate in those things and over those things which are measured by time".[36] Thus the Emperor, like Pope has the cosmic purpose and hence he cannot be the subordinate to the papacy.

Like the universe and all the objects in it are created and set in a single movement from a source of motion, that is God, the world is also in need of a single source of order and motion. For this purpose, Dante argues, "there must be one person, who directs and rules mankind, and he is properly called 'Monarch' or 'Emperor'. And thus it is apparent the well being of the world requires that there be a monarchy or empire".[37] Having thus established the cosmic purpose of the existence of the Emperor, Dante proceeds to envision him as the sole restorer of the universal peace, and lawgiver.

All these philosophical endeavors aimed to carve out an independent and legitimate space for the existence of the Emperor. Where Dante differed from the rest of the medieval thinkers was his sense of history. While the rest of the scholars were engaged in the debate of Pope vs Emperor along the theological line, he was the first thinker of the kind, introduced a historical argument in support of the empire. In this sense, he was the initiator of the kind of discourse that is visible and much audible in the domain of today's European integration.

Having argued that monarchy was the divinely ordained cosmic role to play, the original revelation of monarchy happened only in the Roman era. Before it, the Persian Xerxes and Macedonian Alexander tried to erect such a universal monarchy. But they all had miserably failed in their endeavors albeit for different reasons. However, it was only during the Roman imperium that the *real* universal monarchy was established. Dante reasoned it, Romans were the God's chosen people to erect such a universal monarchy in the image of His Heavenly Kingdom. Thus the Roman Empire was the will of God on earth or His providential plan for humanity. Dante has thrust upon the historical Roman Empire a cosmic aura. By sheer potential of his poetic mind, Dante was able to synthesis the politically engrained world of Roman Empire with the cosmology of Christianity. His was the longing of the resurrection of Rome once again, but in the form of *Pax Romana-Christiana*.[38]

The reader of *De Monarchia* may observe the success and versatility of Dante in not only overcoming the diabolical dichotomy of Pope/Emperor, but even more persuasively blended the ancient Roman world with the medieval Christian universe. However, what attracts or surprise us more is Dante's almost effortless but flawless blending of philosophy and politics whose oppositional antithesis made the Greeks and Romans choose either of them. His synthesizing of these two domains is yet another modular example for the current European integration. Even though, his was not a new model, where his uniqueness does matter in the case of present integration is his blending of the earlier Greek and Roman models. In Dante's sense political unity had philosophical purpose.

European Movement: Towards Empire or Federation?

One of the fundamental paradoxes of history is that it repeats itself one way or another. When the 17th and 18th centuries philosophers distinctively strive for the creation of a viable political unity of Europe, out of the numerous billiard-ball states through their philosophical theorizing, Napoleon tried to achieve it by his sword. The same history repeated once again when the intellectuals of Europe of the 20th century, standing in the midst of First World War, cried for European unification, Hitler with the help of his tanks and artilleries, almost brought the entire Europe under his command. The inter war period witnessed two distinguished tendencies which shaped the future European unity movement. On the one hand, there had been attempts to impose unity through hegemony by force; on the other hand, there had also been schemes for a peaceful, voluntary association of states on terms of equality. To put it in nutshell, Europe was destined to choose either Nazi Empire or European Federation. Anyhow, the subsequent World War turned the stream of history towards the second option.

Indeed, after the First World War, there emerged four kinds of discourse aiming to change the future course of European destiny. First was the Wilsonian vision of international system of states based on national self-determination and international law. His fourteen points principles along with the creation of 'League of Nations' were intended to promote and preserve order and security in Europe. The Versailles Treaty of 1919 created new states like Poland, Czechoslovakia and Yugoslavia and redrew the political map of Europe. It was expected that the creation and assurance of national self-determination along with the 'League of Nation' would become an alternative to either empire building or federation.

The second discourse was the idea of European federation. The sheer carnage of 1914-1919 war propelled the European liberal thinkers to dream a kind of European federation. These liberal thinkers thought that the League of Nations was a compromise formula, aiming status quo mechanism and correctly believed that it would not solve the seething trouble Europe facing at that time. They were proved right by the events of 1939, when Hitler emerged triumphantly by collapsing the Wilsonian vision of Europe into dust. On the contrary, they argued passionately for the creation of European federation separately, or at least with in the parameters of the League of Nations.

Walter Lipgens vividly reflects the general ambians and moods of this liberal thinkers of that period as,

> During the war (First World War) several intellectuals embarked on a passionate search for European self-awareness – a look back

> at the past, a thorough investigation into what European civilisation really consisted of, a conscious rediscovery of the unity of European values as an indispensable preliminary to the political unification which was beginning to seem imperative.[39]

Authors like Ernest Barker[40], Walter Alison[41] and Eric Woolf wholeheartedly argued for the creation of European federation. The only rational path that leads Europeans to Heaven, they said, was to federation. Even one thinker went to the extent of warning Europeans to 'Federate or perish'[42].

One of the rallying point or a recurrent theme of this liberal federalist was the issue of decline of Europe. For centuries, the European states dominated and colonised the entire world. But because of their internecine war of 1914 wrecked a great damage to their power and prestige. More pathetic was that the US once their colony had to intervene in the European affairs to set things right. Importantly this war had destroyed the economic superiority of Europe and created massive unemployment and depression of the state, which it witnessed during 1930s. This bleak and gloomy future of Europe compelled these thinkers to declare the 'bankruptcy of nationalism'[43] and announce that 'only the determination to construct a great nation from the group of peoples of the continent would give new life to the pulses of Europe".[44]

Many organisations were started to spearhead the idea of European federation. The most important and somewhat visible one was 'pan-Europe' movement started by Count Coudenhove-Kalergi.[45] He was an Austrian aristocrat of mixed European-Japanese parenthood and met all the European States leaders and mobilised public opinion in favour of federation during 1920s. He wrote a book called "Pan Europa" published in 1923 to popularise the idea of the Union. He staunchly campaigned for the creation of European constitution for the entire Europe like the American experience of 1776. Under his initiation, in November 1926, the famous *Entente Internationale de'l Alier* was signed. This agreement regulated the production of steel by German, French, Belgium and Luxembourg firms on the basis of agreed quotas and thus laid the foundation for the future European Coal and Steel Community Treaty in 1951.

Similarly, in France, during the early 1930s one federalist movement called *Ordre Nouveau* was founded by Arnaud Dandieu and Robert Aron. These federalists declared that Europe was experiencing a crisis of civilisation. In their book *'La Rivoluiton necessaire'*, they expressed 'the present crisis is not simply a social, national or economic crisis; it is a crisis of consciousness".[46] Hence, they pleaded for strong coherent European consciousness, which they believed, would liberate Europe from its current crisis.

Italy too witnessed a surge of Europeanism in this period. An influential book by two Italians Giovanni Angelli and Attilio Cabiatti, "European Federation or League of Nations?"[47] initiated the debate about the desirability of moving federal Europe. The idea of Pan-Europeanism was also percolated into some of the literary works of that time. Robert Briffault's novel[48] "Europe: A Novel of the Age of Ignorance"(1935) and its sequel "Europa in Limbo" (1937) strongly pleaded for a kind of Euro-federation to regain the supremacy and glory of Europe once again.

In Britain, the Federal Union Movement was started more or less at the same time. However, it differed from the other movements in a sense, its aim was not a single European state, rather the division of sovereignty of states and assigning portion of it to different organs of government'[49] . The British federalist criticised their counterparts in other European countries, as their idea of Europe was 'Latin or Cartesian'. Spinelli distinguishes their different approaches as,

> The Latin people always thought that in terms of well-spelled out written constitutions, while the British, whose political system is based on an unwritten constitution, were supposed to apply the empirical approach in the field of international cooperation.[50]

When these two streams of thought – the Descartian Cartesian approach or Lockean empiricist approach, had loggerhead with each other, history surprised them as usually both streams of thinkers and the rest of the world.

Two different but challenging discourses emerged against this European idea in this period. The one distinctively radical communist discourse that had triumphantly emerged after the successful October Revolution of Russia in 1917, challenged the inherently aristocratic, conservative claims to the European federalism. Rather it pitched its voice against both nationalism and Europeanism and invited the 'workers of the world to unite'. Inherently, this international outlook of communism that questioned the backwardness of the European geographical determinism. Thus communists encountered the bourgeois call for Europeanism, with their call for internationalism.

Even before the Revolution, Lenin in 1915 declared that under capitalist conditions the idea of establishing such a federation was either impossible or merely a reactionary manoeuvre. To put it his own words:

> Of course, temporary agreements are possible between capitalists and between states. In this sense a United States of Europe is possible as an agreement between the European capitalists.. but to what end? Only for the purpose of jointly suppressing socialism in Europe, of jointly protecting colonial booty against Japan and America.[51]

Thus Lenin saw two pronged strategy of the creation of European federation: the bourgeois strategy to quell the burgeoning voice of socialism that had been raising in Europe; on the other hand, to pool their energies collectively to enhance the unimpeded colonial exploitation in Africa and Asia and to outpour the American and Japanese challenge in this exploitation.

Nazism and Idea of Europe

The fourth discourse on Europeanism, which had not only been expressed through concrete manifestations but also set Europe into an unbelievable violence and destruction is Nazism. Hitler's constricted racial outlook coloured and contextualised the European movement. Hitler out and rightly attacked both – the European idea and the Asiatic Bolshevism. In one of his propaganda speeches he meticulously linked these two issues to define his notion of what Europe was:

> Europe is not a geographical conception, it is a matter of the blood

> in ones veins; the real frontiers between Europe and Asia is the one that separates Germanic world from the Slav World. It is our duty to place it where we want to be.[52]

Hitler's discourse revolved around two axes: defining Europe from the outside and cleaning it inside. He constructed an identity for Europe by exclusively placing it against the communism. He argued it was the 'common European destiny'[53] that led him to undertaken the 'crusade against Bolshevism'.[54] By defining Europe was different from the rest, particularly from Asia, he further turned into the European soil. For him whoever resided and lived in Europe were not Europeans. He particularly singled out the Jews and condemned them as Asiatic-Semitic people who connived with and propagated communism in Europe.

Hitler, thus, made Europe in a single stroke (with a painter's ability!) a synonym for the "Teutonic Empire of the German Nation".[55] Europe was thus defined as the sum of all those peoples whom Destiny had united under German leadership to ward off the 'Asiatic – Jewish-Bolshevik', threat on the one hand and Anglo-American encroachment on the other.[56]

It is interesting to note that not only Hitler's definition of Europe was different from others but also his means and methodology to achieve it also differed from others. He poked at these Cartesian and empirical methodologies and instead glorified the Greek warrior's sword. Goebbels, the Nazi propaganda Minister once thundered,

> The *Fuhrer* drew the conclusion that the clutter of small nations still existing in Europe must be liquidated as soon as possible. The aim of our struggle must be to create a unified Europe. Only the Germans can really organise Europe…therefore the way to world domination is practically certain. To dominate, Europe will be assumed the leadership of the world.[57]

The ultimate objective of the European unification, as far as the Nazis were concerned, is the universal leadership of the world. European unification was not just for intellectual or spiritual attainment as seemed to be to some enlightenment philosophers. For Nazis, it was for power and domination. That is why Kluke condemned their idea of Europe as,

> Nazi ideas on Europe were never more than a disguise for aggressive aims involving the restoration of a mythicised 'Roman Empire of the German nation'; the Nazi's ultimate objective was not a united Europe but merely the 'Germanic Reich.[58]

It was this racial colour of unification and the abhorring violence employed to achieve this goal, that distanced many of liberal thinkers of that period from the Nazi doctrine even though they were themselves striving to achieve this unification.

The liberal Europeanists were actively engaged in organising Nazi Resistant Movements during the war periods. Particularly in 1941, the *Movimento Federalista Europea*, known as MFN was founded in Italy by Alterio Spinelli and Ernesto Rossi. They issued the famous 'Ventotene Manifesto'[59] in which passionately appealed to the Europeans to resist in all possible ways of the Nazi menace. For them, Nazism represented the hyper-nationalism and to avoid it in future Europe they requested both the people and their leaders seriously consider the sole alternative of federating Europe. In 1943 the MFN held meeting at Milan. In June, a French section of MFN was founded at Lyon. Thus it acquired momentum and spread at least in all the major European countries.

These resistance movements organised people against the Nazis, but at the same time mobilised public opinion towards achieving united Europe; interestingly, the Nazis were using the same slogan and justifying their actions under the garb of this motto. That is why a liberal Europeanist was compelled to differentiate and distinguish him or herself from the Nazi doctrine. In 1943, Henri Frenay, the founder of the resistance movement *Combat* denunciated the Nazi ideology but at the same time pushed what his idea of United Europe was:

> What we are fighting is an attempt to unite Europe by violence by a totalitarian regime. On the contrary we are now fighting the very people with whom, after liberation, we will have to work together to build a free and democratic Europe.[60]

Thus, the liberal Europeanists differentiated themselves on two grounds: their method of reaching their goal was consensus and constitutional; and the future united Europe would be a democratic not authoritarian one. They said so far there has been attempts, from Romans to Hitler, to unit Europe by violence and transform it in to totalitarian empire. Instead, they argued that the need of this hour was to aim a united Europe through democratic means.

This liberal Europeanist ideology seemed to be attracting many people after the Second World War. Spinelli captured the general mood of that immediate post-war period:

> This elementary experience (that is Second World War) penetrated the minds of all..and it brought about a situation which has made possible the spreading of the movement for European Unity, that is, the attainment or order which would replace the discredited and obsolete formulae of national states.[61]

That is why, person of the stature of Winston Churchill a staunch supporter of British Empire where sun never sets, made a clarion call for 'United States of Europe', in his now famous Zurich speech[62] on 19th September 1946. His political rivals of labour camp Attlee reverberated and echoed this call and even declared 'Europe should federate or perish'. We can hear this appeal from almost all leaders of other European countries-in the voice of Schuman in France, Adenauor in Germany and Degasperi in Italy. The ambience was created where almost all the leaders of different national denomination were ready to see through some kind of unity in Europe to avoid any future war in the continent. Now the history moved to the phase of how to construct this unity.

REFERENCES

1. Lucien Febvre, "Civilization: Evolution of a Word and a Group of Ideas", in John Rundell and Stephen Mennell, ed., *Classical Readings in Culture and Civilization* (London, 1998), p. 160.
2. This quote has been taken from his "Forward" to his book, *Culture and Society* (London, 1993).
3. Ibid., p. 3.
4. Immanuel Kant, "An Answer to the Question: What is Enlightenment?", in Paul Raabe and Wilhelm Schmidt-Biggemann, ed., *Enlightenment in Germany* (Bonn, 1979), pp. 9-15. Most of my arguments regarding the relationship of Enlightenment and Germany have been traced from the article,

Rudolf Vierhaus, "The Historical Interpretation of the Enlightenment: Problems and Viewpoints", in Paul Raabe and Wilhelm Schmidt-Biggemann, ed., *Enlightenment in Germany* (Bonn, 1979), pp. 23-36.

5. I owe this point to John Rundell and Stephen Mennell. See John Rundell and Stephen Mannell, "Introduction: Civilization, Culture and the Human Self-Image", in John Rundell and Stephen Mannell, ed., no. 1, p.13.
6. A.L. Kroeber and Clyde Kluckhohn, *Culture: A Critical Review of Concepts and Definitions* (New York, 1950), pp. 25-52.
7. Silvia Federici, "The God That Never Failed: The Origins and Crises of Western Civilization", in Silvia Federici, ed., *Enduring Western Civilization: The Construction of the Concept of Western Civilization and Its "Others"* (London, 1995), p.70.
8. John Rundell and Stephen Mannell, ed., no. 1, p. 7.
9. Lionel Gossman, "The 'Two Cultures' in Nineteenth Century Basle: Between the French 'Encyclopedie' and German Neo-Humanism", *Journal of European Studies*, vol.20, no.78, June 1990, p. 101.
10. For a detailed analysis of the methodological significance of the concept of culture and civilization in the social sciences see, "Culture and Civilization", *Encyclopedia Britannica*, vol.5 (London, 1969), pp.824-33. And "The Relationship Between the Concepts 'Civilization' and 'Culture'", *Social Sciences* (Moscow), vol.15, no.4, 1984, pp.147-64.
11. For an elaborate discussion of Freud's notion of civilization refer, Sigmund Freud, *Civilization and Its Discontents*. I owe my further and better understanding of Freud to Herbert Marcuse's, *Eros and Civilization.*
12. Oswald Spengler, *The Decline of the West: Form and Actuality*, trans. Charles F. Atkinson (London), p. 20.
13. Albert Salomon has excellently dealt with the issue of how the antithesis of *kultur* and *zivilisation* structured the foundations of the early German Sociology. See, Albert Salomon, "German Sociology", in George Gurvitch and Wilbert E. Moore, ed., *Twentieth Century Sociology* (New York, 1945), p. 587.
14. Quoted in Anouar Abdel-Malek, *Civilizations and Social Theory*, Vol.1: *Social Dialectics* (London, 1981), p. 100. Especially the Chapter 6 titled "Marxism and Sociology of Civilizations", pp. 97-117 would be useful for further study.
15. For further elaborate analysis refer, Alfred Weber, "Culture-Sociology: Social Process, Civilizational Process and Cultural

Movement", in John Rundell and Stephen Mannell, ed., no. 1, pp.191-215.

16. See, Norbert Elias, *The Germans: Essays on Power Struggles and the Formation of Habitus,* trans. Dunning and Menell (Oxford, 1989).
17. Louis Dumont, "Are Cultures Living Beings? German Identity in Interaction", *Man,* vol. 21, no. 4, 1986, p. 588.
18. Norman Hampson, *The Enlightenment* (Harmondsworth, 1968), p.15.
19. Alex Roney, ed., *The European Community Fact Book* (London, 1993), edn.3, p.14.
20. Douglas Johnson, "Epilogue: Historians, Nations, and the Future of Europe", in Marry Fulbrook, ed., *National Histories and European History* (Boulder, 1993), p. 286.
21. Lord Gladwyn, *The European Idea* , quoted in Douglas Johnson, no. 20, p. 293.
22. Braudel, quoted in Douglas Johnson, no. 20, p. 293.
23. Immanuel Kant, *Perpetual Peace,* Lewis Beck White, ed., (Indianapolis, 1957).
24. See the Penguin Special Publication of the year 1939 of the works of Norman Angell, *The Great Illusion;* W.B. Curry, *The Case for Federal Union;* H.G. Wells, *The Common-Sense of World Peace;* and J.M.E. Joad, *Why War?*
25. Karl R. Poper, *The Open Society and Its Enemies, Vol.1: The Spell of Plato,* 5th ed., (London, 1966). Peter J. Euben and Josiah Ober, ed., *Athenian Political Thought and the Reconstruction of American Democracy* (Ithaca, N.Y., 1994).
26. H.A.L. Fisher, *The History of Europe* (London, 1941), reprint, p.1.
27. Hegel, "Philosophy of History", in Carl J. Friedrich, ed., *The Philosophy of Hegel* (New York, 1954), p.73.
28. Friedrich Nietzsche, *Birth of the Tragedy* (London, 1968).
29. Deleuze and Guattari, *What is Philosophy?* (London, 1994).
30. The popular comic series "Asterix" subtly expressed, perhaps in a parodical inversion, the cultural conflicts that had ragged the otherwise generally presumed category of united Roman Empire. These comic books successfully bring forth the internal contradiction of the Roman imperial arena at least on three ethnic divisions: Romans, Gauls, and Goths. On this aspect see, Goscinny and Underzo, "The Asterix and Goths" and "Asterix the Gladiator" (London, 1995).
31. Hannah Arendt, "Philosophy and Politics", *Social Research,* vol. 57, no.1, Spiring 1990, pp.73-103.

32. Bertrand Russell, *History of Western Philosophy* (London, 1950), reprint, p.304.
33. Ibid., p. 307.
34. For an elaborate discussion on this point refer, Robert Folz, *Concept of Empire in Western Europe* (Boulder, 1962).
35. For further discussion see, St. Thomas Aquinas, *Selected Political Writings*, trans. J.G. Dawson, and ed., by A.P. D'entreves (Oxford, 1981), 8th ed.
36. Dante, *Monarchy*, trans. Prue Shaw (Cambridge, 1996), p. 4.
37. Ibid., p.11.
38. I owe this point to Charles Till Davis, "Dante and the Emperor", in Rachel Jacoff, ed., *The Cambridge Companion to Dante* (Cambridge, 1993), pp. 67-79.
39. Walter Lipgens, ed., *Documents on the History of European Integration*, Vol. 1, *Continental Plans for European Union*, (New York, 1985), p. 5.
40. Ernest Barker, *The Confederation of Nations* (Oxford, 1918).
41. Walter Allison Philips, *The Confederation of Europe* (London, 1914).
42. C.R. Attle quoted in John Pinter, " Federalism in Britain and Italy: Radicals and the English Liberal Tradition", in Peter M.R. Strik, ed., *European Unity in Context: The Interwar Period* (London, 1989), p.203.
43. E.H. Carr, *The Twenty Years Crisis, 1919-1939* (London, 1939).
44. Ibid., p. 52.
45. See Ralph White, "The Europeanism of Coudenhove-Kalergi", in Peter M.R. Strik, ed., no. 42, p. 23.
46. Quoted in John Loughlin, "French Personalities and Federal Movements in the Interwar Period", in Peter M.R. Strik, ed., no.42, p.190.
47. Quoted in Walter Lipgens, ed., no.39, p.30.
48. Quoted in John Loughlin, no.46, p.191.
49. Altiero Spinelli, " The Growth of the European Movement Since the Second World War", in Michael Hodges, ed., *European Integration: Selected Readings* (Harmondsworth, 1972), p.45.
50. Ibid., p.44.
51. Quoted in Walter Hallstein and Hans Barker, "European Economic Community", in C.D. Kering, ed., *Marxism, Communism and Western Society: A Comparative Encyclopedia* (New York, 1972), Vol. 3, p. 341.
52. Walter Lipgens, "General Introduction", in Walter Lipgens, ed., no. 39, p. 12.
53. Michael Salewski, "Ideas of the National Socialist Government

and Party", in Walter Lipgens, ed., no. 39, p. 48.

54. Ibid., p.48.
55. Walter Lipgens, no. 52, p. 12.
56. Michael Salewski, no. 53, p. 48.
57. Quoted in Walter Lipgens, no. 39, p. 12.
58. Kulke, quoted in Michael Salewski, no. 53, p. 37.
59. See Walter Lipgens, no. 39. p. 27.
60. John Loughlin, no. 46, p. 190.
61. Altiero Spinneli, no. 49, p. 49.
62. Quoted in Max Beloff, "Churchill and Europe", in Mortin Holms, ed., *The Eurosceptical Reader* (London, 1996), p. 270.

CHAPTER III

European Integration and Institutional Historiography

What is European Union?[1] Any non-professional, newspaper reading layman would get bewildered on reading about the Union: On the one hand, it is a conglomeration of some institutions and organisations working under formal and informal networks. On the other hand, it represents a supranational state formation, having its own executive, legislative and judicial bodies with separate flag and embassy staff-attaché in non-member countries. Again some argue that the treaties establishing the Union are nothing but the international treaties signed by some sovereign states to collectively achieve their common interests. On the other hand, some consider the treaties as constitutional provisions of emerging European superstate. This notoriously elusive nature of the Union tempted Perry Anderson to chide it for being "an unfathomable mystery", "a film of mist even in the mirror of scholars".[2]

However, the same author tries to define it as,

> Mathematically, the Union today represents the largest single unit in the world economy. It has a nominal GNP of about $ 6 trillion, compared with $ 5 trillion of the US and $ 3 trillion for Japan. Its total population, now over 360 million, approaches that of the United States and Japan.[3]

Instead of concretely defining the Union, he further mystified or magnified it, as mathematics would always do. But Anderson is not the one who relays solely on some economic statistics to define the Union. Invariably all the scholars try to understand the Union by defining it with some economical categories. There are two major streams of tradition in this line of thought: One stream portrays the Union as a single market with standardized tax system and a common currency circulated cutting across the national boundaries of the member states. The other stream considers it as a trade bloc intended to negotiate with the non-member states and multilateral agreements with GATT and other international bodies. Thus there are two broad tendencies developed over the years in defining the Union: One that has emphasized its internal structure (of single market); and the second one giving more stress on its external activities (as trade bloc) and contrasting it with others say USA or Japan or some other regional organizations.

But considering the Union either as a single market or as a trade bloc is to reduce the multi-layered, complex dynamics of its institutional nuances and activities to a monochromatic and one-dimensional perspective. Take for example the case of single market argument. The Union has no power to create or levy taxes; it depends on the member states for its revenue. This has created a peculiar situation where the Union has a single market and soon going to have a common currency but without a common tax policy. That is why, one of the Union's publication on this subject clearly explains and certainly refutes the arguments of the single market school as: "its [*Sic*] aim is not to standardize the national systems of compulsory taxes and contributions but simply to ensure that they are compatible with each other but also with the aims of the Treaty establishing the European Community".[4] Similarly considering it as a trade bloc is not without contradiction. During the recent round of WTO negotiation, we witnessed that before entering a negotiation with the non-member countries, there were multipronged negotiation carried on even within the Union, among its member states before arriving at a common approach to be made before the WTO. This indicates the possibility of considering the Union itself as a multilateral forum and not a cohesive entity to be reckoned with. These contradictions may well expose the confusion over the issue of whether treating the Union as an international organization or a federal set up; the treaties establishing the Union as international treaties of multinational agreements or a constitution aiming for the creation of a federal political structure.

These confusions and contradictions prodded one scholar to recommend abandoning of any such move to define the Union, because for him, "It (*Sic*) remains an 'experiment'...a hypothetical and a matter for conjecture: clearly, being axiomatic or predictive about the shape or content of Europe in 1990s would be foolhardy".[5] It is true that the seemingly eclectic and even sometimes the eccentric nature of the Union elude any simple and convincing explanation. But then, how is one to comprehend the Union? In a simple procedural understanding, one can define the Union as a group of fifteen states[6] coming together under one unifying, overarching organization to preserve and promote their common and collective interests - economic, political as well as cultural. However, at the same time, one should aware that a host of countries, majority of them Eastern European are waiting to be incorporated in to the Union. That is why one scholar exhorts, "the European Union is itself not yet a finished product; it is in the process of evolving and the form it finally takes still cannot be predicted".[7]

Irrespective of these problems, the official documents of the Union proceeds to define it in terms of its institutional structures and functions. "To give simple and precise answers to the most frequently asked questions", one of the publicity booklets of the Union circles out "two particular aspects of the union: its institutions and its budgets".[8] Thus, over the years, there are two but interrelated approaches to study the European Union evolved: explaining the Union either solely on the edifice of its institutional structures or by concentrating on its supposed economic oriented functions. However, in this chapter, I would develop a critique of this predominant structural-functional approach to the Union; instead I would rather focus on the process of its institutional evolution and the historical context of this process.

I
EUROPEAN UNION AND ITS INSTITUTIONAL ARCHITECTURE[9]

Architecture is the most prevalently used metaphor both in the official Union documents and rhetoric to explain the institutional foundations of the Union. Normally, it is presumed that the Union is a three pillars structure: The European Coal and Steel Community (ECSC), European Economic Community (EEC) and Euratom all three come under the first pillar; the second pillar is the Common Foreign and Security Policy (CFSP); the third one is the Justice and Home Affairs Co-operation. These pillars signify the functional aspects of the Union. While the first one exclusively concentrates the issues of economic importance like common market and common currency; the second one focuses the external affairs and the third one covers the internal matters such as immigration, terrorism, drug trafficking and internal security. To carry on these functions a hierarchy of organisations has been erected over the years: European Council, Council of European Union, European Parliament, European Commission, Court of Justice, Court of Auditors and apart from these institutions, two advisory committees such as Economic and Social Committee and Committee of Regions.

European Council

It is the apex and superior body among the other Union institutions. It includes all the Heads of State or Government of the Member States and the President of the European Commission. It is this council which actually sets the guidelines for the rest of the Union institutions. By providing the necessary instruction to the Council of Ministers to make up certain policy decisions regarding economic and monetary union, common social policy, common foreign and security policy and enlargement, the European Council acts as an axis of the wheel of the Union. Any amendments to the previously concluded Union treaties could only be done during the regular European Council Summit or by specially convened Intergovernmental

Conference (IGC) for this purpose. It must meet at least twice a year and in practice regularly meets three times every year. The presidency of this council passes over to the every member states once in a six months.

Council of European Union

It is popularly known as Council of Ministers. Normally, it consists of the Foreign Ministers of the Member States; but depending upon the issues under consideration the respective ministers of the concerned matters of the member states would assemble at every six months to make the policy proposals in tandem with the European Council's guidelines. All the decisions will be taken under the qualitative majority voting. Every country has its voting power depending upon its relative size. For a decision to be adopted in the Council, it needs at least sixty-two votes. Also it will scrutinize the policy and legislative initiatives submitted to it by the Commission and as well as the Parliament.

European Parliament

The European Parliament is the only democratically elected international institution. It has 626 members who exercise democratic control at European level. From 1979 onwards, it has been elected by universal adult suffrage. The most important powers of the Parliament fall into three categories: legislative power, power over the budget and supervision of the executive. Thus it helps to draft, amend and adopt European laws and budgets and make political proposals. The successive treaties have extended the Parliament's influence in amending and even adopting the legislation so that both the Parliament and the Council of Ministers share power of decision in a large number of areas. The Parliament approves the Union budget each year. The budgetary procedure allows Parliament to propose modifications and amendments to the Commission's initial proposals and to the position taken by the member states in the Council. Again the Parliament exercises overall political supervision of the way the Union's policies are conducted.

European Commission

It is said that the Commission is the executive branch of the Union. It actually puts before both the European Council and Council of Ministers any policy proposals to be undertaken. It further ensures that the treaties, the community rules and programmes are correctly implemented. It also puts before the European Parliament and the Council of Ministers the legislative proposals; and enforces the decision taken and the community law. It consists of twenty commissioners headed by the President. The Heads of State or Government choose the President by consensus. The rest of the Commissioners are appointed by the each member states in consultation with the President. They are obliged to be completely independent of their national governments. Finally, thus created Commission should get approval from the European Parliament. The Commission meets once a week to conduct its business, which may involve adopting proposals, finalising the policy papers and discussing the evolution of its priority policies. The decision will be taken by the majority. The Commission is divided into 26 Directorates-General (DGs) with an additional 15 or so specialised services. Each DG is headed by a Director-General, reporting to the Commissioner who has political and operational responsibility for the work of the DG.

Court of Justice

It is the judicial institution of the Union. It consists of 15 judges and 9 Advocate Generals. They are appointed by the government of member states and hold office for a renewable term of six years. The judges select one of their members to be President of the Court for a renewable term of three years. The Advocate Generals assist the court in its tasks. The role of the court is to provide the judicial safeguards necessary to ensure that the law is observed in the interpretation and application of the treaties, and generally in all of the activities of the Union. The court may be called upon to decide cases brought by the Member States, by Community institutions and by individuals and companies. It ensures uniform interpretation of Community law through out the Community by close co-operation with the national courts and tribunals through the preliminary ruling procedure.

European Court of Auditors

It is the taxpayers' representative, responsible for checking that the Union spends its money according to its budgetary rules and regulations. It is considered as a 'watchdog' over the Union's money. It is a 15-member body from each country. The task of the court and the auditors is to check that revenue and expenditure observe the regulations and are in line with the Union's budgetary and accounting principles. At the same time, the court is also concerned to make sure that the Union is getting vale for its money by checking whether and to what extent financial management objectives have been achieved.

The Economic and Social Committee

It is basically a consultative or an advisory body. It provides institutional representation for the various categories of economic and social activity: employers, workers and interest groups covering the other forms of activities including agriculture, transport, commerce, consumer affairs, protection of environment and co-operatives all are represented on the committee. Its total members are 222. They are divided in to three groups: employers, workers and other interest groups. Opinions delivered in plenary session are drawn up by specialised section, whose members may be accompanied at meetings by assistance appointed by experts.

Committee of the Regions

It is the youngest institution of the Union created as a consultative body under the provision of the Maastricht Treaty. It is said that this committee has been set up to involve regional and local bodies in the development and implementation of the Union policies. As regional presidents, mayors of cities or chairman of city and county councils, the 222 members of the committee are elected officials from the levels of government closest to the citizens.

It should be noted that these above discussed institutional

structures were not constructed all at once and as smooth as one could expect. Rather, they have been created gradually through a strenuous process which in turn been determined by the historical context and constrains. The next section would attempt to survey in a bird's eye view on the different historical explanations of the evolution of the institutional edifice of the European Union.

II
EUROPEAN INTEGRATION AND HISTORIOGRAPHY: A SURVEY

In the historiographic tradition of European integration, there are two broad tendencies emerged: on the one hand some historians argue that the origin of European integration was indeed a very ancient one and cite examples from as ancient source as of Charlemagne to as recent of Napoleon as the precursors of the integration agenda. The core of their historiographical writing revolves around their belief in the existence of the idea of Europe from the ancient Greek period and assumes the successive European history as a movement towards achieving a tangible political form of this idea. For convenience's sake, we would call this stream as traditional historiography. On the other hand, some historians consider the integration process as a modern one and that too only as a mid-twentieth century phenomenon. Ernst Hass expressed this sentiment in clear words as "it appears to me that European unity under Roman, Frankish and mediaeval Roman-German imperial realms has no more analytical importance".[10] And instead he believes "a series of traumatic events [i.e. Second World War related] vividly remembered by a generation subjected to integration may launch and spur the process".[11] Again we would term this kind of approach as modern historiography. Since the first stream of historiography has been elaborately dealt with in the Chapter 2, here the focus will be on the second stream of history writing, that is the modern historiography.

Though there is a consensus over rejecting the

historiography of the first variety, the historians of the second stream are themselves divided over the issue of placing the exact year of the starting of the integration process and its causes. For majority of them, the scale of destruction witnessed in the Second World War and the subsequent emergence of cold war situation had actually fuelled the drive to integration. However, Walter Lipgens, who by collecting the various documents of the inter-war period declares confidently:

> The documents ...refute the idea that the movement towards European federation in the first ten years after the war [*sic*] was only a product of East-West conflict, of Soviet threats and American pressure. It was, indeed, the attitudes of the superpowers which induced West European governments to set about making European union a reality, *but the concept itself had taken shape in Europe long before.*[12]

Thus, he pushes the period of the starting point of the process further back and placed it in the immediate years after the First World War. He specifically attributes the causes of the integration to the emergence of one *Pan-Europa* movement in the inter-war period and its momentum carried on by the Europe wide federalist movement during the Second World War. By this prompt move, Lipgens traces the motive force for the integration not in some out side forces, say, Soviet Union or United States but solely within the Europe.

In spite of Lipgens' magnificent efforts in collecting documents and placing them under a cohesive narrative, the popular or the official historiography of the European integration starts with the end of Second World War. For this historiography, the sole cause or the driving force behind the integration was the destruction that Europe faced during that war. The official historiography maintains that even though "the idea of Europe is an old one, the will to create institutions leading to an ever-closure union among the people of Europe, however, arose out of the ashes of the Second World War".[13] The core premise of the official historiography may be summarised like this: On seeing the destruction wreaked by the two successive world wars, the founding-fathers of the Union, even under the adverse and mutually suspicious condition "consciously sowed the seeds of greater European integration".[14] Thus, it is the story of heroic adventure and sacrifice of some visionary leaders who were determined to transform the Europe into a single political unit.

The quintessential example of this line of historiography is Holland's. It was, "the psychological and material effects of intra-European conflicts", Holland argues, "propelled the minds of politicians in the 1945-50 period"[15] towards integration. His was a story of metamorphosis of Europe "from civil war to interdependence". However, for him, this transformation was not a smooth one. The dynamics of integration was and is interrupted intermittently by "plateau and stagnation".[16] That is why, any historical writing on European integration, he emphasises, should invariably reflect upon both these dynamic and as well as stagnating phases of integration. He diagnoses the reason for this periodically accelerated and decelerated momentum in the integration process as the result of conflict over the desirability and possibility of achieving a true federal set up in Europe.

> In this survey of the community's history, the idea of federalism is the reorganising principle. The tensions between the intergovernmental and *communautaire* elements within the community are used to delineate specific periods of integration.[17]

Thus, his heroic institutional historiography revolves around two axes: one that the ultimate and final destination of the European integration process is the achievement of a federal political set up in Europe and the belief that the history progresses toward that culminating point; second, the history of European integration is understood and divided into periods of cyclical dynamic and stagnant phases caused due to the conflict between intergovernmental and federal approaches.

However, Holland was criticised for his stress and emphasis on the adventure of federal spirit and the determination to achieve it at any cost. His failure or his seemingly visible negligence in taking into consideration of the post-war political and economic conditions of Europe, particularly the dawning of cold war situation and the division of Europe into West and East zones hardly brings any substantiation to his mode of historiography.

Unlike Holland, De Porte[18] gives importance to the post-war political condition of Europe, which was virtually divided into East-West blocs under the leadership control of Soviet Union and United States, respectively. The clearly emerged bipolar system and the consequent crippling cold war situation, De Porte argues, had necessitated the Western European countries to come close and unite themselves under some formal institutional structures. He understands this move on the part of these countries as a deliberate attempt to check and contain the zone of influence of the Soviet Union on this side. For this reason alone, the United States stressed and supported the integration move wholeheartedly. Thus the history of European integration, as far as De Porte is concerned, should be understood in the broader and contextual history of cold war and its dynamics.

Contrary to De Porte, but sharing some points with Holland, Andrew Barry understands the move towards the integration as "(seeking) to establish the possibility of European government".[19] But he differs from Holland in attributing the nature of the integration: while Holland stresses the federal goal, Barry sees it merely as a "project of harmonization".[20] To drive his point he focuses fully on the economic aspects of the integration and traces the history of this harmonization from the economic history of Europe dating before the two world wars.

Completely different and more controversial is the historiography of Alan Milward. He too rejects the idea of the long run historical trends and instead prefers to stick to the period of post-1945 years. This is the only point he shares with the modern historiography and the rest is complete polemics with it. He reserves his staunchest criticism to the federal-institutional historians for their notion of progress towards a post-national federal political set up of Europe. He accuses them of propagandists of US, since for Milward the unity of Western Europe becomes the US foreign policy objective and forces it up on Europe. Thus, he sees a nexus between the American foreign policy establishment and the historians and theorists of post-national integration. On the contrary, he claims "to set out to look at the history of European integration from the European view point and to test an alternative theory".[21]

But at the same time, Milward's intended European viewpoint is not the kind of one that De Porte has portrayed. Here too, Milward rejects all the cold war based history of European integration. He openly pitched his tone against them:

> For many political scientists, the process of European integration as now seen... as a process directly by interplay of foreign policy of great and medium sized powers in search of traditional objectives of influence and security.[22]

Similarly, he attacked the official historiography of European integration which emphasises the thematic idea behind the move as the ultimate achievement of federation. By rejecting the idea of federal spirit behind the history of integration, rather he saw,

> The process of integration was deliberately conceived and developed to preserve the nation-state by supporting a range of new social and economic policies whose very purpose was the resurrection of the nation-state after its collapse between 1929 and 1945.[23]

Thus, Milward rejects the two prominent historiographies that dominate today in the field of European integration: the offspring of American disillusionment with the dangerous political disunity of the European continent and naïve progressivist optimism.[24] Rather, he understands the integration within the history of post-war nation-state. His history conceptualizes integration as a post-war international framework, in which the European nation-states reassert themselves as the fundamental organizational unit of Europe as vigorously and securely as possible.

In this chapter, I would trace the history of post-war history of European integration by making use of the above discussed three varieties of writing history. For me, any particular deterministic view would seriously impair our understanding of the complex process of integration of Europe. And what it requires rather is to comprehend holistically. However, in this chapter, I am merely content with to outline the general and popular historical outlook of the European integration. In so doing, I have posed some questions: how far the cold war situation propelled the European integration? Is this integration process was an attempt to solve the East-West confrontation? Or is this mere a Franco-German alliance compelled by the two successive world wars? Seeking an answer to these questions will give meaning and context to the integration. This is one way of writing the history of European integration.

In this venture, I have taken the idea of Holland's periodical divisions of dynamic and stagnation phases while at the same time placing them in the broader context of cold war and bipolar system as emphasised by De Porte. At the same time cautioned by Milward's criticism, I would concentrate on each national unit of European Union and its actions and reactions towards integration.

III
EUROPEAN INTEGRATION: MAPPING THE TERRAIN AND MEASURING THE DIRECTION

Like Versailles Treaty of the First World War, the Yalta and Postdam Conferences of 1944-45 tried to redraw the 'new Europe'. Out of the chaos created by the Second World War both the United States and the Soviet Union were in a bid for a European settlement that would be more suitable and secure for their intended future hegemonic role. However, this was also a period when both these countries co-operated, though for a short period, to structure the New World Order and assure peace and security in future. This was evident from the resurrection of the old League of Nations, under the new garb of United Nations Organisation with some modifications. In addition to this, the wildly spreading and tremendously successful national liberation movements in Asia and Africa not only collapsed the imperial edifice of the Old World Order but challenged to envisage a broader vision of future world order.

Roosevelt, the then American president – a staunch supporter of his predecessor Wilson's ideology of liberal internationalism, strongly argued for setting up of a series of international organisations which would assure not only peace and security, but also economic stability and growth. In the same spirit the Bretton Woods System was created in 1944 for promoting a new and stable international monetary system. An international organisation, International Monetary Fund (IMF) was created for this purpose. Similarly it was felt at that time, an unimpeded trade and frictionless trade relations were important conditions for any future stability and peace. To assure of this, the dismantling of trade barriers was seemed to be a logical one and again an international organisation named General Agreements of Trade and Tariff (GATT) was set up in 1947 exclusively for this purpose.

While America was on the spree of forming wide ranging international organisations covering matters on security, trade and economic issues, its war ally, Britain had pressed for the decentralisation of the projected world body in the form of regional associations. However, as Keylor pointed out "it had been overruled by an adamant Roosevelt who had insisted on the Wilsonian concept of single Universal Organisation without regional subdivisions".[25] But contrary to Roosevelt, another towering personality of that period, Winston Churchill argued for a special and specific treatment for Europe and its peace, through some regional mechanisms.

Indeed it was Churchill[26] who set a paradigm for understanding the nature and future of Europe in the coming years, through his two subsequent famous speeches delivered in 1946. Even before the American realisation of the presumed Soviet threat, Churchill on March 1946, Fulton Speech declared the falling on of the so-called 'iron curtain', which would divide Europe into two camps. In such case, he argued the only possible and desirable move to rescue Europe from this situation was to form a federation. This was the gist of his another famous speech on September 1946 in Zurich. However, Churchill's idea of federation was different from what the liberal Europeanists of that time demanded. His federal ideas were only meant for continental countries and he consciously excluded Britain from it. As a vanguard of the Victorian legacy, he saw bigger and wider role of Britain in future. Actually, his strategy was to create three concentric circles of alliances to be made in order to check the communist danger: the prime and principal circle was Britain and its commonwealth; the second was the United Federal Europe; and the third was United States. Though Churchill expected America would retreat into its traditional isolationist policy, he was firm that it would extend its power to contain the Soviet threat.

With this understanding, in March 1948, Britain, France and the three Benelux countries signed a Treaty of Economic, Social and Cultural Collaboration and Collective Self-defence in Brussels. This Brussels Treaty was the founding document for the establishment of the popularly known 'Western European Union'. While move was on to achieve some kind of collaborations among the Western European states, the leaders of the 'Resistance Movement' of war period pitched their voice for the ultimate creation of United States of Europe through constitutional means. Fed up with the same old tactics of alliance formation, they argued that it was through uniting Europe on federal set-up, a semblance of peace could be brought on to Europe. Hence, they assembled at The Hague in May 1948 to plan a strategy for achieving European unity. This Conference was known as 'Congress of Europe'. However, in this Congress, two different and opposing streams of thought emerged: On the one side, some argued in favour of establishing an institutional set-up that would promote a kind of intergovernmental co-operation among the nations. On the other side, the strong federalists argued for a settlement of not less than a federal union. The former stream was under the influence of Churchillian outlook, while the latter was personified by Alterio Spinelli, the Italian leader of the Fascist resistant movement. The Britain, more particularly Churchill, turned this Congress into a replica of the previous one – the Congress of Vienna of 1815 where the leaders were hell-bent to preserve the existing *status quo* and organised some sort of collaboration of the kind witnessed as 'Concert of Europe'. The same was repeated again in 1948.

Britain took initiative in organising an intergovernmental

summit in London and formalised a treaty, which established the Council of Europe in 1949. It was established with a body of parliamentary assembly with intergovernmental ministerial committee. The federalist welcomed the initiative and thought of transforming this Council into an assembly responsible of drafting the future constitution of united Europe. But, the 'Unionists' of Churchillian variety actually transformed it into merely a consultative organ devoid of any power and prestige that the 'federalists' specifically vied for. Spinelli[27] accused British as betraying the European cause and lamented that a golden chance was missed to see the European unification through.

Meanwhile, the international scenario changed rapidly as the immediate post-war co-operation between America and Soviet Union was latter heading on towards a confrontationist posture. With the announcement of Truman Doctrine in 12th March 1947, virtually the so-called Cold War era began. The European integration had acquired different meaning and colour under this circumstance. As Spinelli expressed, now Europe had but four options:

> ... [*Sic*] integration with either the Soviet Union or the United States or of a restoration of the old national state system, or of a free union of existing European states under a new supranational body superior to that of national states.[28]

But the irony was that instead of choosing any one of these four options, Europe attempted to traverse in all these paths. Consequently, Europe was divided into East-West blocs under the overarching suzerainty of the Soviet Union and the United States respectively; and the western part was further mired over the conflict of intergovernmentalism and federalism. Indeed, the East-West division, and intergovernmentalism versus federalism shaped and drove the subsequent course of European destiny for over four decades.

Atlanticism and Marshall Plan

The famous or infamous George Kennan's telegram and the subsequent announcement of the 'Truman Doctrine' had actually clamped cold war situation in the coming years. While his colleague Kennan was preoccupied with the question of how to 'contain' the Soviet power, George Marshall, the Secretary of State announced on 5th June, 1947, an 'European Recovery Programme', popularly known as Marshall Plan to help European countries recover from the present gloomy economic conditions caused by the massive war mobilization and reconstruct their economic base afresh. Apart from its seemingly visible humanistic overtures, the United States' hidden and covert agenda behind this plan was to cripple the expanding influence of the Soviet Union in Europe. Thus, the rationale behind and the reason cited for formulating this plan was that of the American perception of economically weak and vulnerable Europe would inevitably become prey to the wooing communist ideology. As one author argues,

> The continued impoverishment of the countries of Western Europe seemed an open invitation to the Soviet Union to extend its political dominion over them with the connivance of the powerful communist parties and communist-controlled labour organisations in countries such as France, Italy and Belgium.[29]

That is why the Americans pumped their dollars into Europe as aids so as to check the threatening 'red menace'. Between 1948-1952, the Marshall Plan supplied massive grants and credit totalling around $13.2 billion.

Another presumed strategy behind this plan was to encourage the European countries to come closure and form a relatively a single or coherent unit. Hence, it sought to encourage the integration move by insisting that the recipient countries should formulate a joint approach to aid solicitation and distribution. Even at some point, the United States put integration as a prerequisite to the disbursement of its funds. To meet this US prerequisite for the Marshall Plan assistance, the recipient countries formed an 'Organisation for European Economic Co-operation' (OEEC) and 'European Payment Union (EPU)', two overarching bodies to utilise the funds effectively and efficiently. In this sense, Keylor argued that the Marshall Plan played a pivotal role in promoting European integration by indirectly inspiring the subsequent Schuman Plan. However, it should be noted that the OEEC was not a supranational or a federal set up but purely an organisation meant for intergovernmental co-operation and consultation. Precisely, this overt intergovernmentalism disappointed the federalists, and they rejected the idea of OEEC because they believed that it did not manifest any "concrete expression of European Unity".[30]

However, the succeeding events like the Soviet invasion of Czechoslovakia in 1948, and the Berlin blockade (1948-49) had confirmed the western powers' paranoia of the communist devil looming large over Europe. As a counter measure, the Soviet Union had brought the entire eastern part of Europe under its fist and prohibited them in participating in Marshall Plan. Instead, it organised its own 'Communist Information Bureau' in 1948 to organise these countries under one banner. Thus, at the beginning of 1948, as Keylor puts it, the "European continent had been reorganised into political and economic blocs, the one dependent on the United States, the other subservient to the Soviet Union".[31]

The cold war thus dashed the federalists' hope of attaining a united federal Europe after the Second World War. Instead, an Atlantic organisation was formed under the leadership of the United States. Contrary to Roosevelt's universal outlook, the succeeding Truman administration arranged for insertion of Article 51 in the UN Charter, which preserved the right of member states to establish regional security organisation outside the perimeter of the United Nations. As a consequence, Senator Vandenberg[32] introduced a resolution in the Congress supporting the idea of promoting an organisation that was exclusively meant for European security. On 4th April 1949, North Atlantic Treaty Organisation (NATO) was created. It was an integrated defence system under one supreme command of the United States. Under the provisions of this treaty the USA sent their troops to Europe to be stationed permanently there.

The Soviet Union retaliated with the creation of Warsaw Treaty Pact and 'Comecon' in the subsequent years. With these moves, the federalist dream of United Europe was completely shattered and instead of Europeanism, Atlanticism had taken root.

Europeanism and Schuman Plan

Even though the Western Europe moved into a broader Atlantic umbrella, the urge for federal union did not dissipate as yet completely. Monnet, the supposed conscience keeper of the federal spirit, time and again emphasised, "the countries of Western Europe must turn their national efforts into a truly European effort. This will be possible only through a *federation of the west*". [33]

Monnet frequently complained that the various organisations that had been created over the years like OEEC, WEU, Council of Europe and NATO were all based on the intergovernmental approach and did not provide any scope for bypassing the national sovereignty. Instead, drawing inspiration from the Benelux agreements of 1940s, he campaigned for a gradual and incremental pooling of national sovereignty and building of supranational solidarity. For him, "Europe will not be built all at once, or as a single whole: it will be built by concrete achievements, which first create *de facto* solidarity".[34]

To create such a *de facto* solidarity, the France took initiative in 1950 to pool the coal and steel production of France and West Germany along with the three Benelux countries. On 9th May 1950, the then French foreign minister Robert Schuman declared a proposal for setting up of a supranational body which "will lay the first foundation of the European federation, which is indispensable to the maintenance of peace".[35] It was presumed that any outright move to erase the rigid national identity was not possible in the cold war dominated scenario; the alternative method adopted was a gradual and sectoral unification of Europe. Thus, the aligning of coal and steel production by the six signatory states was considered as a stepping stone in this direction. The Chancellor of Federal Republic of Germany Konrad Adenauer vividly reflected this idea latter in his memoir as "that morning [*Sic*] I had no idea that the day was going to bring the news of such a decisive turning point in the development of Europe".[36] Based on this declaration, later a treaty was concluded in 15th April 1951 at Paris by the six countries, thereby created the European Coal and Steel Community (ECSC). It was a new supranational entity endorsed with a political organisation to complement its economic apparatus: an executive body called High Authority, a Parliamentary Assembly and a Court of Justice.

The creation of ECSC was hailed as "a leap in the dark"[37] and set "Europe on the move".[38] However, this initial move of six member states was not considered as unification in literal sense, rather an attempt to guarantee their people that war would not be possible once again in their soil and preserve peace and security for ever. That is why one scholar was more inclined to consider the formation of ECSC as "a significant episode in the diplomatic history rather than the political history of Europe".[39] On the contrary, Monnet was exalted over this formation and expressed, "I have never doubted that one day this process will lead us to the United states of Europe: but I see no point in trying to imagine today what political form it will take".[40]

While some had cast their doubt over the ECSC's potential in transforming the Western Europe into a federal unit in future, there were two different conflicting interpretations put forward around its formation. On the one side, some people argued that at a time when the rearmament of West Germany seemed immanent and got support from both USA and Britain, the France had no other option but to engage West Germany's industry which would be more crucial for any future military mobilisation. This perception was strengthened by the statement of Adenauer:

> Any form of rearmament would first of all be reflected by an increase in the production of coal, iron and steel. If an organisation such as the one he [*Sic*] imagined were to be created, which allowed the two participant countries to detect the first sign of any such development, this would go a long way to easing the minds of the French.[41]

On the other hand, some had argued that it was a deliberate move on the part of French to strengthen Franco-German axis, thereby creates a third powerhouse in a bipolar world system. They cited the statement of Monnet to substantiate their argument:

> We went to turn what divided France from Germany – that is,

> the industries of war – into a common asset, which would also be European. In this way *Europe will rediscover the leading role which she used to play in the world and which she lost because she was divided.*[42]

While there was a thick debate going on about how to interpret the creation of ECSC, in the mean time, the subsequent events happened in Europe in the following years shattered the hope of moving towards a United Europe. As Holland observed, this phase of dynamic integration was interrupted by a stagnating period of conflicts.

The Korean War in 1950 convinced the United States that the Soviet threat was imminent both in Europe and Asia. So, it wanted to consolidate its position in Europe and strengthen the prowess of its allies both in economic and military terms. When USA, through Acheson proposal, revealed its determination of rearming the Federal Republic of Germany (FRG) and granting full sovereignty to it, France was in a dilemma over this issue. For French, the fully armed sovereign Germany meant nightmare since Germany invaded France three times previously since 1870. So, it was hesitant and reluctant of rearming Germany. But both USA and Britain were adamant over this issue because for them the immediate and threatening danger was the Soviet Union not Germany. Indeed, they thought that the armed Germany would strengthen their position vis-à-vis the Soviet Union.

Under such conditions of the cold war, France did not have any option but to accept this proposal. But in order to cripple the Frankenstein German, the then French Prime Minister Rene Pleven came out with what was called as Pleven Plan. It envisioned a united integrated European military force, equipped and financed by the member states. That means, no necessity of organising separately any German army. Rather, as Keylor put it, the Germans would work in the 'European army', wearing a 'European uniform' and taking orders from 'European Commanders'.[43] Based on this plan, on May 27, 1952, after long and tiresome negotiations, the representative of the six ECSC nations singed the treaty establishing "European Defence Community".[44]

However, after the decisive and humiliating defeat of its army at Dien Bien Phu, in Indo-China war in May 1954 and its engagement with the suppression of the raising Algerian militant nationalism, the French feared that the proposed EDC would dilute their ability to fight for keeping their overseas, colonial territories. Similarly, the other countries were reluctant of handing over an important power of state to some supranational body. Finally, the France refused to ratify the EDC treaty and thus the prospect of forming a federal defence community evaporated. Critics[45] interpreted the failure of EDC as the six nations were ready to pool their powers only in matters of 'low politics', say in the field of coal and steel, but they were reluctant over the high politics of defence and foreign policy matters.

In the mean time, the foreign minister of the Netherlands, John William Beyen submitted a proposal to the six nations for establishing a Common Customs Union and Common Market. He expressed his dissatisfaction over the concentration of integration only in some sectors. Rather, he insisted a multipronged approach to integration. At the same time, disappointed with the failure of EDC, Monnet formed 'Action Committee for the United States of Europe – a sort of pressure group in 1955. Through this organisation, Monnet started mobilising public opinion for establishing a kind of European atomic energy co-operation.

Relaunching the project of Europe: EEC and Euratom

In the face of the defeat of EDC and under the tremendous pressure from the federal lobby, on June 1-3, 1955, the six foreign ministers of the ECSC met at Messina to decide the future course of the integration process. At the end of the meeting they jointly issued a statement reiterating their commitment to integration and further declared,

> If Europe is to maintain her position in the world, regain her influence and prestige and achieve a continuing increase in the standard of living of her population, *it is necessary to work for the establishment of a United Europe by the development of common institutions.*[46]

The same conference appointed a committee under the chairmanship of Spaak, the foreign minister of Belgium to propose some concrete measures to be undertaken to further the integration process. This committee submitted its report, known as Spaak Report, at Venice Conference in 1956. This report suggested a two-prong strategy: focussing on both sectoral as well as broader fields. It suggested of implementing the Beyen's idea of Customs Union and Common Market (emphasising the broader outlook) and Monnet's idea of atomic energy organisation (focusing on specific sectoral area).

The Venice Conference studied the proposal and decided to convene an intergovernmental conference to take further actions on this direction. A year later, in 1957 at Rome, the Heads of State and Government of six member states of ECSC met and finally signed a famous treaty, popularly known as Rome Treaty. This treaty established two supranational bodies: the European Economic Community (EEC) intended to achieve a Common Customs Union and Common Market; and European Atomic Energy Community, known as "Euratom" for pooling their atomic energy sources. Thus, the Spaak report once again relaunched the aborted European integration project.

This Rome Treaty was considered as a first and foremost constitutional measures undertaken towards a federal Europe. It declared its aim as "to establish the foundations for an ever closer union among the peoples"[47] as a substitute for age-old rivalries. Again it had established the core supranational bodies such as Council of Ministers, European Commission, European Parliament and Court of Justice, thus covering all the branches of government – executive, legislative and judicial. And yet it was not a true federal set-up and did cover only some sectoral economic matters. As Keylor noted, the goal of political federation was still much more elusive.[48]

However, it was expected that the merging of respective member state's essential interests by establishing an economic community would provide a solid basis for a broader and deeper community sense among the European peoples long divided by the bloody national conflict. That is why one author while commenting on the Rome Treaty said,

> Measured realistically against the European past rather than against dreams of the future, its (i.e. Rome Treaty) accomplishments have been more striking. *The European* glass *may be half empty, but it also helpful – no small achievement.* [49]

The EEC was successful in a short span of time in dismantling all sorts of Quantitative Restrictions (QRS) – tariffs and quotas within the community. Also it was very much successful in establishing series of – Common External Tariff (CET), Common Commercial Policy (CCP), Common External Trade Policy and Common Agricultural Policy (CAP). In addition to these policies, the European Investment Bank was created in 1958. Its main task was to contribute the balanced development of the common market in the interest of the community by financing projects.

It should be noted that all these initiatives of the Rome Treaty were, what Pinter[50] calls, 'negative integration'. That means, easing and finally dismantling the internal restrictions for the free movement of goods and people. It was aimed to expedite the economic growth. As Stephen George noted, "by the time (i.e., 1958) the motivation had moved beyond economic recovery of post-war depression to ensuring economic prosperity"[51] ; but when other matters except economic came to fore front, or say 'any positive integration', the EEC bungled pathetically. Dahrendorf has vividly expressed the mentality at that time as,

> The fiction of an uncontrolled European government, free from national direction as well as parliamentary doubts was bearable to the member states as long as very little was to be decided at a European level.[52]

Though the EEC was successful and achieved its goal of Customs Union well before the deadline prescribed in the Rome Treaty, it was not successful in creating a Common Market or Monetary Union. Even the other provisions like introducing 'qualitative majority votes' in the Council of Ministers became impossible. With the advent of General De Gaulle into the French Presidentship, the integration process headed towards yet another conflicts and crisis.

De Gaulle and 'Europe of States'

As Holland noted, despite successive reforms and the progressive communitarisation of European activity, intergovernmentalism has remained the real alternative and challenge to the community experiment.[53] De Gaulle who vehemently opposed the formation of both ECSC and EEC, later transformed himself as a reluctant supporter after becoming French President. However, his idea of European integration was different from federalist. For him, the European integration meant for two things: On the one side, it was to strengthen the bond existing among the six member states so as to create a solid 'Europe of states'; it was precisely on this point he differed from the federalist. He poured scorn on the idea of Federal United Europe. Duroselle dramatised this situation in the catchwords of "Europe of De Gaulle versus Europe of Monnet".[54]

On the other side, the European integration, for De Gaulle[55], meant for 'European Europe'. That means independent of American dominance in the matters of security and foreign policy. In fact during 1960s, the general mood in France was against any unwarranted American influence over European matters. In addition to this, French saw the increasing American economic might at the cost of Europe. In a very popular and controversial book at the time, "The American Challenge', the author Jean – Jacques Servan – Schreiber[56] demonstrated that how American industrial and economic powers destroyed and paralysed the growth of European industries. Further he cautioned about the rapid growth of Japan, particularly its successful stride over the electronic revolution. He warned his fellow Europeans as, "if Europe continues to lag behind in electronics, she could cease to be included among the advanced areas of civilisation within a single generation.[57] In this context, De Gaulle argued for creating, although through intergovernmental means, economically strong, politically assertive and militarily independent Europe. Strategically also he thought of creating Europe a 'third force' between the two superpowers.

To promote and realise his vision of Europe, De Gaulle

proposed a plan, what was later called as, 'Fouchet Plan'. The six member summit at Bonn on 18th July 1961, asked Christian Fouchet, the French ambassador in Denmark to prepare a draft proposal on the means of giving the union of some statutory political character. Fouchet submitted a plan recommending the formation of a Confederation of European States with a common foreign and defence policy as well as co-operation on cultural, educational and scientific matters. It failed to take off because of an unenthusiastic response from other member states. There are two conflicting interpretations about the plan's failure. One school argued that other states, particularly FRG and Italy saw in this plan a French hegemonial ambition whereas the other school said that the other member states who were loyal to the federal union, rejected this plan because it only aimed to set up a confederation.

Any way, the rejection of this French backed plan disappointed De Gaulle very much. He squarely blamed it on the federalist of Monnet kind. In a press conference on 15th May 1962, De Gaulle said, "at present there is and can be no Europe other than a Europe of the states – except, of course, myths, fictions and pageants".[58] Thus, his vision of Europe was completely different from the federalist and he expressed it in two rather catchy words: 'Europe of States' and 'European Europe'. By the first one he defied Europe as confederation of states not as some supranational entity. He did not conceal his disgust over the building of technocratic supranational institutions in Europe. Rather, he was at loggerhead with the Commission, particularly with the then president of the Commission Walter Hallstein, over granting some budgetary power to the European Parliament. Latter, he withdrew the French representative from the Council of Ministers, what was known as 'Empty Chair Crisis' in 1965 over the issue of implementing the Rome Treaty's provision of Article 148 which envisaged introducing qualitative majority voting in the Council.

At the same time, De Gaulle wanted to carve out a separate, identity for Europe independent of the United States' shadow. He expressed time and again that the Atlantic Community did mean the US hegemony in Western Europe. As long as these countries remain within the NATO, they will not have their own independent outlook and always subservient to the US policy decisions. Therefore, his vision of 'European Europe' longed for a distinct, confederated European states, as a third force to check the hegemony of the two superpowers, not only within Europe, but also throughout the world.

De Gaulle's independent and visionary posture was correctly understood by the US and its then president John Kennedy as a threat to its power and influence in European affairs. The 1962 round of GATT negotiation exposed the united power of six over the matters of trade and tariffs. In order to ease the friction, Kennedy through his policy 'Grand Design' came out with a strategy of two-pillar theory where 'Atlanticism' and Europeanism' would coexists side by side. But De Gaulle rightly deciphered Kennedy's overtures as a strategy of re-emphasising American hegemony once again and he even withdrew France from the integrated military structure of NATO in 1966.

Thus throughout 1960s, De Gaulle dominated and actually shaped the course of integration process. Both his inward looking and outward looking policies were severely criticised and he was blamed for the stagnation of the integration. He vetoed twice the entry of Britain into the EEC. He considered Britain as what Hoffman calls, 'American Trojan Horse'[59] whose entry would help only the Americans not the Europeans. Hoffman beautifully captures the enigma of De Gaulle and his rather ironic position vis-à-vis the integration as:

> De Gaulle's was the emergence of a "European Europe' but his tactics and his conceptions prevent the emergence of the only kind of Europe that could theoretically speak with one voice – a federated Europe. The General wants to speak for Europe, but it is a Europe which politically does not exist yet and which is often repelled by his imperious way of acting alone, of rejecting supranational integration, of promoting purely of French policies and of upsetting the unwritten rules of the Community by restoring the vetoes and threat.[60]

For most of the scholars, De Gaulle's period was doldrums era in the history of European integration. The realist school of theorists quickly took this issue and argued that their theoretical foundation, that is the impossibility of moving away from the nation-state, was once again proved and verified by the events of 1960s. The dark mood of this period provoked one scholar to proclaim "the end to European integration".[61] Though the integration process had not stopped as expected, the De Gaulle's period inflicted an intelligible wound that had killed the high-flying idealist spirit associated with this movement.

Cold War Détente and European Integration

The year 1968 was in many senses a turning point in the contemporary history of Europe. The post war consensus, liberal worldview was completely shattered, and the previous decade economic boom slackened and exhausted its potential. The all-round disappointment with the present system was amply reflected in the organised protest against both the US and the Soviet hegemonies. The Asian and African continents caught in the trap of debt crisis, started demanding a just world order in which their economic backwardness should be addressed and cared.

The American involvement in Vietnam and the Soviet atrocities in Hungary exposed the demonic faces of both these superpowers. It was increasingly believed that world peace and stability could no longer be relieved into the hands of these two powers. In the mean time, new leaders came and occupy positions in both France and Germany. Pompidou of France and Willy Brandt of Germany extended olive branch to their eastern neighbours. Particularly Brandt through his *Ostpolitik* was determined to ease the tension in East-West relations. Under this détente syndrome, naturally one can expect the European integration would get accelerated. With the resignation of De Gaulle, as Holland said, 'the Europe was diverted from its intergovernmentalist cul-de-sac and re-routed back on the *communautarie* road'.[62]

By the time, the Common Customs Union was completed eighteen months ahead of the schedule: customs duties between members states were removed and the common customs tariffs replaced national customs duties in trade with the rest of the world. Now time has arrived, as far as the six are concerned, to decide the future direction and nature of the integration. As Hoffman asked "whether they are going to move further towards integration in high politics or use their economic strength gained by the previous customs union to strengthen their individual national bases?"[63] Under this situation the six met at The Hague in 1969 to define the broad lines for the future course of action. At the end of this summit they issued a statement affirming their commitment to integration:

> Entry upon the final stage of common market not only means confirming the irreversible nature of the work accomplished by the communities, but also means paving the way for a United Europe capable of assuming its responsibilities in the world of tomorrow and of making a contribution commensurate with its traditions and its missions.[64]

But on the crucial question about the nature of integration, that is, whether it moves beyond the national boundaries and towards a federated Europe, this summit was non-committal and vague. It just simply announced: "They have common conviction that a Europe composed of states which, while presenting their national characteristics, are united in their essential interest assured of internal cohesion".[65] Anyhow, under the so-called 'the spirit of The Hague', they had decided to relaunch the European integration once again.

The Hague Summit decided to push the integration further towards political and monetary union. It appointed two committees: one for making proposal on political union called 'Davignon Report'; the other one for economic and monetary union called 'Werner Plan'. Dahrendorf welcomed these initiations on seeing this as "the most important beginning towards a second Europe and a starting point of a significant new development".[66] The Davignon Report proposed a plan to set up European Political Co-operation (EPC) to integrate the member states' foreign and security policies but not through some federal body but through the intergovernmental mechanism. Similarly the Werner Plan presented an ambitious seven-stage plan to achieve European Monetary Union (EMU) by 1980. Thus, the issue of European integration moved as Dahrendorf sarcastically said, "from the subject matter of beef, labels on mayonnaise jars and free moving mid wives – to more serious talks, political and economics".[67]

To achieve the recommendation of Davignon Report, that is the European Political Co-operation, the member states asked their foreign ministers to find ways and means to attain this goal. They, under the chairmanship of Walter Scheal, submitted two reports: Luxembourg Report in 1970 and Copenhagen Report in 1973. These reports recommended setting up of an intergovernmental body called 'European Council', which would meet at least twice in a year and would co-ordinate the foreign and security policies of the member states. Accepting this recommendation, the Paris summit in 1973 established the European Council consisted of the Heads of six member states. The federalist strongly criticised this creation of EPC instead of federal united set up. However others welcomed this move saying "certainly voluntary agreements on important matters is at least more valuable than technically binding agreements on insignificant ones".[68]

Apart from this EPC, there was strong support to create European Monetary Union (EMU) also. Indeed, the international economic situation compelled them visualise such a union. The collapse of the Bretton Woods system and ending of convertibility of dollar in 1971 brought down the post-war US hegemony in international monetary system. In addition to this, the 1973 OPEC induced oil crisis and the increasing debt crisis of the third world developing countries all created chaos in world economic conditions. These conditions encouraged the hitherto expanded nine-member community to look for a possibility of forming EMU. As Stephen George said, "it was a move to establish a zone of monetary stability in Europe at the time of international monetary instability".[69] However, the move towards this EMU was blocked by the Britain, the new entrant into the Community in the previous year.

Despite the tall claims about the move towards EPC and EMU, actually the achievement of the Community in 1970s was nil and blank. As Keohan put it emphatically "this was a period of Doldrums and Dark Age".[70] On the contrary to the Community principle, each member state resorted individually to impose long-range non-tariff barriers as recourse to reserve domestic market for domestic producers because of world economic crisis. Helmut Schmidt, the former Chancellor of FRG, captured the then condition of Community as,

> The French telephone system will not buy German telephones. British rail will never buy French rail cars, the German federal rail road system will not buy British locomotives and so on. *It is said to be common market, but it is not really very common!*[71]

However, in 1974, the Community recovered from its slumber somewhat by the leadership change happened in the three important member states: Valery Giscard' Estaing in France, Helmut Schmidt in Germany and Harold Wilson in Britain came to power. They were faced with, to put in Hoffman's words a paradox: all the statesmen of the six agreed on the need to crown economic with some kind of political association and yet no progress had been in that direction'.[72] So when they met in European Council Summit in 1974, they directed Tindeman to prepare a report on European Union. At the same time Monnet actively campaigned for the formation of 'provisional European Government' from 1973 onwards.

Under these conditions, Tindeman submitted its report in 1976, recommended that the 'federal Europe' should be the goal and priority. For this, he demanded "drastic measures (to be undertaken by the community) to make a significant leap forward". To regain the lost air of adventure, Tindeman proposed a radical change in the outlook of community building: "No one wants to see a technocratic Europe. European Union must be experienced by the citizens in his (sic) daily life".[73] Thus he wanted to build Europe through democratic and holistic approach not be limiting it to a series of functional economic agreements.

The long détente (1967-79) between the USA and the Soviet Union indeed helped a lot and indirectly encouraged the European leaders to put the derailed integration process again in the track. Actually the 1967 'Hamreal Report' outlined a two-track philosophy: strengthen the Western alliance deeply; and extend limited co-operation to the Soviet Union on the basis of assured security. Based on this philosophy, both the USA and the Soviet Union signed SALT I Treaty in 1972. Encouraged by this major achievement, both Eastern and Western European countries came together and formed a single organisation called "The Conference on Security and Co-operation in Europe (CSCE) in 1973. The following CSCE at Helsinki, known as Helsinki Conference, all the thirty-five European states of east and west along with the USA and Canada signed a declaration to bring about a peaceful atmosphere to ease the tension in east-west relations.

Under this prospective and congenial atmosphere, during Bremen European Council Summit on 6th and 7th July 1978, both France and Germany decided to launch 'European Monetary System' (EMS) as a first step towards the monetary union. This summit rekindled interest in the earlier Werner Plan which envisaged the first stage of economic monetary union. The EMS was agreed in principle by the Council through a resolution passed in the Brussels Summit on 5th November 1978. Hereby, it was proposed that all the currencies of the Member States would participate the exchange- rate mechanism, which operates on the principle of stable, but flexible exchange rates. The core idea behind the establishment of an Exchange Rate Mechanism (ERM) was that the member states' money would be allowed to fluctuate vis-à-vis other community currencies only within the predetermined bonds of +/- 2.5 per cent of the currency's value'.[74] On political side, direct election to the European Parliament was implemented in 1979. This was done to promote the democratic face of the community and popularise it among people thereby get legitimated. By this time, the détente period was over and a phase of new cold war started which in turn adversely affected the integration process.

New Cold War to Single European Act

The Soviet invasion of Afghanistan and the Iranian Islamic revolution in 1979 and the subsequent second oil crisis along with the coming to power of the right-wing, conservative establishment, under the leadership of Reagan in the USA and

Thatcher in Britain, all vitiated the international situation and a new phase of intensive cold war. This in turn created a tension in East-West relations in Europe. The series of fresh deployment of American Crussie missiles and Soviet SU20 missiles on both sides of Europe created an ambience of nuclear war once again in Europe.

In this moment of tension, on November 1981, Dietrich Genscher and Emilio Colombo, the foreign ministers of Germany and Italy presented to European parliament (EP) their governments' proposal for a 'European Act'. This Genscher-Colombo proposal advocated far reaching institutional reforms like dissolving the gap between the EPC and the EC's external relations; and stressed the need for closer link in foreign and security policy. However, this move was construed as dangerous and threatening one by Reagan administration. Regan expressed his displeasure and conveyed to his European partners in no uncertain words that it was unnecessary to have an independent foreign and security policy at a time of heightened cold war. In the face of strong American resistance, the EC countries backtracked from their earlier move and simply affirmed their inclination only in words at Stuttgart Council meet in 1983.

In the mean time, the USA unilaterally withdrew from the INF treaty negotiation in 1982 and announced its intention of promoting the 'Strategic Defence Initiative' (SDI) popularly knows as Star Wars. Helmut Schmidt, the then Chancellor of FRG expressed his displeasure over the American action as "the total lack of consultation prior to the American rejection of the compromise formula was clearly an act of unwarranted American dominance".[75] Even at the peak of opposition, the US insisted deploying its Crussie missiles in Western Europe and pressurised the seemingly hesitant colleagues. Again, Helmut Schmidt, a staunch opponent of the missile deployment in his soil cautioned his European partners: "obviously the US is not going to change its military thinking and its order of priorities in the short run. Therefore *the Europeans themselves ought to look at their situation*".[76] But it is an irony that the same Schmidt buckled under the US pressure and latter accepted the deployment of the missile despite the strong protest from the people.

When the European Council failed to accept the recommendations of Genscher – Colombo proposals and carried away by the US manipulation, the European Parliament, under the able leadership of Alterio Spinelli adopted a 'Draft Treaty Establishing the European Union'. Under the pressure from the European Parliament and from the pan-European popular peace movement, the newly emerged leaders of France and Germany – Francois Mitterand and Helmut Kohl decided to initiate the integration process afresh. During the Fontainbleau Council Summit, under the initiative of Mitterand, two *ad hoc* committees were appointed: Committee on People's Europe and Committee on Institutional Affairs.

The first one known as Adinnino Committee emphasised the basic thrust of both Genscher-Colombo plan and European Parliament's draft treaty and recommended "to translate [*Sic*] wide range of existing views on the nature of European integration into politically accepted reform" in its report called 'Citizen's Europe'.[77] Further, the report recommended abolition of border controls, granting mutual recognition of diplomas and examinations and allowing citizen of one member state to reside and work in another. Similarly the other committee called Dooge Committee recommended far reaching changes in the institutional set up of the European Community. Both these Committees recommended to the Council to convene an intergovernmental conference to amend the Rome Treaty so as to accommodate their concerned recommendations.

The Milan European Council meeting in 1985, accepted the recommendations of these committees and decided to convene an intergovernmental conference to amend the Rome Treaty. The gradual disappearing of the cold war tension and Gorbachev's policy of 'Common European Home' helped move closer in that direction. Later, in Luxembourg, the member states signed 'Single European Act' (SEA), which entered into force on first July 1987. Its preamble reiterated the broad objective – the creation of a European Union. It also laid down the legal base for establishing a single market by 1992. Also for the first time, the European Political Co-operation was brought under some treaty provisions. Although the EPC was kept within the bounds of intergovernmental set up, the act brought the foreign policy issues under the treaty provisions.

For the federalist, the SEA was not up to their expectation. They accused it of still treading on the path of intergovernmentalism. However, the general mood was appreciative and considered it as a major achievement after the Rome Treaty in 1957. Helmut Kohl, the Chancellor of West Germany reflected this perception when he gave statement to the *Bundestag* on 18 March 1987 as "the people in the member states of the Community must develop a common political awareness: let us call it a European Patriotism".[78] But there were dissenting voices also; it was Britain and its leader Margaret Thatcher. She opposed the act as abridging the national sovereignty. When the then Commission president Jacques Delors[79] came with his two future plans to implement the provisions of the SEA, she vehemently opposed the move, more particularly his plan of creating a European Monetary Union (EMU) by 1993. Once again the Community witnessed the old rivalry between nationalism and supranationalism: this time represented by Thatcher and Delors respectively.

Delors, a committed Europeanist, tried to push the integration process deeper. He set the political agenda – known as 'Programme 1992', to achieve a full-fledged Single Market and Monetary Union by the year of 1992. He commissioned a group of economists under the leadership of Paolo Cecchini to study 'the cost of non-Europe'.[80] Cecchini came out with a report on the same title; and the gist of the report was that the existing physical, technical and fiscal barriers to trade cost the community around 3 to 6 per cent of GDP annually. Delors utilised this report to mobilise the public opinion in favour of deeper integration. But Thatcher, as a countermove to Delors, in her famous Burges Speech in 1988 argued for 'Europe of Nations' instead of United Europe.[81] Thus, once again the integration process was heading towards stagnation but fortunately the sudden and unexpected events happened in the Eastern Europe rescued the Community from the impasse.

Birth of New Europe: Maastricht and Amsterdam Treaties

1989 was the year of revolutions. Nobody predicted that the course of history would change at that pace and momentum. One after another all the East European countries rebelled against their totalitarian regimes and freed themselves from the Soviet imperialism. At this historical moment, the special European Council met at Dublin in 1990 and directed their foreign ministers to produce a proposal on European Political Union to be achieved. As to show their commitment to EPU, the three Benelux countries, Germany and France singed the Schengen Agreement whereby they resolved eventually to remove all sorts of broader controls, both for goods and citizens.

On October 1990, the East and West Germany unified. This unification created a psychological pressure on the other European countries because for them a unified Germany means a nightmare. To alley the fear of Germany, Kohl announced his commitment to put Germany in the European mould. In this context, the 12 member European Council met at Rome in December 1990 and decided to launch two special intergovernmental conferences: one for EPU and other for EMU. After prolonged negotiations, finally they signed a treaty called 'Treaty on European Union' in February 1991 at Maastricht.

But before its final ratification and entry into force on 1 November 1993, the Treaty had to face severe hurdles. In a first referendum, the Danish people rejected the treaty. It was only after getting some special concessions to Denmark, the Danish people accepted it. Similarly it had to come over a rough weather both in France and Britain. In Germany the treaty was challenged in the constitutional court and finally the court justified the provisions of the treaty.

The Maastricht treaty was indeed a major turning point in the history of European integration. It introduced a radical shift in the objective outlook both in terms of institutional change and policy goals. It was evident from the dropping of the word 'economics' from the treaty. As one official document portrayed "it (Sic) can be taken to symbolise the intention that the EC should gradually become transformed from an economic community into a political union".[82] This treaty outlined two projects- Political Union and Economic Union to be undertaken in the near future to set momentum to the integration process. For this, new institutional foundations have been laid. The Political Union is expected to be constructed around three pillars: one, the old European Communities (including ECSE, Euratom and EEC); second, the Common Foreign and Security Policy intended to achieve co-ordinated and cohesive foreign and security policy for all the member states; the third one, co-operation in the fields of Justice and Home Affairs. While the second one looks after evolving a common approach towards the non-member countries, the third pillar intends to create a common agenda for member states in the issues of immigration, asylum, drug trafficking and other aspects of internal crimes.

As far as the second project, the European Monetary Union is considered, the Maastricht treaty outlined the measures to be undertaken to achieve the monetary union by the end of 20th century. Based on the first stage initiative of European Monetary System (EMS) of 1970s, the recent treaty set the second stage initiatives. The principal goal in this second stage is to secure broad convergence between the economic policies of the member states. To this end the European Council formulated economics policy guidelines with the main focus being on price stability and sound public finance. As a final stage, the treaty envisioned the establishment of an independent European Central Bank, which will manage the money supply of the European currency 'ecu'.[83] Under the special provision of the treaty, the European Central Bank will have the right to authorise the issue of notes and coins in the Union.

Apart from these two projects – EPU and EMU, the Maastricht Treaty introduced far-reaching measures of 'Union Citizenship'. The Article 8 of this treaty affirmed that every national of the member states "shall be a citizen of the Union" and "shall enjoy the rights conferred by this treaty and be subjected to the duties imposed thereby".[84] It was expected that the supposed Union citizenship would create a direct link between European integration and the people whom it is meant to serve. Thus, the treaty finally provided the required legal foundations to what Tindeman and Adinnino committees argued for over two decades. The treaty confers four crucial rights to its citizens: to move and reside freely within the territory of the member states; to petition the European Parliament on a matter directly affecting them or to take their problems to an Ombudsman; to vote and stand as a candidate in local and European elections of the member state in which the citizen resides; and in the territory of non-member countries, the right to enjoy the diplomatic and consular protection of all member states represented there. Despite the lofty claims about Union citizenship, as John Pinter[85] argues, "the rights would have remained a pious aspiration had they not been enforced throughout the Community by the rule of law". However, at the same time, it was expected that the citizenship clause would create the necessary solidarity of people required to set the integration moving.

However, the spirit of the Maastricht agenda evaporated over the years. The initial euphoria of the immediate post-cold war period slowly dissipated into new kind of scepticism over the integration move. The much acclaimed 'convergence process', said to be initiated by the Maastricht Treaty, and did not lead the Union to expected new hights. Rather, " by the summer of 1996, it had become obvious that the drive for monetary union, intended to be the occasion of a new and deeper phase of European integration, had become the almost the opposite – a clear sign of the inadequacy of European institutions".[86] The situation was further aggravated by some member states that vied for to be excluded from early participation in the key projects of the Union especially from EMU.

The abject apathy shown by the common people during the Maastricht referendum and some member state's reluctance in accepting some of the provisions of the treaty compelled the Union leadership to summon a Special Reflection Group to consider future reforms. Based on this group's recommendations on June 16 and 17, 1997 at Amsterdam, an Intergovernmental Conference (IGC) was organised to review the earlier Maastricht Treaty. As a result, Amsterdam Treaty was signed on 2 October 1997. The member states declared in this treaty that "it is intended to make the European Union more relevant and appealing to its increasingly sceptical and apathetic citizens and to prepare the EU for the challenge of enlargement to the east".[87]

The new treaty while amending and adding some provisions to the old one, it concentrated on three main areas: expansion of citizenship concept, creation of an identity of the Union on international stage and institutional reforms. On the first issue, the Amsterdam Treaty fairly extended the concept of Union citizenship. The initial European Treaties gave citizens a range of individual rights based essentially on freedom of movement between the member states. The Treaty of Maastricht added the right to vote and stand as a candidate in European and local elections. The Treaty of Amsterdam, on the other hand, focuses on the fundamental rights. Under this treaty, the Union has adopted the Council of Europe's 'Convention for the Protection of Human Rights and Fundamental Freedom' for itself too and there by extended the scope and range of the individual rights enjoyed by the citizens of the Union. Further, this treaty has given the Union right to act against any kind of discrimination based on sex, race or ethnic origin, religion or beliefs, disability, age or sexual orientation. In addition to these matters, the Union has made a pledge to promote equal opportunities for men and women in all its policies, above and beyond the existing treaty rules on equality in the spheres of social affairs and employment. In employment the new treaty opens the door to 'positive discrimination' if one of the sexes is clearly disadvantaged.

As far as the second issue is concerned, so far the Union has power to deal with foreign trade and development aid but not in diplomacy and defence. The Maastricht Treaty introduced for a first time a single set of rules for a Common Foreign and Security Policy (CFSP) including a Common Defence Policy. The Amsterdam Treaty further expanded the scope of CFSP by setting out guiding principles such as: to safeguard the common values, fundamental interests, independence, integrity and security of the Union; to protect peace and strengthen international security and co-operation, and to consolidate democracy, the rule of law and fundamental rights. Thirdly, the new treaty has increased the powers of both the Commission and the Parliament.

Thus, over the years, the European Union has gradually assumes greater role for itself in the daily affairs of European politics and economics and stealthily encroaches the powers and prestige monopolistically enjoyed by the nation-states so far. Now the Union has its own legislative, executive and judicial branches of government with wielding power over internal security and external foreign policy matters. Even in a year or two, it will soon have a common currency circulating through out the Union territories irrespective of the national boundaries. Then, can we presume the Union as a formation and consolidation of a super- state on a European scale? Milward has cautioned us to compare the Union formation with a state formation. However, the current situation and the evolutionary direction would support both the arguments. But one crucial aspect of the integration has been neglected by both the protagonists and opponents of state formation arguments, that is, whether the common people have shifted their loyalties from the age-old nation-state to the Union.

Shifting loyalties from one point to another is not an easy process since they have been erected on some cultural legitimisation. If then, what are the cultural legitimisation that the Union has built for its own consolidation? Has it succeeded in penetrating and finally overtaking the reified national cultural traditions? These are the question to be answered before one could arrive at any decisive conclusion about the nature of European integration. Strangely, this aspect has been continuously neglected by the historiographies that predominate today in the field of integration studies. Aware of this shortcoming, I would turn towards the cultural aspects of the integration before venturing on my own narration of the European integration process. The next chapter will undertake such an attempt.

REFERENCES

1. The name 'European Communities' had been used before the Maastricht Treaty. After this treaty, it is common to denote the

institutionalization of the European integration process by the term 'European Union'. However, in this study I have used both these terms as interchangeable.

2. Perry Anderson, "Under the Sign of the Interim", in Peter Gowan and Perry Anderson, eds., *The Question of Europe* (London, 1997), p. 51.
3. Ibid., p. 51.
4. Union's publicity booklet titled "Tax Policy in the European Union" (Luxembourg, 2000), p. 5.
5. Martin Holland, *European Community Integration* (London, 1993), p. 5.
6. They are: Austria (1995), Belgium*, Denmark (1973), Finland (1995), France*, Germany*, Greece (1981), Ireland (1973), Italy*, Luxembourg*, Netherlands*, Portugal (1986), Spain (1986), Sweden (1995), and United Kingdom (1973). The star mark indicates original six member states of the Rome Treaty; the years in the brackets indicate the accession of that country into the Communities. However, the number was and is not a fixed static one. The membership was increased over the years and going to be increased soon; indeed a whole bunch of countries waiting in a queue to be incorporated into the Union in the near future.
7. Klaus-Dieter Borchardt, *The Community of European Law* (Luxembourg, 2000), p. 25.
8. A publicity booklet titled "How Does the European Union Work?" (Luxembourg, 1998), edn. 2, p. 5.
9. To understand the institutional structures of the Union, I have relayed much on the publicity booklets, "Serving the Union: A Citizen's Guide to the Institutions of the European Union", (Luxembourg, 1996); "How Does the European Union Work?" (Luxembourg, 1998), edn. 2; and Emile Noel, "Working Together - The Institutions of the European Community" (Luxembourg, 1994).
10. Ernst Hass, "International Integration: The European and Universal Process", in Michael Hodges, ed., *European Integration: Selected Readings* (Harmondsworth, 1972), p.92.
11. Ibid., p. 92.
12. Walter Lipgens, ed., *Documents on the History of European Integration, Continental Plans for European Union 1939-1945* (New York, 1985), vol. 1, p. xi. Emphasis added.
13. The Union's publicity booklet titled, "How Does the European Union Work?" (Luxembourg, 1998), edn.2, p. 6.
14. Ibid., p. 6.

15. Martin Holland, no. 5, p.22. For a comprehensive outline of Community history, see the second chapter "The Community experience: From Civil War to Interdependence".
16. Ibid., p. 23.
17. Ibid., p. 22.
18. A.W. De Porte, *Europe Between the Superpowers: The Enduring Balance* (London, 1979). Particularly the topic on 'Unity of Europe', pp. 220-29.
19. Andrew Barry, " The European Community and European Government: Harmonization, Mobility and Space", *Economy and Society*, vol. 22, no. 3, Aug 1993, p. 314.
20. Ibid., p. 314.
21. Alan S. Milward and Vibeke Sorensen, "Interdependence or Integration? A National Choice", in Alan S. Milward and others, ed., *The Frontier of National Sovereignty: History and Theory 1945-1992* (London, 1994), p. 5.
22. Alan S. Milward, *The European Rescue of the Nation State* (London, 1992), p. 6.
23. Ibid., pp. 9-10.
24. Ibid., p. 5
25. William R. Keylor, *The Twentieth-Century World: An International History* (Oxford, New York, 1984), p.283.
26. For Churchill's role in the European integration see, Max Beloff, "Churchill and Europe", in Martin Holms, ed., *The Eurosceptical Reader* (London, 1996), pp. 269-84. Also see John Pinter, "Federalism in Britain and Italy: Radicals and English Liberal Tradition", in Peter M.R. Strike, ed., *European Unity in Context: The Interwar Period* (London, 1989), p. 203.
27. To get the federalist account of this event and for their own integration history refer, Alterio Spinelli, "The Growth of the European Movement Since the Second World War", in Michael Holms, ed., *European Integration: Selected Readings* (Harmondsworth, 1972), pp. 43-68.
28. Ibid., p.54.
29. Keylor, no.25, p.273.
30. Jean Monnet, as quoted in Holland, no. 5, p.24.
31. Keylor, no.25. p.278.
32. For an elaborate historical account of the formation of NATO, see, Keylor, no.25, p.200.
33. Monnet, as quoted in Holland, no. 5, p. 5. Emphasis added.
34. Ibid., pp. 5-6.
35. Ibid., p. 8.

36. Konrad Adenauer, *Memoirs*, Gainer, trans, (London, 1969), p.323.
37. Robert Schuman, as quoted in Holland, no. 5, p. 25.
38. Monnet, as quoted in Holland, no. 5, p.25.
39. John Gillingham, "The European Coal and Steel Community", in Desmond Dinan, ed., *Encyclopedia of the European Union* (London, 1998), p. 179.
40. Monnet, as quoted in Holland, no. 5. p. 26.
41. Adenauer, no.36. p. 325.
42. Monnet, as quoted in Holland, no. 5, p. 25. Emphasis added.
43. Keylor, no. 25, p. 293.
44. For the emergence and collapse of EDC, refer, Edward Fursdon, *The European Defense Community: A History* (London, 1980).
45. A good example is : Stanley Hoffman, "Obstinate or Obsolete? The Fact of the Nation State and the Case of Western Europe", *Daedalus*, no.95, 1964, pp.862-915.
46. Quoted in S. Patijin, ed., *Landmarks in European Unity* (Leydon, 1970), p.101. Emphasis added.
47. *Treaties of the Communities*, Abridged version (Luxembourg, 1995), p. 11.
48. Keylor, no. 25, p. 301. Emphasis added.
49. De Porte, no.18, p. 224. Emphasis added.
50. John Pinter, "Positive and Negative Integration: Some Problems of Economic Union in the EEC", in Michael Hodges, ed., no. 10, pp. 124-49.
51. Stephen George, "The European Union, 1992 and the Fear of 'Fortress Europe'", in Andrew Gamble and Anthony Payne, ed., *Regionalism and World Order* (London, 1996), p.22.
52. Rolf Dahrendorf, "A New Goal for Europe", in Michael Hodges, ed., no. 10, p. 74.
53. Holland, no. 5, p. 24.
54. J-P. Duroselle, "General de Gaulle's Europe and Jean Monnet's Europe", in C. Cosgrove and K. Twitchett, ed., *The New International Actors: The UN and the EEC* (London, 1970), pp. 187-200.
55. For de Gaulle and the integration debate, I have extensively used the sources from Charles de Gaulle, *Memoirs of Hope: Renewal and Endeavor* (New York, 1971) and Stanley Hoffman, "The European Process at Atlantic Cross-Purpose", *Journal of Common Market Studies*, vol.3, 1965, pp. 85-101.
56. Jean-Jacques Servan-Schreiber, *The American Challenge*, Ronald Steel, trans. (New York, 1979), p. 12.
57. Quoted in Stephen George, no. 51, p. 31.

58. Quoted in Holland, no. 5, p. 34.
59. Stanley Hoffman, no. 45, p. 92.
60. Ibid., p.98.
61. R. Inglahrat, "An End to European Union?", in Michael Hodges, ed., no. 10, pp. 91-105.
62. Holland, no. 5, p. 38.
63. Stanley Hoffman, no. 45, p.88.
64. "Communiqué of the Heads of State and Government of the Member-States of the EC, The Hague Summit, 2 December 1969", in *European Political Cooperation* (Bonn, 1988), edn.5, p.22.
65. Ibid., p.23.
66. R. Dahrendorf, no. 52, p.78.
67. Ibid., p.78.
68. Ibid., p.80.
69. Stephen George, no.51, p.27.
70. Robert Keohan and Stanly Hoffman, "Institutional Change in Europe in the 1980", in Keohan and Hoffman, ed., *The New European Community: Decision Making and Institutional Change* (Boulder, 1991), p. 8.
71. Helmut Schmidt, *A Grand Strategy for the West: The Anachronism of National Strategies in an Independent World* (London, 1985), p.43. Emphasis added.
72. Stanley Hoffman, no. 45, pp. 91-92.
73. L. Tindeman, quoted in Holland, no. 5, p. 61.
74. Kathleen R. McNamara, "European Monetary Union", in Desmond Dinan, ed., *Encyclopedia of the European Union* (London, 1998), pp. 206-209
75. Helmut Schmidt, no.71, p. 61.
76. Ibid., p.42. Emphasis added.
77. P. Adinnino, "A People's Europe: Reports From the *ad hoc* Committee", *Bulletin of European Communities* (Luxembourg, 1985), supplement 7/85, pp. 1-20.
78. Helmut Kohl's statement to the *Bundestag*, 18 March 1987, published in, *European Political Cooperation* (Bonn, 1988), edn. 5, p. 378.
79. "Programme of the Commission for 1986", Statement by J. Delors to the European Parliament, *Bulletin of European Communities*, supplement, 1/86, 1986, p.30.
80. Paolo Cecchini and Others, *The European Challenge 1992: The Benefits of a Single Market* (Aldershot, 1988).
81. Margaret Thatcher, "Europe of Nations, Bruges Speech", in Martin Holms, ed., *The Eurosceptical Reader*, pp. 76-82.

82. Klaus-Dieter Borchardt, *European Integration: The Origins and Growth of the European Union* (Luxembourg, 1995), edn.4, p.59.
83. It is an abbreviation of 'European Currency Unit'. It comprises a basket of the currencies of the Member States, each currency accounting for a proportion fixed according to the economic strength of the country in question.
84. *Treaties of the Communities*, Abridged version (Luxembourg, 1995), p.67.
85. John Pinter, "European Citizenship: A Project in Need of Completion", in Colin Crouch and David Marquand, ed., *Reinventing Collective Action from the Global to the Social* (Oxford, 1995), p.113.
86. To get a clear picture about the immediate post-Maastricht period, refer, Sam Aaronovitch and John Grahl, "Building on Maastricht", in Peter Gowan and Perry Anderson, ed., no.2, p. 181.
87. Quoted in the Unions publicity booklet titled, "Treaty of Amsterdam: What has changed in Europe?" (Luxembourg, 1999), p. 3.

CHAPTER IV

Culture and Community: European Union's Cultural Policy and the Dynamics of Europeanization

For many, it may sound odd or even perhaps over-ambitious when one begins to talk about the cultural aspect of European integration. After all, they would reply, European integration was and is an instrument of economic co-operation and a mechanism of pooling of their collective economic interest and nothing more. For some others, the European integration is exclusively a political issue. They would reduce the matter as a political problem of having to achieve a federal set-up among some group of states in Western Europe. They would say the European integration deserves to be analyzed only along with some past historical events such as making of federal set-up in the USA and German unification of 1870 under Bismarck. Their line of argument runs like this: how the organization of *Zollverin* in the late nineteenth century led to the final unification of Germany, the current European Economic Community will culminate in the said objective of the European unification. Thus, so far only two approaches dominate in the arena of the understanding of European integration process: economic and political aspect of the integration; cultural issues are almost marginal.

From the very beginning of the integration process, economics dominated both theory as well as practice. Under the influence of the functional approach at an early stage, the Community leaders believed that the market integrated through Common Customs Union would have its spillover effects on other areas such as social, political and cultural. This crude economic determinism dominated the EC's integration philosophy. The another reason frequently cited for this economic emphasis was that the relying on some other alternative mechanisms such as cultural phenomenon would ultimately hamper and derail the very process itself. For them culture is so sensible and sentimental one and bringing it into the radius of integration would create unnecessary complications in the initial formative periods. Rather, it could be tackled only through the logic of economics.

On the contrary, the federalist strongly criticized this functionalist approach. For them, there exists a concrete essential cultural foundation of Europeanness to be exploited to achieve the federal Europe on that basis. This argument has been reemphasized vividly by one leader as,

> This vision (Sic) is really of an economy rather than a civilization. It is not therefore a vision of Europe. It could apply in principle to anywhere in the world that embraces a similar economic ideology. It derives little or nothing from *any sense of European heritage.*[1]

The realization of the common heritage and the civilizational unity of the Europe time and again resurfaced in the discourse of integration but at the periphery. Though there were some momentary expositions on cultural aspect of integration within the Community initiatives, they had all been reluctant and rudimentary gestures. However, this tendency has got changed after the Maastricht Treaty.

In this chapter, the cultural aspect of the European integration would be taken up. By focusing on the cultural policy of the European Union, I would intend to extract what kind of cultural notion that the Union entertains in its approach towards the issues related to culture. Here, my methodology would be both historical and structural analysis. In the first part, I would sketch out the evolutionary gradient of the cultural developments happened within the Community orientation of integration. In the second part, by exclusively concentrating on certain specific policy proposals, I would try to capture the conceptual shifts occurred in the Community's interpretation of culture.

DOES CULTURE MATTER IN EUROPEAN INTEGRATION?

Indeed in the history of European integration culture was not a banished one. It seemed so because of the high-profile activities of the European Community in economic matters. But actually the matter that had attracted the Western European countries much after the immediate post-war period was the shared cultural heritage and common destiny. To foster cooperation in the field of culture they formed Council of Europe[2] in 1949 well before the formation of other economic organizations such as EEC and EFTA. In the midst of destruction and devastation of the Second World War, the leaders of the West European countries disparaged the nationalism as the reason for their downfall and proclaimed that the future peaceful Europe rest on the transcendence of this destructive nationalism. For this they stressed the civilizational and cultural unity of all the nations of Europe.

The Council of Europe was formed as a main forum for day-today cultural co-operation at the regional West European level. Culture is expressively included in the Council's field of activities according to the Article 1(b) of its statutes. The Council serves as a forum to address the specific problems in the field of culture. The important aim of the Council has been to provide an institutional framework to facilitate the free flow of culture across the national boundaries. Before any visible and decisive move towards economic unification, all the Western European countries of both EEC and EFTA groups signed in 1954 *'European Cultural Convention'*. Its Article 3 provides that "the contracting parties shall consult with one another within the framework of the Council of Europe, with a view to concerted action in promoting cultural activities of European interest".[3]

For this purpose a number of intergovernmental bodies such as Council for Cultural Co-operation, Conference of European Ministers of Education and Steering Committee on Mass Media have been setup to undertake these concerted activities. This kind of institutional setup provided a forum for the exchange of views and sharing of experiences in the field of culture. The output consists of mainly of studies, conferences, exhibitions and publicity and sometimes also of formal but non-binding rules like resolutions and declarations what are described as 'soft laws'. Since the Council of Europe was more like an intergovernmental organization, its role was restricted only to agenda setting for national governments and a coordinating body for their policies. As one of its reports said "There by remains a very real justification for European cultural co-operations on the basis not dictated at the outset by economic considerations, as in the Council of Europe and reflecting existing national structures rather than imposing harmonization".[4]

On the contrary to the Council of Europe, the European Economic Community, popularly known as the EC[5] had concentrated fully on economic aspects of integration rather than cultural in its initial decades. Even though it proclaimed "to establish the foundations for an ever closer union among the peoples",[6] its sole area of interest was restricted only to maters related to economics. It was expected that the pooling of respective member states' economic interest by establishing an economic community would provide solid basis for a broader and deeper community sense among European peoples long divided by bloody conflicts and destructive wars.

This economic functional determinism did not provide any scope for the word 'culture' under the provisions of the Rome Treaty of 1957, which laid foundations for the creation of the EC. However, in the coming years culture in a material sense had been covered under the terms of economics of culture. The free moment of goods and persons as assured under the Articles 30-36 of the EC Treaty made applicable to cultural goods such as works of art, audio records and tapes, films and video tapes, books and periodicals. Similarly the freedom to provide services extended to the areas of cross border transmission of broadcasts and persons engaged in cultural activities like fine arts, theatre and architecture. In this sense, culture not in abstract meaning but more in a material form, particularly the culture industry structured the EC's cultural approach to integration in the early formative periods.

All these provisional initiations of the EC regarding culture were part of what Bruno de Witte[7] called the *negative integration* where the aim was to eliminate the national obstacles against the free flow of cultural goods and activities within the territory of the Community. Even though these cultural initiatives undertaken by the European Community had indeed affected culture in its material form but they did nothing either in mobilizing people or change their consciousness towards Europe. It was realized later that the mere 'cultural flows' of goods and services was not enough for eventually attaining the set goal of United Europe, by creating "a rapprochement between peoples of national cultures".

Despite the Federalist claim of a common cultural heritage of Europe, the term culture did not find any place both the ECSC and EEC treaties. Indeed, it was after the completion of Common Custom Union in 1968, when the question raised what next, did the term culture emerged. More particularly, when Federalist engaged debate with the Gaullists over the nature of Europe, a distinctive discourse of independent, essential European identity appeared its head in integration issues. The declaration made on the occasion of the achievement of the customs union in 1 July 1968, the six members EC issued a statement emphasizing the cultural aspect of integration. Outlining the move beyond the economic perimeter of the integration, it emphasized "we must take a step towards in the field of political union....The moment has come to call the young and creative forces of Europe to union and hope".[8]

When the EC successfully created the Common Customs Union by the turn of 1968, it had to face two problems: How to carry on further the integration from the so called "low politics" of market integration to "high politics" of common security and foreign policy, in short towards political union; secondly the functional spill over from one sector to another did not happen as indicated by the neo-functionalists. Despite of its one decade endeavor in having to achieve its set goal of European integration in all fields, the EC had come to realize its failure in promoting a collective sense among the peoples of six member states even though it had succeeded in achieving the Common Customs Union well before the deadline.

So it is natural that both the EC officials and leaders of European Movement perplexed to see that why people were not ready to identify with Europe or as Wistricht, the former president of European Movement in Britain asks, "What has failed to make people identify with Europe".[9] They felt that the primary obstacle to European unification was the indomitable presence of nation states. According to them, European integration requires not simply the erosion of national barriers to trade or free moment of capital and labor, but elimination of all those barriers that actually constitute the nation state. Thus, the precondition for the emergence of a true Peoples' Europe, for them, is the dismantling of the nation state and its associated ideologies of nationalism. In this background, the Brussels based Community leadership realized the fact of impossibility of achieving their goal by merely sticks to some economic variables. Slowly it was dawned on their heads the importance of exploiting the hitherto untapped potential of cultural sentimentality to substantiate and sustain their integration drive. It is in this context, Jean Monnet's - the high priest of functional theology of European integration, supposed statement assumes significance: "If we were to do it again, we would start with culture".[10]

From 1970s onwards and more particularly during Delors' presidentship of the Commission, the EC did visibly stride into a cultural terrain. Each and every summit of European Council started issuing statements or declarations emphasizing the cultural unity of European people; and the Commission started drafting different cultural policies. Before venturing to analyze these cultural policies of the EC, let us first capture the unfolding of the cultural aspect of European integration since it is imperative to gauge the shifts and shades in the later day cultural policy orientations.

CULTURE AND EUROPEAN INTEGRATION: A HISTORICAL SURVEY

The year 1968 was the year of revolution. Unlike the previous revolutions, it was not directed against this or that political establishment; neither against nor in support of any particular ideology. It was indeed a Cultural Revolution. The upsurge of the unprecedented student unrest through out the Western Europe was not merely directed against the academic establishment but the ossified, sedimented worldview. That is why, that year is being considered as a year at which "all that is solid melt into air".

In this ambience of overall brimming discontent, the Nine Heads of State and Government of the Member States of EC met at The Hague on 2 December, 1969 issued a communiqué whereby they had declared "the Common Market is about to enter upon its final stage, to draw up a balance-sheet of the work already accomplished, to show their determination to continue and to define the broad lines of the future".[11] In this mood of introvert investigation and a longing for a misty future and as well as to carry forward the goal of political Union, the Heads of State and Government instructed their Foreign Ministers to examine the question of how to progress further towards Political Union.

The Foreign Ministers prepared a report called "Luxembourg Report" under the chairmanship of Walter Scheel and submitted on 27th October 1970. This report stressed the necessity of moving beyond what had been generally perceived as an excessive obsession with economic affairs. Instead, it had argued for the pragmatic co-operation in the sphere of political union and insisted "the spirit of Paris and Rome Treaties (should be) continued to political union so that Europe will be able to speak in one voice".[12] The intention of speaking in one voice had prompted the ministers to declare "A united Europe must be founded upon the common heritage".[13] Of course this was the first time a semblance of cultural idea of integration seeped into the official minds and got expressed in concrete words in the official document. Based on this report, the Paris Summit of

Heads of State and Government on 21st October 1972 announced their intention "to transform before the end of the present decade the whole complex of their relation into European Union".[14] The final declaration of the Paris Summit while acknowledging the economic aspect of the integration but at the same time emphasized, perhaps for the first time "special attention will be paid to non-material values and wealth".[15] Even though the word culture did not find its place in the declaration, indeed it indicated a definite shift in the perception of integration from material connotation to non-material values. This expansion of scope has helped bring issues of culture into the integration debate later.

Mandated by this summit, again the Foreign Ministers drew up a second report called Copenhagen Report on 23rd July 1973. By the time the Britain, Ireland and Denmark joined the EC. Collectively the nine member states signed 'Declaration on the European Identity'[16] at Copenhagen, on 14th December 1973. In this declaration culture was acknowledged, at least in the highest political level, to be one of the basic elements of European identity. This was the first significant step towards defining the cultural basis for European integration. The declaration announced that the "time has come to draw up a document on the European identity and this will enable them to achieve a better definition of their relations with other countries and of their responsibilities and the place which they occupy in world affairs".[17]

They have decided to define the European identity with the dynamic nature of the Community in mind. Defining the European identity involves, according to this declaration:

- Reviewing the common heritage, interests and special obligations of the Nine and as well as the degree of unity so far achieved within the Community.
- Assessing the extent to which the Nine are already acting together in relation to the rest of the world and the responsibilities, which result from this.
- Taking into consideration the dynamic nature of European Unification.

One should note that there is no specific way of defining

European culture in this declaration. Instead they said that the nine member European states might have pushed towards disunity by their history and by defending selfish misjudged interests. But they have overcome their past rivalries and have decided that unity is a basic European necessity to ensure the survival of the civilization they have in common. This declaration further proclaimed that 'they are determined to defend the principles of representative democracy, the rule of law, of social life and of respect for human rights'.[18] They said all of these were the fundamental elements of the European identity.

A year later at the 1974 summit, the European Heads of State and Government agreed to study into special rights which could be granted to citizens of the member states as members of the Community. The subsequent Tindaman Report of 1975 recommended measures of protecting the rights of Europeans and a specific policy for transforming what the report called 'the technocrat's Europe into Peoples' Europe'[19], through concrete manifestation of European solidarity in everyday life.

This Tindaman's Report argued that the very success of the EC had meant that the Community should have become an everyday reality and regained its lost air of adventure. He wanted to build Europe in the fullest sense and not to limit integration to a series of functional economic agreements; he categorically stated, "No one wants to see a technocrat Europe. European Union must be experienced by the citizen in his every day life. *It must make itself felt in education and culture, news and communication*".[20] Thus Tindaman advocated a Pan-European culture and identity to raise a greater global voice for Europe and the dissemination of European ideas internationally to challenge the hegemony of the super powers. Europe, his report argued, must recover some control over its destiny. It must build a type of society which is *ours alone and which reflects the values, which are the heritage and the common creation of our peoples*.[21]

Meanwhile the European Parliament passed a resolution in which it stressed the EC to concentrate on the cultural sector. This resolution and the earlier Tindaman Report, both compelled the European Council - the apex organization of the

EC to do something concrete in the field of culture. In Rome Summit of 26 March 1977, it had directed the Commission to prepare a report on the scope, structure and financing of a European Foundation to look into the cultural aspect of integration as recommended by the Tindaman Report. On the same line, the London Report on 13th October 1981 and the subsequent policy proposal forwarded by both Federal Republic of Germany and Italy on "European Act", outlined new areas of cooperation especially on cultural matters to be developed.

Based on these reports and acts, the nine member states passed a "Solemn Declaration on European Union" on 19th June 1981 at Stuttgart European Council Summit. In this summit, the Heads of State and Government, on the basis of an awareness of common destiny and the wish to affirm the European identity, confirm their commitment to progress towards an ever closer union among peoples and member states of the EC. So far the culture was out of Community treaties' framework. Now that this declaration brought culture under informal procedure by saying, "to protect closer cooperation on cultural matters, in order to affirm the awareness of a common cultural heritage as an element in the European identity".[22] Then the question would arise: what sort of identity that the culture can give to Europe? Indeed the 1973 declaration on identity had already outlined some basic characteristic of such an identity based on culture:

> The diversity of cultures within the framework of Common European Civilization, the attachment to common values and principles, the increasing convergence of attitude to life, the awareness of having specific interest in common and the determination to take part in the construction of a united Europe, all give the European identity its originality and its own dynamism.[23]

To identify the cultural areas where the cooperation is to be carried out, an *ad hoc* committee known as Adinnino Committee was set up under the direction of European Council Summit at Fontainebleau on 25-26 June, 1984. Its main task was to further European cultural integration by promoting the EC's identity and its images both for its citizens and for the rest of the world. This Committee produced two reports under the title, 'A

People's Europe'[24], each of which suggested a sense of practical measures designed to give the Community a new political, cultural and social dimension. While the Solemn Declaration gave the much needed legal foundation to the cultural aspect of integration, the Adinnino Committee had in terms of practical measures paved the way for future cultural policies.

A People's Europe: Cultural Emphasis of Integration

The cultural aspect of international relations has come to the forefront when the UNESCO organizes a World Conference on Cultural Policies in Mexico on 26 July to 8 August 1982. This conference brought for the first time the cultural aspects of development and co-operation. While acknowledging the role of cultural industries in the economic development of the individual countries, at the same time it had emphasized the role of culture in reducing the conflict situations and promoting peace. In this sense, the intercultural communication was identified as the need of the time. Most importantly, the same conference underlined the necessity of strengthening of regional co-operation with the parallel affirmation of new cultural identities.

Drawing inspiration from the principles set by this conference, the Adinnino Committee sets its aim as 'to propose arrangements, which will be direct relevance to Community citizens and which will visibly offer them tangible benefits in their everyday lives'.[25] For this, it outlined a broader cultural policy to be undertaken by the Commission:

- Refers to a collective structure for society's activities to support and promote culture.
- Its successful implementation requires clearly defined objectives, working methods, procedures for follow-up and evaluation, responsible political and administrative organs plus financial resources.
- Covers the fields of education, the arts, youth, sports, the media and the cultural heritage.

The Committee submitted its report during the European Council meeting at Milan in 1985. In its recommendation, it re-emphasized Delor's slogan of *Europe Without Frontiers*[26], and extended this concept from market to education, media and tourism. It stressed the importance of cross-border, transnational cooperation in these fields and directed the Commission to frame policies to achieve concrete result from these prime areas of culture. In addition to these areas, it further recommends to activate the institution already set up called, 'European Foundation' to encourage in the fields of culture, communication, information and education and to create European Academy of Science, Technology and Art to highlight the achievement of European Science and the originality of European Civilization in all its wealth and diversity'.[27]

The spirit of the Adinnino Committee did not produce any tangible result in the field of culture. Even the much acclaimed Single European Act of 1987 did not envisage any scope for the cultural aspect of integration despite its tall claim in its preamble: "the will to continue the works undertaken on the basis of the Treaties establishing the European Communities and to transform relations as a whole among the states in to a European Union".[28] On the contrary, its main focus was on to create an economic and monetary union. Once again the economic issues dominated the agenda of the integration. The cultural angle of integration had to wait for some more years to make audible.

Maastricht and the Cultural Turn of Integration

In the midst of changed global scenario of the early 1990s, the twelve member states decided to strengthen their political and monetary bonds and negotiated a new treaty at the meetings of Heads of State and Government held in the Dutch city of Maastricht on December 9 and 10, 1991. The negotiated agreements called as 'Maastricht European Union Treaty' (in short Maastricht Treaty), was signed in February 1992. This treaty was a watershed in the history of European integration process in many senses. Specifically this treaty had not only dropped the word 'economics' by amending the earlier treaties but also for the first time brought the term 'culture' under the treaty provisions. As seen before, though the EC has already come out with some policy proposals concerning cultural issues, the cultural provisions of the Union had been deliberately kept

Treaty on European Union, 1992
Title IX

CULTURE

Article 128

1. The Community shall contribute to the flowering of the cultures of the Member States, while respecting their national and regional diversity and at the same time bringing the common cultural heritage to the fore.
2. Action by the Community shall be aimed at encouraging co-operation between Member States and, if necessary, supporting and supplementing their action in the following areas:
   — improvement of the knowledge and the dissemination of the culture and history of the European peoples;
   — conservation and safeguarding of cultural heritage of European significance;
   — non-commercial cultural exchange;
   — artistic and literary creation, including in the audiovisual sector.
3. The Community and the Member States shall foster co-operation with the third countries and the competent international organizations in the sphere of culture, in particular the Council of Europe.
4. The Community shall take cultural aspects into account in its action under other provisions of this Treaty, in particular in order to respect and to promote the diversity of its cultures.
5. In order to contribute to the establishment of the objectives referred to in this Article, the Council:
   — acting in accordance with the procedure referred to in Article 251 and after consulting the Committee of the Regions, shall adopt the incentive measures, excluding any harmonization of the laws and regulations of the Member States. The Council shall act unanimously through out the procedure referred to in the Article.
   — acting unanimously on a proposal from the Commission, shall adopt recommendations.

outside of the succeeding treaties of Paris, Rome and Single European Act.

For the first time, the Maastricht Treaty clearly stated that one of its principal objectives was to, "deepening the integration process by emphasizing the cultural aspect of integration through the principle of 'flowering of cultures'.[29] This emphasis of cultural aspect of integration in the treaty brings significant changes for the action undertaken by the Community in the cultural sector. To create an ever closer union of the People's Europe notably through the introduction of a citizenship of the Union is given substance through the conferment of specific powers in sectors such as culture. Indeed, the Article 128 of the treaty elaborately outlines the cultural part of integration and a legal foundation for future community initiatives and actions in the cultural fields. The Article 128 has not only made culture as an integral part of future integration process but also by its elaborate provisions set some directive principles to be implemented by the Commission.[30]

The Article 128(4) clearly put in words that the Community here onwards should take into consideration the cultural aspects of integration. Thus it has made culture as a mandatory domain of integration that cannot be skirt or pushed to the periphery. This new legal provision under this article enables the Community to undertake initiatives and promulgate future laws in the field of culture. For this purpose the Article 128(1) laid down the principle to be adopted in the course of cultural integration. Actually the EU aims a two-track approach to the culture: On the one hand, it encourages the Member States to promote and preserve their respective national and even subnational cultures; but at the same time it tries to propose an overarching European culture where these diversified national and subnational cultures mingle or melt into a holistic European culture. To carry forward such a cultural endeavor, the Article 128(2) further delineates the areas to be covered in the Community's future policy agenda. The shared cultural history of the European peoples, their common cultural heritage, artistic creation and the audiovisual sectors are some of the fields that have been given importance under this provision of the article.

The guiding methods for Community intervention in the cultural field are subsidiary and co-operative regionalism. Through the principle of subsidiary, the Maastricht Treaty envisages to redefine or rebalance the respective cultures of subnational, national and supranational levels so that the loyalty and legitimacy of the community be increased among the people. The second method is co-operative regionalism, which gives subnational governments legislative powers in the EC's policy-making process. In order to facilitate this, the treaty proposes a "committee of the Regions". It would advice both the Council and the Commission on matters of cultural importance.

II
CULTURE AND POLICY: A DEBATE

Nowadays Policy Sciences is a major interdisciplinary branch of study.[31] From the elected governments to non-governmental organizations, from small firms to larger corporations all have their own policy proposals to be carried out and implemented. In this sense "a policy is a guide for carrying out action".[32] Like any organizations, whatever may be their scale and range, have their own policy agenda; similarly all the subject matters irrespective of their nature and scope can have their own policy studies. International Relations too has its own share in the form of foreign policy study. In fact, there is a strong argument circulating among the International Relations' scholars that their subject field is nothing but a foreign policy study. Such is the legitimization that these Policy Sciences command in these years!

If then what is a policy? Steiner's definition may help us in this regard: "A policy is the general statements of purpose and objectives, plans to carry out those objectives, and practices and institutions for activities that are detailed or technical in nature".[33] Before venturing into an analysis of what are those purposes and objectives of the cultural policy of the European Union, we have to concentrate on a debate over the possibility or desirability of having such a policy proposal in the matters related to culture.

For Rajni Kothari, the term culture and policy cannot be concurrent and collateral; when policy means a centralized and focused approach to an issue, the very word culture conveys the idea of vicissitude and diversity. That is why, he would say "Any policy on culture which will lead to further centralization and bureaucratization, or any tightening grip of some entrenched power group, will in fact be an negation of culture".[34] On the other hand, Dube would argue that having a holistic cultural policy is inevitable in the period of constant flux and flow. In order to prevent completely cut off from our past tradition we have to have a policy approach towards the culture not only to preserve it but also to pass it over to the next generations. His logic is simple and prosaic:

> Fundamental alternations in the structure of society and in the relationships of production are inevitable. Along with them a cultural transformation is also imperative. It is our conviction that this transformation can be planned and guided. A cultural policy, thus, becomes necessary.[35]

While Dube supports the making of policy proposals to keep culture intact in the conditions of continuous change, Kothari opposed the very move by declaring that "culture is neither agriculture nor economics".[36] It is fundamentally a creative expression and highly an individualized opinion. Hence, for Kothari, any attempt to propose a cultural policy would ultimately kill the diversity of culture. In a precautionary tone he warns us "culture is not a matter of policy - except the policy of leaving it alone".[37]

Whatever may be the debate over the desirability of having such a cultural policy, the EC, contrary to the popular belief, has its own cultural agenda from its initial formative period onwards. So it is imperative to analyze its cultural policy in order to have a better understanding of the nature of the integration and its future course. To carry on this purpose, first of all there is a need to put forth in clear term what is meant by cultural policy. Conceptually, we would agree with Saberwal's notion of cultural policy: "A cultural policy has to be concerned not only with the content of culture so defined but also with the key domains wherein it is expressed and the channels through which it is transmitted".[38]

However, my intention would not rest with the content of culture, rather focus on the interpretation of culture. It is this interpretation which lends a specific status to the cultural policy. Unlike the other policies which are content with analyzing the present conditions and chart out its supposed planned projection of future orientation, the cultural policy in addition to these two tendencies has to interpret the past so as to set clear what the culture is. It is through this process of interpretation only that a cultural policy might be able to sense what should be preserved and transmitted. With this reasoning, one can analyze any cultural policy along three axes: interpretation, preservation and presentation of future purpose. And exactly this is the method that will be employed in the analysis of European Union's cultural policy.

EUROPEAN UNION AND INTERPRETATION OF CULTURE

To interpret what is culture is a highly challenging task. It is one of the modern words that have still had a diffuse and even elusive meaning. Nevertheless, one can outline three broad mode of conceptualization of culture: First, it means the artistic achievements say in paintings, sculpture, music, literature and architecture. In this sense, culture is predominantly associated with what is known as 'high arts'. It is this material manifestation of individual expression and skill that have been collectively articulated as culture. Second and the most prevalent meaning is the anthropological one; here culture has invariably been linked with a particular community say tribal, ethnic or national. It is said that each and every community has its own culture, which means a collective way of living; a pattern of common cognition and behavior. The third one is a recent articulation when compared with the above two streams of definition. Here culture means an ideology, more specifically a discourse. Having understood thus, this line of reasoning underlined the nature of constructedness inherent in the notion of culture. Its prime focus is on the interrelationship of power and culture. In this aspect, it is a critical engagement with the other two streams of thought.

Out of these three modes of interpretation of the term culture, the first two streams, that is, the high art and the anthropological mode have found their place in the European Union's understanding of culture. Indeed, when we closely analyze the Union's cultural policies we can catch hold of the shift that had happened in the conceptual terrain: from the presumption of 'high arts' to the anthropological perception. This has been well demonstrated in the speech given by Viviane Reding, the Commissioner in charge of Culture in the European Commission: "The Community...seeks to use an *organic definition* of the word 'culture' to ensure that new forms of cultural expression have access to support, alongside more 'traditional' forms of creativity".[39] Her explanation revolves around the organic definition along with her stress on the inclusive interpretation of the word 'culture'. However it is enough here to note that the Union has started treading along the anthropological conception of culture. In this section, the study intends to capture the shift in the interpretation of the Union's idea of culture. For this purpose, it would delineate three catchwords from the Union's policy documents: "Europe without Frontiers", "Flowering of Cultures", and "Common Cultural Area".

Europe without Frontiers

The economic enthusiasm of the Community made it give primacy to market. In a true liberal spirit, it was expected that the invisible hand of the market could not only regulate internal affairs of the societies but also their external relations among themselves. The underlining logic that governed the minds of the leaders of the Community at that time was to link the different national societies under one common market expecting that the rest of the thing would be managed by the internal dynamics of the market. In this philosophy of market naturally culture could have no other meanings but for the economic category. It was well reflected in the supposed cultural policy of the Community in the 1960s. Reducing culture as artifacts the Community emphasized the cross boarder free movement of the 'goods' of high arts such as paintings, sculptures and books etc. In addition, the Community supported the free and unhindered movement of artists across the borders.

Armed with the provisions of Articles 30-36 of the EEC Treaty, the Community for over two decades treated culture in a material sense, that is, one of the goods and services that could be circulated in the market. The underlying principle, as one Council resolution emphasized, was to establish "transnational cultural itineraries".[40] But however this does not mean that the Community did not know the other possible meanings of the word culture; rather sticking to the material aspect alone was their favored approach. It had been well expressed by one official of the EC as,

> We certainly regard culture in purely material terms or as a commodity, but it would be unrealistic to look upon it purely as an abstract product of mind. The least we can do in this respect is to attempt to remove the economic, legal and political barriers to international co-operation where such production can be source of mutual enrichment. The Community, at any rate, favors this approach.[41]

However the supposedly purely abstract notion of culture did slowly creep into the visibly materialistic minds of the Commission officials. More particularly during the Jacques Delors' presidentship of the Commission, the Community gradually got transformed into the notion of culture in the anthropological mode. His famous slogan '*Europe sans frontiers*' had not only meant for making the borders meaningless with respect to the material goods but also for the mental barriers. This perceptible change was in turn reflected in the cultural policy of the Community in the coming years. Delors announced in the European Parliament that the European Council intended to devote some time in 1986 to a discussion of the Community's role in the cultural sector and the Commission would be drawing up proposals to this end. As an indication to the new orientation, he declared enigmatically on the floor of the Parliament,

> Awareness of the European dimension presupposes familiarity with Europe's culture. The Commission will support and encourage initiatives at *rediscovering the history of our continent*.[42]

For this rediscovery of Europe without borders, later he came up with concrete policy proposals covering cultural areas such as,

- Common broadcasting policy
- Common education policy
- Promoting European tourism
- Encouraging specific measures like translation, architectural heritage, support of cultural events of European interest, European cinema and theatre.

Thus Delors' initiative was the major intervention in the cultural policy orientation of the Community. From then onwards had the cultural policy come out of its decade old materialistic outlook and instead look for some new potential avenues both conceptual as well as material. This was discernible when the Community turned to concentrate on the hitherto neglected fields such as media, tourism and heritage sites.

Flowering of Cultures

With the signing of the Maastricht Treaty the economic over-determinism has come to an end. This has been symbolically demonstrated by dropping the very word economics from the treaty provisions. By taking the Article 128 as the reference framework for its activities in cultural fields, the Commission sent a policy proposal to both the European Parliament and the Council under the title "New Prospects for Community Cultural Action" for approval on 29 April 1992. The Commission in this new proposal, popularly called as "First Report on Culture", while acknowledging the earlier cultural considerations however criticized them. "Although considerable means are devoted to cultural activities or activities with a cultural dimension", the Commission lamented, "the operations implemented rarely correspond to specific Community objectives in the cultural field".[43] As a way out, the Commission in this new proposal has outlined some areas of cultural interventions at the Community level. These are: (a) dissemination of European Culture and History, (b) conserving, publishing and safeguarding European Heritage, (c) promoting creative arts, and (c) promotion of electronic media for the dissemination of European identity.

The Council approved the Commission's initiatives in its meeting on 2 November 1992. While welcoming the policy agenda the Council once again emphasized the necessity of concentrating on the cultural aspect of the integration. Without mincing words, the Council clearly announced "the relationship between cultural and other domains (*Sic*) should be made visible... A Better balance must be created between the cultural, economic and other dimensions of the policy of the Community so that these dimensions supplement and support each other".[44] The same Council meeting further directed the Commission to study the potential future areas to be covered and to come with individual and area specific policy outlines. The Commission prepared its second report on culture under the title "European Community Action in Support of Culture". In this report the Commission set forth the preliminary ideas and suggestions for where emphasis should be placed in the cultural actions of the Community.

After getting the mandated approval from the Council when it met on 10 November 1994,[45] the Community, based on these policy outlines, has proposed some programs. The *Raphael* program in the field of cultural heritage has been initiated since January 1996. Under this program, conservation of cultural heritage, restorations of historical monuments are being identified as an irreplaceable means of increasing European awareness and of spreading knowledge about European culture. In order to achieve the said objective the Commission came out with certain programs by which the preservation of polychrome religious sculptures and restoration of baroque arts were given prim importance. Further to take the cultural heritage at the popular level the Commission adopted a two prong strategy: by starting a campaign program under the name "Europe, a Common Heritage"; and by proposing a scheme called "Schools and Museums" each school was encouraged to adopt a work of art, a monument for its exemplary educational quality.

Another program called *Kaleidoscope–2000* has been formulated for performing arts such as dance, music, theatre and opera. It has thus aimed to encourage artistic and cultural creation and co-operation of a European dimension. In 1995, the Commission adopted a program *Ariane*, for support in the fields of books and readings, including translation. Further it was intended especially to promote the dissemination and translation of literacy and dramatic works of European origin. These programs have been designed on the rationale that it would help to bring the cultural heritage to the wider audience across the linguistic and regional barriers.

The major challenge that the Community has to face in the cultural sector is to make sense of all the peoples of the Community irrespective of the social and class division about their shared cultural tradition. This has compelled the Council to make the Commission aware of the fact that "the geographical, physical, educational, social, economic obstacles may make it more difficult for many citizens to gain access to culture and may increase the incidents of exclusion, particularly among the less-favored groups of the population".[46] To remedy the situation the Council meeting of 20 January 1997 asked the Commission to prepare a new proposals to carry forward the cultural aspect of integration without any disparity and division.

A Common Cultural Area

The Commission encouraged by the response to its cultural initiatives taken specifically after the Maastricht period and the support it has got in this endeavor from both the European Parliament and the Council, envisaged a new program for the new millennium, officially called as Culture-2000 program.[47] It has established for a period of five years (2000-2004), with a total budget of 167 million EUR. This financial instrument will grant support for cultural co-operation projects in all artistic and cultural sectors including performing arts, visual and plastic arts, literature, heritage and cultural history.

The policy outline of this document has clearly specified its objectives as to promote a "Common Cultural Area" characterized by both cultural diversity and a Common Cultural Heritage. The new idea is different from the Community's earlier stand on culture in at least two ways: in the chosen objectives and the intended methodology to achieve them. In the immediate post-Maastricht period, when the Community was reluctantly entered into the cultural aspect of integration it was so cautious not to offend the national sentiments of the Member States. That is why its rallying slogan of that period was the flowering of cultures rather than promoting a unified European culture. It was mere content with introducing and making familiarize one national culture to another by methods of translation and mutual exchange and collaborations.

The entire policy agenda of the Commission was preoccupied to promote this strategy in a successful manner. But the Culture- 2000 program differs from this tested strategy; in a one big leap it declared that the Community's new millennium strategy would be to create a "Common Cultural Area". Anybody familiar with the discourse of the Community would immediately acknowledge the subtle turn happened in the sphere of cultural integration. Whenever the Community announced its intention of creating some common area, say, common market or common agriculture, in actuality they meant for harmonization or standardization in the said area. If that be the case, then the common cultural area would also mean the standardization of culture through out the Union territory, that is, promoting a single unified culture for the entire Union.

Similarly, in the case of methodology also the new program differs from the earlier approaches. While the mobility (i.e. public access to culture and the dissemination of individual national culture and arts across the national boundaries) was the methodological mantra for the Community for over a decade. This has been changed in the new policy proposal by stressing the necessity of concentrating upon the creativity instead of mobility. The creative aspect of the culture has been dawned on the Community by realizing the fact that merely sticking to the strategy of encouraging the cross border movement of artistic materials would not sufficient enough to achieve its said goal of cultural unification.

On the contrary, the Community starts believing that it needs some ideological grounding so that it can, not only extract some legitimacy for its actions in this field, but also reach the entire segments of the society from top to bottom of the rung. Knowing well that the artistic creativity is the encoded ensemble of some ideology, the Community in its new policy outlook gives much importance to the artists and their creations. The seemingly simple logic behind this shift (from mobility to creativity) is to convince the artistic minds, which in turn through their artistic expression could bring the people close to the projected unified European culture.

In addition to this, there is yet another logic which propels the Community to focus its attention circularly on creativity. Historically, the artists of different denominations would normally not restrict themselves within their national boundaries and used to have dialogue and comradeship with colleagues across the boarder or otherwise settle in some other territories. This genetically trans-border mentality of the artists attracts the Community more towards them. This attitude was well reflected in the speech given by Viviane Reding, the Commissioner of Culture in the European Commission, in her recent speech,

> Much of the European cultural tradition stems from constant dialogue between artists, a dialogue, which does not respect national frontiers. The European Union, with its unique position as regards co-operation within Europe, is perfectly placed to ensure the continuation of this dialogue in an often uncertain future.[48]

This understanding of the usefulness and utility of artists and their creation to propagate and promote the integration among the peoples of Europe has prompted the Community to give them primacy in the new policy approach to cultural action. This has been re-emphasized by both the European Parliament and the Council when they approved the Commission's new Culture-2000 program and put it in terse words as

> To bring to life the cultural area common to the European people, it is essential to encourage creative activities, promote cultural heritage with a European dimension, encourage mutual

> awareness of the culture and history of the peoples of the Europe and support the cultural exchanges with a view to improving the dissemination of knowledge and stimulating co-operation and creative activities.[49]

The discernible shift from the materialistic connotation of culture to creative aspect could be gauged from the 219 projects, which have been approved for the year 2000-2001 at the cost of 32 million EUR. Out of these total projects, majorities of them have been allocated to the creative fields.

From the above discussion one can realize that since the Rome Treaty there was much water has flown in the stream of European integration process. It is not only the economic determinism of integration receded back but cultural aspect has taken its place instead. Equally important to notice that within the cultural domain the idea of culture continuously got sharpened and transformed over the years: from the cultural economy of trans-boarder mobility of the artists and artistic goods (the period of Europe without Frontier) to familiarizing the discreet national cultures in each others' territories (the Flowering of Culture phase) to a common cultural area where the promotion of cultural dialogue, creativity and sharing and highlighting, at the European level, the common heritage of European significance.

So far this chapter has tried to characterize the cultural aspect of European integration and its unfolding in time; here the emphasis was not only on the chronological sequence of the emergence of the cultural integration but the shifts happened at both conceptual as well as at methodological levels. However in this section attempt has been made to outline these shifts within the general contours of the policy principles. In order to capture the nuances of the shifts, in the next section, the chapter would focus on some selective domains where the cultural policy of the Union has its direct effects.

CULTURAL POLICY AND ITS DOMAINS OF EXPRESSION

To make a policy for culture is a daunting task. In the case of other specific fields say agriculture or environment, which has precisely focused and limited scope and range, the making of any policy proposals would be more easy and effortless. But the notoriously elusive nature of culture, that has laid hand on every thing under the sun, from the most abstract category of collective structure of feelings and symbolic meanings to the visibly concrete manifestation of the works of art, languages and images. This octopus character of culture challenges any simple and systematic policy orientation towards it. If one dares to make such a policy on culture, he has to set his feet on so many diversified fields covering language, symbols, media and even tourism. Hence, I have isolated some specific fields in order to highlight the Community's cultural policy and more particularly the shifts happened in the conceptual domain of the culture itself.

Television without Frontiers: Media, Culture and the EC

The Community for over three decades carefully thought about that the creation of a market or opening up of a single economic space was a primary precondition for European integration. But in mid 1980s, when the EC realized the necessity of having to substantiate the integration process with some cultural orientation, one of the sectors, which immediately attracted attention, was the audio-visual product. The reason for this is of course understandable. Media is perhaps the best example that suits both ways; it has economic utility as well as cultural efficacy. That is why one policy proposal of the Community sets its objective as "to promote the exposure within the Community of each Member-State's broadcasts, thus advancing mutual economic, social, cultural and political interpenetrating of Member States and their peoples".[50]

The EC determined to defend its cultural identity saw reason to believe that the audio-visual sector was not only of major economic importance but also on activity loaded with cultural meanings. Therefore, the EC perceived the audio-visual products like cinema and television as cultural codes of symbolic meaning deserved to be consumed by wider European audience so as to act as an essential instrument to consolidate the European integration. The project of creating a European audio-visual space with "a minimal common cultural currency of the moving images"[51] produced by Europeans and addressed to European audience received much attention in the Commission.

In the European context, public service broadcasting is controlled more directly by the national states and is generally considered as the cultural arm of nation building or protecting. Radio and television have been, thus, conceived as the source of common meanings and of cultural cohesion. It is this national conception of television that has been transposed to the supranational level through the concerted efforts of EC's audio-visual policy. Indeed the EC wanted to create a European television channel and possibly a financial participation of the Community in one such intended channel 'Europe TV'.[52]

If the EC's intervention in the cultural field is examined, it is clear that, its action have been directed at setting up of a unified 'European Cultural Space' with the help of advanced communication technologies. It was the basic idea behind the envisioning of programs like MEDIA and Eureka audio-visual projects. In a policy document of 1984, *Television without Frontiers*, a close link was drawn between the working of mass media and the creation of European identity.[53] The actual idea behind this policy was to consider the transmission and consumption of television programs, to put in a Hebermasian terminology, as 'a culture-imparting or identity-confirming process'.[54] However, this policy did not mention any decisive mechanism to be undertaken to shape and sharpen the integration process further.

Under the broadcasting policy of 'Television without Frontiers', the EC rather tried to guarantee minimum quotas of European produced programs for national networks. Through "Edfo' program[55] (which covers off-setting, dubbing and marketing), the EC has set up a distribution network for European low-budget films to reach European-wide audience. Also through script fund, the EC encourages and rewards new script writing. In October 1989, the EC enacted a Television Directive aimed at standardizing measures relating to the support of television production, and advertising rules. The underlying principle behind these initiatives is 'transnationlisation of television' which means that ensuring equality of access to market freedom applied to television broadcasting across national frontiers. As a subsequent move, both the EC and the much broader regional grouping – the Council of Europe have encouraged the development of European television programming via regulatory measures and convention. Indeed, the Council of Europe has created 'Eurimages Fund',[56] to promote European Cinema.

Further it has set up European audio-visual observatory and organized European Convention on Cinematographic Co-production. These programs have been created aiming at stimulating the production and distribution of audio-visual products throughout member states. The best known of these in the case of EC are the successive MEDIA 92 and MEDIA 95 programs[57], which have sought to strengthen the EC's internal market across national boundaries. These overarching programs are divided into numerous subprograms that have had some impact in creating a European audio-visual market by stimulating new products and in enhancing cross-national collaboration.

Schlesinger rightly observed that there has been a double rationale behind this EC's audio-visual project. On the one hand, the production of European films and television programs has been conceived as a kind of cultural defense activity. The US television fictions and films are widely popular in Europe. The American products circulated in European in the last fifteen years have risen from 35 to 80 percent on average while European products today only account for one per cent of American market. This American popularity has been contemptuously seen as posing a threat of increasing 'Americanization of Europe'. The Baget-Bozzo Committee rightly identified this trend as a result of 'profound European cultural identity crisis'.[58]

To check the overflow of American audio-visual products into European market, the EC has tried to impose quotas and allocate considerable subsidies to indigenous production and distribution networks. This triggered off a major controversy between the US and the EC in the Uruguay Round of GATT negotiations. What has become obvious after the Uruguay Round victory, as one Commission report claims, is that of "defending Europe's cultural identity, forgotten over the centuries by rich mosaic of its many languages but whose common trait has always been universality, its inseparable from recapturing the European market and therefore its audience".[59]

On the other hand, in theoretical sense, it has been assumed in official circles that it is possible to create a common culture through television and cinema production and consumption. They expect that a European audio-visual space might operate as a kind of public sphere that could confer an European identity upon the various people living within it.[60] In this regard cinema has been given a specific treatment. As one Council resolution emphasized, "Cinema is a unique record of the life, customs, history and geography of Europe". It is not just the cinema's cultural authenticity attracts the Community. Rather the Community expects that its "inherent reproducibility and mobility of the cinema medium make it an excellent vehicle for the reciprocal spread of knowledge among peoples".[61] This realization of the cultural potential of cinema compelled the Community to spend considerable amount of its energy as well as money in this sphere so as to make it as both memory and message, mirror and window of the collective European identity. On the eve of the centenary celebration of the cinema the Community has adopted a two-prong strategy: first, through a program called "Lumier Project" a close co-operation among the film archives of the Member States was mooted; second, to promote the dissemination of this common cinema heritage both within the Europe and abroad, the Community has envisaged celebrating a combined European festivals of cinema.

With these media initiatives, the EC believes that Europe can attain its glorious peak once again when it is able to speak for the larger and wider European culture and its civilization, where the English Shakespeare, the German Mozart and the French Picasso are liberated out of their respective national boundaries and portrayed as geniuses and torch-bearers of broader European culture. It is this task that the EC considers important and strives to promote through its audio-visual policy.

But in practice, European-produced programs have limited scope for audience identification due to Europe's linguistic diversity and this diversity prevents any kind of uniform consumption or interpretation. This is clearly manifested in the empirical studies done by Liebes and Katz[62] as well as by Schlesinger.[63] What these studies suggest is that it is something impossible about asking people to consume television or cinema as if they already had a European dimension or imagination. The Europe's language diversity poses serious problems for EC's efforts to achieve a single audio-visual space. The EC is well aware that any attempt to homogenize Europe through a single language, be it English, German or French, is simply impossible and conceived by others as a threat to their cherished languages and their diversities. De Swaan correctly observed that the "robustness of European states and their languages make it extremely unlikely that further political integration will be accompanied by language unification".[64]

The language problem - the virtual impossibility of having one unified language for Western Europe, compelled the EC to concentrate on education. Instead of striving for creating a unified language zone, it reconciled to the idea of making every language familiarize with the entire Community zone. For this purpose the EC drafted an education policy to which we will turn now.

Language and Culture: Europeanizing Education

Language is generally considered as a cultural and symbolic entity. It is said to be the bearer of cultural ensembles. Both the language and culture are thus closely integrated and intertwined. It is through the language only people could recollect their past, and reinterpret it for future. Anderson has ably demonstrated that how language plays a crucial role in imagining any kind of community.

The major impediment that the EC faces in its project of constructing the broader European Political Union is the impossibility of organizing any future Europe-wide Community along a single language. The nation – the modern political community, has been effectively constructed around and through a particular language. Such is the inter-connectedness of the concepts - ethnicity, national and language, without which one might not be able to imagine, let alone constructing an alternative community.

The language diversity of any community always poses threat to its very existence as a community. The best example is Canada. The French speaking Quebec is demanding autonomy from the English-speaking Canada. Even the supposed more flexible and elastic federation could not have pacified the French-speaking people. They see the present dispensation in Canada is not conducive to the prosperity and development of their native French language and culture. If the French and English speaking people, despite their coexistence of more than a century under a single political establishment, could not carry on further on the same line, how could the EC succeed in establishing a single, unified Pan-European political community covering such a multi-linguistic varieties of different shades? Exactly what the EC proposes now, Canada has already disposed of: What Canada tries to do in the name of multiculturalism to keep intact their national structure, the EC treads on the same path, but paradoxically in the name of post-nationalism.

In order to highlight the EC's strategies with regard to language, I would single out one specific field - education. Here, my aim is two fold: not only to pinpoint the interconnection of culture and language, but to expose whenever there was a shift in EC's notion of culture and its interpretation, there was equally a change of outlook happened in the field of education. Since I have already demarcated three kinds of perceptible shift in the interpretation of culture, now I would emphasis how these shifts in turn modified and structured the EC's conception of education and its policies.

When the EC understood culture as a part of 'trasnational itineraries', the same was reflected in the field of education too. Unlike culture, the subject matter education found its place even in the earlier treaties. The ECSC Treaty (Art 56) provides for vocational training; similarly the EEC Treaty gives scope for mutual recognition for diplomas in the Member States (Art 57) and vocational training of workers (Art 118) and farmers (Art 41). These examples of the treaty provisions would amply demonstrate where does actually the interest of the Community lie as far as education is concerned: the technical and vocational aspect. But once the necessity of making the people of Europe aware of their respective cultures and mutually understand them, the EC came with a more participatory aspect of education whereby it gave much stress to the trasnational movement of both students and teachers. As a sequence to this change of perception, the Community using Art 9.2 of the EAEC treaty established European University Institute at Florence in 1976. The idea that drove the Community to establish such a centralized university was to not only achieve congregation of students and teachers of different national background assemble at a single place but also it was expected to impart a European dimension of education.

Thus in the initial formative period when culture was hardly matter in the discourse of integration, education was content with imputing technical skills and instigating trans-boarder mobility. When integration reached a stage whereby it had to have come out of its earlier economic determinism and looked for some new avenues to deepening its process, in short with the cultural turn of integration, the educational policy of the Community witnessed a new shift. That is to make the citizens of the EC aware of their common cultural tradition. Here comes the peculiar problem that the EC has to face squarely: both practical and theoretical. In the practical domain language gives the severe headache to the Community: could it possible for the Community to find a language suitable and acceptable for all the linguistic groups residing within its boundaries? Even more is the pressing problem when it comes to have a common history textbooks satisfying the cultural sentiment of the different national groups. How could it be viable to write a history book, which would do justice to all the nationalities whose histories unto the last century were in direct opposition to each other? Or otherwise, how could be possible to portray the Hundred Years War between the English and the French or the Napoleonic wars (Napoleon, the supposed national hero of the French was definitely the villain for the rest of Europe) in such a way as to convince and pacify the warring sentiments of both the parties concerned?

In this context the multicultural education is presumed to be the correct response to the challenges of creating European Community. As one Council document put it vividly, "interculturalism embodies the principles which inspired the Council of Europe since its creation".[65] The same document recommended to the EC to make ensure that the younger generation of the Community countries in future is familiar with at least two other languages of the Community area. To promote this, the Commission came out with the policy program called "Erasmus", whereby the students of one country can be avail the educational facilities of another. Further as an additional strategy, the Community made initiative to make available the books written in one language be translated into other languages and have a free and unhindered access to other linguistic areas. Indeed in 1985 itself the Commission in its communication to the Council stresses the necessity of what it called "European dimension with regard to books".[66]

The second strategy of the EC is to stress the unity of these national cultures: 'in spite of the wide diversity of national traditions, the existence of cultural unity within Europe is a fact which is no where called into question'[67], the EC declared emphatically. To stress this aspect of unity the educational policy should not only accommodate each other's national cultures but also underlie the cultural unity of Europe. This aspect of education emerged clearly when the Commission sent a policy proposal to the Council, in which it lamented: "the profession (i.e. education) have become cut off from each other and locked within the individual countries in spite of the existence of a common cultural heritage from which each of them continue to draw".[68] To inculcate a sense of Europeanness among the younger generation, the education policy of both the EC and Council of Europe argued for Europeanization of national education. Its object is to bring the peoples of Europe closure together and make them aware of their common cultural heritage.

The discipline, which received much attention for importing Europeanization, is history. "History is our common memory and I believe that the time is ripe for new initiatives by Council of Europe on history teaching and text books",[69] says Secretary General of the Council of Europe. So far history of Europe has been written as the sum total of the histories of nations. To make the people come out of their national sentiment needs primarily a writing of history whose nature and scope must be inclusive of the entire Europe. The resolution of Committee of Ministers of European Cultural Identity points out that "our traditions and European identity are the product of common cultural history and are not delimited by the frontiers separating different political systems in Europe".[70]

In the post-Maastricht phase, the Council gives much importance to the cultural history of Europe. That is why in the "Culture 2000" proposal the priority has been given to the writing of the cultural history of Europe. It is expected that "the knowledge of the shared experiences and memories strengthens the bonds between European citizens and contributes to the development of a European awareness".[71] To write and promote this 'European history', the Commission organized a series of seminars and symposium, inviting the professional historians and teachers to carry on this project. So far the Europe's history has often been written as that of the sum of national histories. But the Council insists that the Commission should fund project concerning the writing of the history of Europe so as "to ensure that such projects are as Pan-European as possible in order to improve the knowledge and the understanding of the history of the European peoples and thereby making a significant contribution to European co-operation and integration".[72] On the basis of this idea the Commission funded years back to write such a history: Duroselle wrote European history under the title of *Europe: A History of Its People*.[73] Thus the cultural turn of integration has prompted the EC to prod and poke into the matters so far unimaginable: form translation to writing a common European history.

Cultural Tourism as Pilgrimage

In a modern industrial society tourism is a leisure and pleasure seeking activity. It is basically an individualistic adventure; and its sheer potential of economic transaction has endowed it as one of the crucial economic activities. Above all its potential of generating cross boarder mobility of both men and women is incomparable. On both these accounts tourism is well suited within the provisions of Rome Treaty. That is why, the Adinnino Committee which was set up to look for some cultural sectors for promoting integration specifically singled out tourism as a potential area to be concentrated necessarily. Yet tourism is not simply an asset to be exploited for the economic activity and job generating method. As happened with the other fields, tourism too gradually acquired more ideological underpinnings, rather than merely content with the economical purposes. As one EC document rightly observed that "tourism's importance in a multicultural, multi-national Community like ours lies in its function as a promoter of mutual knowledge, understanding and awareness of the Community dimension".[74]

The EC thus over the years, is fully aware of the cultural aspect of tourism that would provide the much needed vehicle for propagating the European culture. The EC has come with a policy proposal on tourism, what it calls, 'cultural tourism', which aims to "improve general knowledge of history, art and social customs of great importance to the Community... (because) it brings Europeans face to face with the reality of their shared heritage".[75] The EC's 'cultural tourism' policy was conceived as a double-track strategy: by providing and enhancing the infrastructure facilities, determined to boost the inter-European tourism and thereby mobilize considerable employment generation and capital resources; and at the same time, by encouraging Europeans to visit the member states' culturally important places and monuments, it believes, could inculcate a sense of Europeanness among its people. In no other fields than this tourism sector that the Community's gradual but decisive shift in the perception of culture can be gauged. From the initial conception of the "transnational itineries", tourism has acquired over the years a depth of meaning, which signifies the parallel thick description of culture.

In the post-Maastricht phase of integration, tourism is considered with some positive connotations apart from its usual economic viability. It has now become a strategy to promote the expected "flowering of cultures". In a traditional sense, to make their community people to undertake a pilgrimage to the European cultural heritages. The underlying strategy of the EC is to transform the mere individualistic, hedonistic activity of tourism into a culturally determined collective pilgrimage. This is evident from the statement of European Union's Commissioner of Tourism, Christes Papoutsis, in his speech:

> A couple of years before 2000, at the threshold of a new era, we should undertake a cultural and spiritual self-questioning... cultural and religious tourism could be excellent means to achieve this goal.[76]

The above-discussed media, education and tourism policies of the EC made us aware of the internal dynamics and the shifting conceptual interpretation of culture within the Community's policy orientations. As a surface manifestation, the Community seems to have employed two-prong strategies. First, culture as an economic category where the cultural industries and the cross border mobility of the so-called cultural goods received at most attention. Second, in the anthropological understanding of the term culture, the Community has undertaken the project of promoting the supposedly existing European cultural unity. As a part of this project, the Community has evolved a strategy based on the effective mobilization of people around some symbols, which would signify essentially the European Spirit.

Culture and Integration: Symbolizing Europe

Cris Shore rightly identified the symbolic gestures of the Community as 'motivational dynamics relating to Europeanization'.[77] With this thematic idea the EC has created a number of Euro-symbols believing that these symbols of Europe would mobilize sentiments and public opinions in favor of it. Among these new symbols of Europe, the 'European Flag' and 'European Anthem' deserve mention. The European flag - twelve gold stars on a blue background and the European

Anthem taken from the prelude of Beethoven's "Ode to Joy" which the Commission insists must be displayed and performed respectively wherever the EC sponsored public ceremonies are being held. According to one Commission report, this anthem is "representative of the European idea and should therefore be played at appropriate events and ceremonies. Other symbolic measures included the standardized passport, the harmonized European driving license and numberplates.[78]

Along this line there is another symbolic measure, which has been employed form 1985 is the "European Capital of Culture".[79] Under this program all the important cities associated with the development of European culture will be selected by a rotational system thereby ensure that each Member State will have one of its cities chosen at regular intervals. It is expected that by promoting this symbolic gesture of announcing a city as a cultural capital of Europe for a year or more would bring the citizens of Europe close to each other and inculcate a sense of belonging together.

In the previous chapter, I have exclusively concentrated on the general course of the historical evolution of the formation of the European Community in the post-Second World War years. After highlighting the various historical explanations given to the process of European integration, in this chapter, I have circled out one particular issue of whether culture has any role to play in the integration drive. Affirming the cultural aspect of integration by extricating the cultural policy of the European Union, I have singled out three conceptual shifts that had happened in the interpretation of culture - from material connotation to a more abstract and symbolic definitions. Presuming that the shifts in the conceptual domain of culture indicate the parallel shift appears in the imagination of political community that is from national community to some broader post-national community; or to put it in other words, from nationalism to Europeanism.

Precisely this dynamics of Europeanization would be the focal point of the next chapter. In the second chapter, I have already explained that the Europeanization was conceived as a way out or solution to the philosophico-historical condition (which I called 'Europe at the antithesis of culture and civilization') in which Europe caught hold of in the post-Enlightenment era. In the next and last chapter, my intention is to draw attention to the imperial tendency of the Europe and its causal relationship with the integration process. This task will be carried on with the help of the recent postcolonial theoretical ventures.

REFERENCES

1. Senator Joe Lee in *The Irish Time*, 2 July 1996. Emphasis added.
2. However one should not confuse this Council of Europe with European Council or Council of Ministers of the European Union institutions. The Council of Europe is completely a different set of organization, which would not come under either any provisions of the European Union Treaties, or under any of the European Union institutions. It is basically an intergovernmental organization exclusively concentrating maters of European culture and identity.
3. Gunther Muller, "Report on European Cultural Cooperation", *Parliamentary Assembly of the Council of Europe*, vol. 1, 3 February 1988, Doc.5871, p.9.
4. Ibid., p.14.
5. In this chapter, I would use the term EC to denote all the institutions carved out by the Rome Treaty such as European Coal and Steel Community, European Economic Community and Euatom. When I use the term EU, it signifies all these institutions after the Maastricht Treaty. However I treat both the EC and EU as interchangeable terminologies.
6. "Statement by The Heads of State and Government at The Hague Summit in 1969", in *European Political Cooperation*, edn.5, (Bonn, 1988).
7. Bruno de Witte, "Cultural Linkages", in William Wallace, ed., *The Dynamics of European Integration* (London, 1990), p. 193.
8. "Declaration on the Occasion of the Achievement of Common Customs Union", 1 July 1968, in *European Political Cooperation* (Bonn, 1988).
9. E. Wistricht, *After 1992: The United States of Europe* (London, 1989), p.36.
10. Monnet quoted in Cris Shore, "Inventing the 'People's Europe': Critical Approaches to EC's Cultural Policy", *Man*, vol. 28, p. 787.

11. Communiqué of the Conference of the Heads of State and Government of the Member States of EC, The Hague, 2 December, 1969, in *European Political Co-operation* (Bonn, 1988), p. 22.
12. First Report of the Foreign Ministers submitted to the Heads of State and Government on 27 October 1970, in *European Political Co-operation* (Bonn, 1988), p.26.
13. Ibid., p. 25.
14. Statement of the Conference of the Heads of State and Government of the EC, Paris Summit, 21 October 1972, in *European Political Co-operation* (Bonn, 1988), p. 32.
15. The statement quoted from "Europe Today: State of European Integration, 1980-1981", European Parliament Secretariat, Director-General for Research and Documentation (Luxembourg, 1981), p. 4.72.
16. See "Copenhagen Report", in *European Political Co-operation* (Bonn, 1988), p. 36.
17. Ibid., p. 37.
18. Ibid., p. 38.
19. L. Tindaman, "Report on European Union", *Bulletin of the European Community*, supplement 1/76, (Luxembourg, 1976).
20. Ibid., p.6. Emphasis added.
21. Ibid., p. 11. Emphasis added.
22. "Solemn Declaration on European Union", 19 June 1981, in no. 6, p. 4.
23. "Document on the European Identity", published in *Bulletin of the European Community*, supplement 1/74 (Luxembourg, 1974), p. 50.
24. P. Adinnino, "People's Europe: Report from the *ad hoc* Committee", *Bulletin of the European Community*, supplement 7/85 (Luxembourg, 1985).
25. Ibid., p. 9.
26. For this see, Jacques Delors, "Statement on the Thrust of Commission Policy to the European Parliament", *Bulletin of the European Community*, supplement 1/85 (Luxembourg, 1985).
27. P. Adinnino. no. 24, p. 22.
28. "The Single European Act, 1987", in *European Union, Selected Instruments Taken from the Treaties*, Book I, Vol. I (Luxembourg, 1999) p. 765.
29. "Treaty on European Union", in *European Union, Selected Instruments Taken from the Treaties*, Book I, Vol. I (Luxembourg, 1999).
30. The Amsterdam Treaty through its modification and

consolidation of the earlier treaties changed the sequential number of the articles, which deal with culture. Instead of put under Title IX, Article 128, the provisions of culture are now placed under Title XII, Article 151 without any change either in words or ideas. However, in this Chapter, I chose to quote Article 128 as originally placed under the Maastricht Treaty.

31. For an initial and trend setting analysis refer, Daniel Lerner and Harold D. Lasswell, ed., *The Policy Sciences: Recent Developments in Scope and Method* (Stanford, 1951).
32. Valliant Higginson quoted in Richard M. Hodgetts and Max S. Wortman Jr., *Administrative Policy: Texts and Cases in the Policy Sciences* (London: John Wilay & Sons Inc., 1975), p. 4.
33. A. Steiner, *Business and Society* (New York, 1971), pp. 268-69.
34. Rajni Kothari, "Policy and Culture", in Satish Saberwal, ed., *Towards a Cultural Policy* (Delhi, 1975), p. 30.
35. S.C. Dube's welcome address printed in Satish Saberwal, ed., no. 34, p. 8.
36. Rajni Kothari, no. 34, p. 30.
37. Ibid., p. 31.
38. Satish Saberwal, "The Theme Paper", in Satish Saberwal, ed., no. 34, p. 3.
39. Viviane Reding, "Which Cultural Policy for the European Union?", Speech Delivered to Conference of the World Association of Newspapers, Hanover, 1 June 2000. Emphasis added. Cited in http:/ / www.europa.eu.int/
40. Resolution of the Ministers responsible for Cultural Affairs, meeting within the Council of 17 February 1986, *Official Journal* No. C044, 26.02.1986, Doc. 486Y0226(02), p. 0002.
41. Statement by Ambassador Mertz on behalf of the Luxembourg Presidency at the CSCE Forum, Budapest, 15 October 1985, in *European Political Cooperation* (Bonn, 1988), p. 219-20.
42. Statement by J. Delors to the European Parliament, "Program of the Commission for 1986", *Bulletin of the European Community*, supplement 1/86 (Luxembourg, 1986), p. 30. Emphasis added.
43. "New Prospects for Community Cultural Action", *Bulletin of the European Community*, supplement 1/92 (Luxembourg, 1992), p.28.
44. Conclusion of the Ministers of Culture meeting within the Council of 12 November 1992 on guidelines for Community Cultural Action, *Official Journal* No. C.336, 19.12.1999, Doc. 492Y1219(01), pp. 0001-0002.
45. Ibid., pp. 0001-0002.
46. Council Resolution of 25 July 1996 on Access to Culture for All,

Official Journal, C.242, 21.08.1996, Doc. 396Y0821(01), p. 0001.
47. Ibid., p. 0001.
48. Viviane Reding, no. 39.
49. Decision No 508/2000/EC of the European Parliament and of the Council of 14 February establishing the Culture- 2000 Program, *Official Journal*, L.063, 10.03.2000, Doc. 300D0508, pp. 0001-0009.
50. See "The Communities Broadcasting Policy: Proposals for a Council Directive Concerning Broadcasting Activities", *Bulletin of the European Communities*, supplement 8/86 (Luxembourg, 1986), p. 5.
51. Commission of the European Community, *Report by the Think-Tank on the Audio-visual Policy in the European Union* (Luxembourg, 1994), p.4.
52. See Commission of the European Community, *Television without Frontiers: Green Paper on the Establishment of the Common Market for Broadcasting* (Luxembourg, 1984).
53. Ibid., p. 8.
54. J. Habermas, *Legitimation Crisis* (Heinemann, 1976), p.118.
55. See no. 52, p. 24.
56. "European Cinema: A Common Future" 8th Conference of European Ministers Responsible for Cultural Affair, Budapest, 28-29 October 1966. Cited in http://www.europa.eu.int/
57. See Commission of the European Community, *Information, Communication and Openness* (Luxembourg, 1994), p.25.
58. Baget-Bozzo, *Report on the Information Policy of the European Community* (Luxembourg, 1986).
59. See, no.57, p. 32.
60. On this aspect refer, Draft Resolution of 4 April 1995 on Culture and Multimedia, *Official Journal*, C.247, 23.09.1995, Doc. 395Y0923(01), pp. 0001-2.
61. Council Resolution of 26 June 2000 on the Conservation and Enhancement of European Cinema Heritage, *Official Journal*, C.193, 11.07.2000, Doc. 300Y0711(01), pp. 0001-2.
62. T. Liebes and E. Katz, *The Export of Meaning: Cross-Cultural Readings of DALLAS (New York*, N.Y., 1990).
63. See Philip Schlesinger, *Media, State and Nation: Political Violence and Collective Identities* (London, 1991).
64. De Swaan, " Notes on the Emerging Global Language System: Regional, National and Supranational", *Media, Culture and Society*, vol.13, no. 3, p. 311.
65. "Report of the Secretary General on Problems of Education and Training in Europe", *Parliamentary Assembly of the Council of*

Europe, vol. 1, 12 April 1988, Doc.5864, p.13.

66. On this aspect refer, "Resolution of the Council and of the Ministers responsible for cultural affairs, meeting within the Council of 9 November 1987 on the promotion of Translation of the works of European Culture", *Official Journal* No. C309, 19.11.1987, Doc. 487Y1119(01), p.0003.
67. "A General System for the Recognition of Higher Education Diplomas", *Bulletin of the European Community*, supplement 8/85 (Luxembourg, 1985), p.5.
68. Ibid., p.5.
69. See no.67, p.15.
70. Ibid., p.16.
71. For this matter refer, "Council Resolution of 28 October 1999, Integrating History into Community's Cultural Action", *Official Journal* No. C.324, 12.11.1999, Doc. 3999Y1112(01), p.0001.
72. Ibid., p. 0001.
73. J. Duroselle, *Europe: A History of Its People* (Viking, 1990).
74. "Community Action in the Field of Tourism", Commission Communication to the Council Transmitted on 31 January 1986, *Bulletin of the European Community*, supplement 4/86 (Luxembourg, 1986), p.6.
75. Ibid., p.10.
76. Christos Papoutsis, *Culture and Tourism: Opportunities and Perspectives* (Luxembourg, 1986), Speech/ 96/52. Cited in http://www.europa.eu.int/
77. Cris Shore, no.10, p.790.
78. P. Adinnino, no.24, p.12.
79. On this aspect refer, Decision 1419/1999/EC of the European Parliament and of the Council of 25 May 1999 establishing a Community Action for the European Capital of Culture event for the year 2005-2019, *Official Journal*, L.166, 01.07.1999, Doc. 399D1419, pp. 0001-5.

Chapter V

Imperialism of European Integration: A Postcolonial Critique

Once we understood Europe as an imaginary construction, aiming the perpetuation of its colonial mastery, one may expect that with the end of colonialism this purposeful imagination would have come to an end. But the story is not as simple as one may expect; Europe does not stop to exist with the end of colonialism. Indeed, it has reincarnated itself in a new *avatar*, as a promoter of world peace specifically in the context of the cold war situation. Interestingly, the discourse of European integration lends a space for such a boasting and keeping intact its earlier *ser-monological* posturing. Had the imaginary land of Europe of rational and universal ideas given moral superior notion to the Europeans in the colonial period, it is now the European integration process that makes survive Europe's earlier superior, moral sense to preach the world.

In this sense, the integration is not a new phenomenon determined by the consequences of Second World War or some internal dynamics of European politics. On the other hand, a continuation of its earlier colonial policy by other means: as a deliberate attempt on the part of the Europeans to actualize or concretize what they imagined earlier in the colonial space; as an attempt to translate the ideality into reality. Moreover this process gives the Europeans a sense of further progress and achievement towards higher morals. It is said that while the rest of the world is fighting among themselves in the name of nationalism, more particularly the newly independent third world countries, Europe boasts of striving to move forward to post-national society and state and thereby creates a zone of peace within Europe. Once again Europe becomes an ideal model and to be emulated by others. Europe thus successfully created the old colonial binary of Europe / Orient in post-colonial situation but in a different terminology: zone of peace / zone of conflict.

What is interesting more is that the subversion of its earlier discourse but at the same time reproducing the same colonial power relationship. In the colonial period it was repeated again and again either in colonial historiography or in literature that the colonized people were not nation in themselves; they were divided along all sorts of primitive identities. It was Europe that united them and brought them under one roof. After centuries of their struggle for liberation through national movement, now Europe condemns nationalism as divisive force and a dangerous one to world peace. What a striking contrast to see that the year 1950 witnessed both the birth of the democratic republic of India and the Schumann plan of bringing Europe under one political unit. If at all any world peace ever possible the rest of the world should follow the path of Europe in relegating the idea of nationalism. Already the East Europeans buying the argument stand in a queue to be admitted into the fold of the European Union. Thus, to be precise, the European integration process gives Europe the status of theoretical, political *avant-garde* and the vanguard of the march of history, where the other people should always and forever follow it.

European integration is a yet another discourse of Europeans to perpetuate their superior power relationship *vis-à-vis* the other people in the post-colonial phase. By comparison, then, and in contrast to the previous colonial project which aimed to inscribe power in the hierarchical order of colonized and colonizer, the European integration discourse produces the same force of power albeit in a different ordering: war and peace; nationalism and post-nationalism. And, after all, is it not perhaps the case that the colonial discourse is no sooner brought under sever criticism, the particular element of power relationship that the third world sought to overcome through the national liberation movements are no sooner accredited and put into circulation in a different set of discourse, i.e. integration? A re-colonization in a different sense?

It may spring surprise to have seen a link between the seemingly internal process of European integration with its old colonial ventures. Even one may get suspicion of my intention of understanding the process and accuse of the familiar criticism the third world scholars face today - of bringing colonial issues in all and sundry. Despite the repeated criticism, the scholars of this side increasingly aware of the fact that colonialism was not as simple as thought of earlier. Having come out of the accepted theories of colonialism - predominantly focusing on the political or economic aspect of colonialism, (what an irony, these theories of colonialism also handed over by the colonizers), these thinkers delineate the much broader ramifications of colonialism. In this sense, nowadays the aspects of cultural imperialism and production of power relationship get greater attention. They have started exploring the hitherto uncharted terrain of the colonialism. The good example of this line is Ashis Nandy who examined the psychological aspect of colonialism exposed the concealed dynamics of colonialism nakedly:

> This colonialism colonizes minds in addition to bodies and it releases forces within the colonized societies to alter their cultural priorities once for all. In the process, it helps generalize the concept of modern west from a geographical and temporal entity to a psychological category. The west now everywhere, within the west and outside; in structures and in minds.[1]

If Europe is a fictitious psychological fantasy, then the hysteria over the integrating such a psychic landscape is nothing but a pathological syndrome. The interrelationship of a pathological condition and the circulation of the discourse of European integration can be well demonstrated when one starts historicizing the integration process itself. That is to presume the integration as a yet another strategy of imperialism in the era of decolonization.

Only within the total framework of the imperial history of Europe and the immediate conditions of decolonization, the integration can be intelligible. So, we are faced with the task of re-fashioning the hitherto uncritically accepted Eurocentric interpretations, which so far successfully concealed the imperialist genealogy of integration. What was overlooked was the inter-relations of 'integration' and 'imperialism' both in economic and political arms. In other words, in this chapter, it will be highlighted that the integration is the inversion of Europe's earlier imperial strategy. In order to set its alternative interpretation, the study would first bring the recent postcolonial theoretical ventures into the field of International Relations. Secondly, by equipped with the postcolonial theoretical tool, the chapter concentrates on the conceptual link that exists between the imperialism and integration.

I
BRIDGING POSTCOLONIALISM AND INTERNATIONAL RELATIONS

In recent times, a sort of revolution is happening in the third world academia: more and more scholars of this area are becoming aware of their colonial past and its influence and impact on their academic theorizing. It was generally believed that with the formal demise of colonialism and the raising tide of national consciousness and the subsequent establishment of independent nation-states, the former colonized countries have finally entered into the history of their own. But this sense of content has evaporated once the academicians, the privileged strata of the national society came to realize the fact that indeed, the colonial discourse of the erstwhile masters did not disappear with the end of colonial rule. On the contrary, it has been prolonged and propagated in the academic arena; and the most disgusting part of it is that it is being done by the third world scholers themselves.

Once this realization dawned on their head, their immediate response was to problematize the each and every subject field as a lineage of colonialism and the site where even today the colonial discourses survived and structured even the minds of the third world scholars. Thus postcoloniality is a condition of a consciousness on the part of the third world scholars of the irretrievable and incorrigible impact of colonialism on their mental structure and the incrusting nexus between the individual disciplines of social science and the discourse of colonialism. As one scholar puts it vividly, "Postcolonial refers to a *process* of disengagement from the whole colonial syndrome, which takes many forms and is probably inescapable for all those whose worlds have been marked by that set of phenomena: 'Postcolonial' is a descriptive not an evaluative term".[2]

This descriptive aspect of postcolonialism has produced incitement to third world scholars to seriously look for alternative theories which would do justice to their historical experience and not mechanically regurgitating the western theories whose main purpose is to legitimize the colonial discourse. One way of doing this, perhaps the visibly predominant one, is to start questioning the very premises of the existence of the subject field itself. The anthropologists, historians and literary theorists started focusing on the nexus between their respective subject disciplines and the colonial discourse. Talal Asad in his path setting article exposed how the birth of anthropology as a separate subject was "dialectically linked"[3] to the ambitions of the colonial masters. Kathleen Gough dares to pronounce that the discipline of anthropology was "the child of western imperialism" and called for new proposals for anthropologists.[4]

In the similar vein, some historians in India, collectively known as 'Subaltern Studies' historians echoed the same critical tone of their counterparts in anthropology. Dipesh Chakrabarty, in his article what is considered perhaps as a manifesto of this school of historians, reflects the condition of historical study as

> Insofar as the academic discourse of history - that is 'history' as a discourse produced at the institutional site of the university is concerned, 'Europe' remains the sovereign, theoretical subject of all histories, including the ones we call 'Indian', 'Chinese', 'Kenyan' and so on... The everyday paradox of third-world social science is that we find these theories, in spite of their inherent ignorance of 'us' eminently useful in understanding our societies. What allowed the modern European sages to develop such clairvoyance with regard to societies of which they were empirically ignorant? Why cannot we once again, return the gaze?[5]

Returning the gaze is thus the sole mantra of the postcolonial theories. By "provincializing the European experiences", the theorists of postcolonialism have shattered the so far indisputable claim of Europe of its universal validity and values. But unfortunately the radical vision and the vigor of demolishing the foundational assumption of old discipline has not let any trace of footprint in the Indian international relations scholars. On the contrary, the Indian scholars of this discipline have accepted unquestionably the theories of west and with a bend of uncritical mind applied them universally; it has thus reaffirmed the universal validity of Europe's experiences even today.

I feel the increasing urgency of dismantling the Europe influenced foundational precincts of International relations; then only, there could be a possibility of envisioning a new critical understanding of European integration process. Hence, the prim objective of this chapter is to bring the issue of postcoloniality within the theoretical questions of International Relations. Before moving towards this direction, as a first step, we have to make clear what does the term postcoloniality mean and what are the different ways of theorizing it.

The term postcolonialism is being employed in the academic parlance in a two but interrelated sense: as a descriptive methodology and as an emancipatory ideology. The first descriptive one denotes the general and generic conditions that prevailed in the former colonized societies. It has been best exemplified in a trend setting book where some group of scholars declared "We use the term post-colonial to cover all the culture affected by the imperial process from the moment of colonization to the present day. This is because there is a continuity of preoccupations through out the historical process initiated by the imperial aggression".[6] Their definition indicates two primary presumptions about post-colonialism: first by putting the prefix 'post' before colonialism, they like to convey literally the sense of temporal break happened with the earlier phase of colonialism. With the 'third world' national liberation movements and the subsequent formation of their own nation-states, the period of formal colonialism had come to an end.

But as a second proposition, these scholars tend to see the continuation of European imperial aggression even after in a changed historical condition. They would say that it is the responsibility on the part of academic scholars to identify and make sense of this continuation and problematize it in their respective studies.

Here one should note that the thesis put forward by the descriptive post-colonialists is not a new discovery imported into the academic fields. Rather the third world people or at least their leaders were well aware of the continuation of colonialism in some other guise even today. And they did not deceive themselves by believing that the achievement of having their own nation-state was a complete tryst with destiny. Unlike the recent entrant, they had understood it and named it as neo-colonialism. But this should not prevent us to identify one major difference that distinctively separates the new post-colonialism from the earlier neo-colonialism. While the neo-colonialism exclusively concentrated on the economic relations and presumed the continuation of the imperial policy only in the economic domain, the later post-colonialism expands its range and scope and exposes the continuation of imperialism in politics, economics and more particularly in cultural fields.

Once this realization of the continuation of imperialism became conscious, naturally as an extension of this realization there must be a discussion about the possible ways of opposing it. In the phase of formal colonialism, there was a discernible center against which the liberationists could focus their attention and struggle. But in the current post-colonial situation there is no such a identifiable center; rather the tentacles of imperialism is so disperse in a sense that it seems to have percolated in all walks of life. The most glaring contrast is to see that the very same third world people and their institutional structures are now the agents of imperialism. This has compelled that any struggle against imperialism in the post-colonial period should be porous and diversified. It has to cover from the international institutions to academic establishment to even its own nation-state. In this sense, post-colonialism is transformed from mere a descriptive methodology to a more radical emancipatory ideology. It is more visible and revealing nowadays in academic theorizing. When commenting on postcolonialism in literary studies, Meenakshi Mukherjee, the noted Indian literary theorist said,

> Post-colonialism is not merely a chronological label referring to the period after the demise of empire. It is ideologically an emancipatory concept, because it makes us interrogate many aspects of the study of literature that we were made to take for granted, enabling us not only to read our own texts in our own terms, but also re-interpret some of the old canonical texts from Europe the perspective of our special historical and geographical location.[7]

I have just above outlined how postcolonialism shaped and sharpened other disciplinary fields particularly anthropology and history in India. Needless to repeat it again, we may concentrate on the ways and methods by which postcolonialism is operating as a liberating force within the academic activities. As Mukherjee herself outlined, there are two modes of doing this: to read our own texts in our own terms and to re-interpret the canonical texts from Europe in our perspective.

Beyond or Within Nation? Postcolonialist Encounter

In order to explicate the intricate nuances of postcolonial theorizing, let us isolate one particular issue which would be more relevant to our scope of study: nation-state. The postcolonial thinkers unlike others are not interested in either the retreat or rescue of nation-state. Rather, their engagement with the concept of nation-state is completely different and radical. For them, the very idea of nation-state as a form of political community was a European one and has been implanted in other non-European territories by colonialism. In this sense, the present nation-state system in the third world countries even though ruled by their own people, is actually the representation of colonialism. Their argument runs like this: one of the consequences of the European modernity project was the universalization of a particular form of political community that is national, organized by the sovereign state. As an identity securing system, the state homogenized the domestic individuals as citizens. Then, the state transformed the citizenship identity into a geographically fixed territorial identity. Though the nationality inscribed on some definite portion of earth had eradicated violence and conflicts within the boundary of nation-state by intense pacification of its people, at the same stroke, it had transposed those violence and conflicts to outside the perimeter of nation, that is among the states. Walker has identified it as a political theory of inside/outside.

When the European expansion came through colonialism, the same violence and conflicts had been transferred into the non-western societies. The struggle against colonialism was indeed against the violence perpetrated by the Europeans on this part of the world and demanded the right to have its own identity defined in terms of 'nation'. The greatest irony of these liberation movements is that they had not only endorsed the universalistic claim of the European model of political community but also integrated those indigenous populations into expanding realm of world market by locating meaning and identity beyond the confines of local cultures. With the abstract positing of subjects as individuals, they were forced to move from 'the fizzy conception of community'[8] to geographically fixed territorial identity. Thus the entry of colonialism not only introduced a set of unfamiliar new institutions into the third world societies, but also a set of colonial discourses on which the functioning of these institutions depended.

The greatest irony of the Indian nationalism was that it not only did not question those colonial institutions, rather it reproduced the same colonial discourse by negating all other local identities to promote a single and compartmentalized national identity. As Gyan Prakash[9] says the modern Indian nationhood was anchored in appeals to a lost ancient belonging and the unity of national subject was forced in the space of differences. Thus both the colonialism and nationalism were embedded in the *primitive accumulation of capitalist modernity.*[10] Thus the international system evolved first by the accommodation of colonial presence and priorities and latter through the historical construction of 'nation-state'. This international system has certainly undergone numerous displacements and destabilization over the second half of the twentieth century; but its dynamics and asymmetric remain recognizably colonialist. The state centric, territorially fixed national identity could not empower India to dismantle the imperial international structures because the Indian state itself is the representative of the same system in which colonial knowledge was constructed and deployed.[11]

Having thus understood the nation-state as an embodiment of colonial legacy and as a site where the colonial discourses are still being reproduced and reactivated this time by the same victims of colonialism, then what would be an alternative that the postcolonialists can suggest? In fact it is exactly over the issue of visualizing an alternative that these postcolonialists differ among themselves. One can broadly classify them under three groups according to their vision of alternative.

The first group of scholars, who at the height of diabolical spirit reject whatever associated with European modernity, both ideas and institutions. As far as they are concerned, colonialism is a disease or more accurately a pathological condition, which could be cured only when the complete annihilation of the colonial discourse made possible. This could be achieved, they would say, through recovering ones own self by recapturing and reactivating the tradition.[12] The revival of religious traditions that has been undergoing on different parts of the world now has this theoretical underpinning. The anti-modern, historically retrograding march towards the past and its glorification draw severe criticism.

The second group of scholars cast their doubt on the possibility of such revival of tradition. They say, there could not be a single tradition that would not have been distorted by the colonialism. As one front ranking postcolonial theorist asks in a more melancholic mood, "Can the Subaltern Speak?"[13] Instead of longing for the past, these scholars in a serene postmodern frame of mind suggest let us celebrate ambivalence and hybridity. Their central hypothesis is that the emancipation from the colonially constructed, imperialist world is possible only when postcolonial condition is achieved, where rigid and homogenous national identity broken and multiple identities flourish and flow across the globe.

When the anti-modern postcolonialists build their hope around the imperative of achieving an authentic identity based on tradition, the postmodern postcolonialists of second variety reject the very idea of authentic subjective identity. Instead, they believe that any successful fight against colonial imperialism could only be possible through decentering the subjectivity by splitting and multiplying it.

Contrary to these two extreme positions, a third group of scholars proposes a middle way. While accepting the impossibility of having an authentic traditional identity, at the same time, this group of scholars rejects the postmodern posturing of promoting ambiguity and multiplicity. In the fight against imperialism this kind of aesthetic posturing alone cannot help solve the problems. The concrete manifestation of imperialism cannot be rectified by mere abstract polemical theorizing. It requires the equally concrete manifestation of spheres of struggle; and that it could be possible only when organizing around a single agonistic identity. This realization has made these scholars talk about strategic essentialization of the subjective identity of the subaltern peoples in opposition to the imperialist oppression.

The best example of this line of thinking is Partha Chaterjee. Unlike his other postcolonial colleagues, he does not see Indian nation as a copied replica of the western notion implanted by the colonial encounter. In contrast, he introduces the categories of inner and outer domains. And he would argue that the Indians have accepted and adopted western modern ideas in their outer domain, while modified and even transformed it in their inner domain.[14] To put it otherwise, he acknowledges that there was a distinct, independent Indian way of imagining of nation. But bringing the nation and the state into a same conceptual plane and giving legitimacy to nation-state as the one and only form of political community in post-independence period, they have accepted and accommodated the imperial notion. Hence he would suggest two ways of overcoming the situation: first to reject the coterminous and coeval western notion of nation-state as the only desirable form of political community; and second by democratizing the nation by accommodating other suppressed voices, say, women, dalits and adivasis. Instead of rejecting the idea of nation completely in the name of either tradition or postmodern hybridity, he calls for to work within the nation.[15]

International Relations as Imperial Relations

Whatever may be the differences over the alternative way of theorizing postcoloniality, the one insurmountable positive contribution of these various postcolonial theories, is to radically transform the scope and nature of the each and every subject fields. Unfortunately International Relations is the rare specimen piece which is so far immune to this kind of thinking. When Jim George labeled International Relations as a backward discipline[16] he has this aspect in his mind. However, in recent times, there is a move on the part of some International Relations scholars to bridge International Relations with postcolonialism.[17]

Exuberating the same reflective critical spirit of their counterparts in the other disciplines, the postcolonial International Relation scholars echoed,

> What is characterized, as 'colonialism' is not merely the experience of western imperialism in the non-European world, which ended at some particular juncture in history. Rather, colonialism has come to signify a continuing set of practices that are seen to prescribe relations between the West and the Third World beyond the independence of the former colonies.[18]

Despite the glaring fact of continuation of the imperial realm, the International Relations still today has not only refused to take it as a problematical issue to be theorized but concealed or even distorted the real fact by helped perpetuate this relation in its various orthodox, conservative theories. Having imagined international relations as an ideal objective sphere where each and every nation-state is sovereign in its own terms and free to promote its national interest, what it concealed is that unto some decades before, most of the nation-states of Asia and Africa were under colonial yoke which had made them completely dependent and underdeveloped. Under this pressing condition, treating the third world countries as equal players and subjecting both the former colonized and colonizer countries under same set of rules and norms is nothing but elimination of their historical colonial experiences altogether from the subject field.

This elimination of difference by treating them as one among the equal members of the international system of states in which each contenting to promote their interest through acquiring power, denied the experiences of third world countries and their colonial past. The realist and neo-realist theories of International Relations, thus virtually erased the history of colonialism there by concealed the hierarchical character of international system. But unfortunately the Indian International Relations scholars still revolve around the realist paradigm. Both the Indian academic and as well as the practitioners of diplomacy have failed to comprehend that colonialism has not vanished with the demise of formal imperialism and still the colonialism's culture is so fundamental to both the larger dynamics of global history and power relations. International relations in actuality is imperial relation.

For realist it is not important to ask how the European form of political community was made universal appeal and how the international system of states came into being. They simply consider the state as a starting point and never go beyond this to explain the historicity of state formation. In their eyes the discipline International Relations primarily concerns with sovereignty of state and external politics which is governed by the irresistible logic of anarchy. Morgenthau[19] declares that objective laws, which are fundamentally different from the principles of domestic politics, govern the international politics. By privileging its epistemology (i.e. Inside/outside), the realism made international politics as "a terrain where progressivist assumptions so important to other modes of social thought have no purchase".[20]

If any attempt to transcend this epistemological division is seen as a crude reductionism blind to the objective external anarchy. With their positivistic epistemological foundation, realist treated International Relations as a field concerned only with inter-state affairs steered by foreign policies. They never take cognition of the other social relationships and their dynamics both inside and outside the state structure. As Rosenberg[21] laments, realism considers state with its policies as a sole agency in international system and denies any other historical agency. This denial of historical agency conceals the colonial hierarchical conditions of the international system.

While the neo-liberal, pluralist school, particularly Nye and Keohane gave scope to transnational and multinational non-state actors in international relations, they still perpetuate the colonial hierarchy through its theory of interdependence and regime maintenance. Similarly, though the world system theory rightly identified the historical agency of capitalism, it still sticks to the structural analysis. By dividing the international space as core and periphery, what Wallerstein gives to the third world countries is only an alternative in priorities of policy making, not emancipation from the asymmetrical set up.

It is very clear that the present day international system came into being through the expansion of Western European state system into the non-Western societies. Rosenberg claims that the actual historical path to the modern global state system lies not through the widening interaction among pre-existing sovereignties, but rather through the construction of the greatest colonial empires the world had ever seen.

Thus the genealogy of international relations lies in the colonial imperial relations. And what postcolonialism taught us is that even today the international relations is in actuality imperial relations. That is why, it is said that "had the discipline directed its attention to the phenomenon, and had it taken account of the developments in imperial historiography, international relations might have taken a substantially different trajectory".[22] Since postcolonialism has already brought the attention to the imperial relations, then what sort of trajectory it has given to International Relations?

Like in other disciplines, postcolonial engagement in International Relations has caught up in the web of theoretical debate bordering around the issue of possibility and desirability of subjectivity and identity. Some scholars, notably David

Campbell, Der Derian, Michael Shapiro and Michael Dillon, in a postmodern bent of mind rejected all possible forms of representations in international relations. The sole motive of their works is to expose the power/knowledge nexus inherent in the disciplinary practice of the international relations. By directing ones gun towards this nexus and deconstructing the foundational precincts of International Relations, they would argue the imperial relations can be challenged. Despite their contribution in opening up of new space for more radical questioning, their denial of subjectivity and agency to the historically subjugated peoples and the vengeful celebration of ambivalence and hybridity have come under thick criticism. Other streams of scholars started exposing, in turn, the postmodernists' inability to propose a concrete political action rather than some rhetorical boasting.

In his criticism of postmodern exploration in International Relations, Sankaran Krishna highlights the fact that "in political terms, the postmodernist suspicion of subjectivity and agency may be a problem for peoples that are not so advantageously placed in the hierarchy of late capitalism".[23] As a way out, he stresses the necessity of "reconstituting subjectivity for a more enabling politics"[24] under the pressing circumstantial context. In a similar line of argument, Phillip Darby opposed the "rejigging of postcolonialism with postmodernism"[25] in International Relations. Rather, he argues for allowing the strategic essentialization of subjectivity to the historically suppressed category of peoples. He identifies one such a strategically useful subjectivity in the 'Third World' identity. For him, the tag of third world "provides a conceptual tripwire against the colonizing tendencies of much contemporary Western discourse". "If today the Third World is at the edge of international relations", he declares, "it is better having a voice there than being silenced through an illusory incorporation into the center".[26]

Darby thus brings North - South relations to the center stage and argues that it should be the paradigm for the study of future international relations. This paradigm setting is not a new entrant to mainstream International relations. The past three decades have perhaps witnessed the emergence of many theories, which undertook 'North-South' relations of world politics, but in different name. Under the influence of dependency and world-system schools, they called it core - periphery relations. However, these scholars' attention was fully focused only on the economic aspect of the North - South relations. Other relational matrixes had hardly drew their attention.

II
IMPERIALISM OF EUROPEAN INTEGRATION

With the exception of Luxembourg, the other five founding members of the European Community were at once the colonial masters and possessed vast colonial empires under their control. This fact is not the only link that makes the current European integration connected with the past imperialism. Nevertheless, there are some striking similarities, if not in location, but at least in ideational characters, between the imperialism of the European past and its present integration. The European imperialism did indeed begin with the matters of economics - trade and investment in the colonised areas and gradually turned into politics with uniting the colonies more and more with the metropolitan core. This process was known as 'empire building'. To protect their economic interests and promote profit, the colonisers constructed empire whereby the centralised, excessively bureaucratic control and undemocratic colonial state were set up to mediate the metropolitan centre and the peripheral colony.

Here, one cannot miss the parallelism that the present integration process has with the earlier imperial venture. European integration too like the imperial project started with issues of economic maters; and gradually transferred to political character by trying to unite some discreet nationalities into a common political umbrella. Like the empire building of the imperial phase, the union building of the integration has created an institution which is equally undemocratic, centralised and completely managed and manoeuvred by bureaucracy. In this sense, there is not much difference between the colonial state and the European Commission. While the former colonial state mediated between the core and periphery, the European Commission mediates between the Union and the respective national states. However, there is one crucial difference that distinctively differentiates the imperialism from the integration: During imperialism the European powers successfully created empires outside Europe, that is, in other continental areas. Whereas in the present integration phase, all the previous colonial powers have come together to erect a foundation for a one more empire in the history; but this time within the Europe and more particularly by bringing their own territories instead of others in to unification. This inversion of imperialism would be identified in the catchword of 'empire looks in'.

Apart from these conceptual and institutional similarities, there is a much deeper theoretical chord that thematically unites imperialism and integration. This could be explicated only when the economical, political and cultural aspects of imperialism compared with the integration.

Imperialism of Free Trade

Gallagher and Robinson in their controversial but path breaking article titled "The Imperialism of Free Trade" declared, "Imperialism, perhaps, may be defined as a sufficient political function of the process of integrating new regions into expanding economy; its character is largely decided by the various and changing relationships between the political and economic elements of expansion in any particular region and time".[27] It should be noted that Gallagher and Robinson give imperialism two pronged strategy: economic integration of new regions with the metropolitan core country; and thus erecting the foundational structure of an empire. Further, they have argued in their article that the economic integration was the necessary function of imperialism, while the political function of empire building was remained optional.

Grounding their arguments based on the experience of British imperialism, they explicated two modes of economic integration of the colonies. First, through the strategy of free trade the British allowed the political autonomy of the colony while simply integrate them into the orbit of its economy by free flow of trade and investment. On the contrary, the second one was the mercantilist use of power to obtain commercial supremacy and monopoly through direct political possession of the colonies. Their logic of argument borders on the differentiation of formal and informal empire. When imperialism brought new regions inducted into the economy of Europe through free trade, Gallagher and Robinson identified it as an informal empire, while with the tactics of mercantilist practice the formal empire was built-up.

From this vantage point, one can clearly discern the relationship that the current European integration has with the imperialism especially employing the old imperial strategies in achieving European integration, both in economic and political terms. Through the strategy of promoting free trade with in its boundaries, the European Union has successfully achieved the required economic integration. Similarly, by assuming it as a single mercantilist trade bloc, the European Union nowadays acts as a united political entity vis-à-vis other non-member countries.

Thus the earlier imperialist strategies are being deployed in the service of integration. Apart from these maters of economics, the nexus that exists between the imperialism and integration is more glaring in the domain of politics and let us turn to this area.

Imperialism of Decolonization

The centuries old European empires built with the meticulous strategies adopted in the colonised space started cracking during the Second World War. The people of the Afro-Asian countries raised their voice against the imperialist exploitation and demanded their independence. The colonial powers' immediate response to these uprisings was to quell the national spirit and keeps intact the empire at any cost. In this context, the colonial powers invented a new strategy by which they tried to incorporate the colonies, this time with federal set up. It should be noted that contrary to the belief, the idea of federal integration was mooted immediately after the Second World War not for the entire Europe but to bring the warring European nationals under one political envelop. And instead the idea of the integrated federal set up was brought into the colonies to tie them for ever with their colonial masters albeit under a new institutional set up.

This point can be explained with the example of France and the Netherlands. During Brazzaville conference in 1944, France rejected the demand for self-government to their overseas colonial territories. Instead, the new 1946 constitution envisioned to replace the French empire into *Union Francaise* (French Union) where the French overseas colonies would become the members of the Union, sending representatives to the Assembly of the French Union at Versailles.[28] Similarly, the Dutch government while refused to grant political independence to their Indonesian colonies, at the same time through the Linggajat agreement of 1947 envisaged bringing the Indonesians under a common federal set up with the Kingdom of Holland under the authority of the Dutch crown.[29]

The same was happened with the Britain also. It was hell-bent to keep its colonial territories at any cost after the world war. And in case of failure, it tried to keep them under the guise of British Commonwealth whereby it could bring the former colonies under the control of the British crown. The successive British governments tried to preserve this edifice of Commonwealth. The British foreign secretary Selwyn Lloyd in his programme on 'Grand Design' clearly spelt out the rational for Britain's emphasis on the formation of the Commonwealth:

> With the Commonwealth behind as and holding, as we should, a balance between France and Germany, Britain would be the unchallenged leader of the European Confederation. This, in itself, would further strengthen our position in the Commonwealth. As the leader, moreover, of both the Commonwealth and Europe, we should be able to establish a more equal partnership with the United States both in the immediate task of containing Russia and in long term.[30]

Further, the Britain initiated in 1947 preliminary talks with the French regarding the possibility of creating Anglo-French customs union. The presumed objective behind this move was to suppress the nationalist movement in Africa by collectively managing their colonial possessions. This rationale was well expressed by Ernest Bevin, the British Foreign Secretary as Britain and France should unite with their colonial possessions by common customs union which would promote free access of African goods into Europe. This was, in turn, expected to encourage the African countries prefer to stick to the metropolitan link intact.[31]

Thus, it has become clear that the real cause for the project of European unification came from the colonial powers' desperate attempt to keep their colonial territory and perpetuate their hold over them. In this sense, one can easily understand that the integration was the precise plan on the part of the European powers to stem the forces of decolonization. Or to put it in the words of Louis and Robinson, integration of Europe is nothing but the imperial coalition to perpetuate their power and position in the otherwise changed world conditions.[32] The understanding of the reincarnation of imperialism as European integration in the decolonizing milieu has made us aware of the fact that what the European Union, in its external dimension, tried hard not to be, is a form of neo-colonialism, old wine in new bottle and that the former colonial powers might try to re-invent themselves in this way. Hence, we would say, if imperialism is conceived to be the latest stage of capitalism, then the European integration is the latest phase of imperialism. This could be well exposed by critically positing the mutually complementing tendencies inherent in both cultural imperialism and integration.

Cultural Imperialism and European Integration

Getting inspiration from the works of Edward Said, the postcolonial International Relations theorists brought their focus fully on the question of culture and power relations into the scope of the subject field. They have zeroed in on the question of colonial discourse, which is the sole bedrock of any relationship that these two blocs developed over the years. It therefore seems to have convinced them that the study of international relations should invariably concentrate on the discourse analysis whose purpose will be to bring forth how the self and others are being produced and circulated. The best example of this kind of work in international relations is David Campbell's discourse analysis of the United States' foreign policy. Here, he brings a method of analyzing foreign policy by exposing how the United States through its foreign policy management is able to construct the self and other identities.[33] In this way he opens up a new space for future foreign policy analysis. Similarly, can we expect that the postcolonialism would help us re-theorize European integration?

Bringing the postcolonial question into the scope of the study of European integration would help us raise the issue of its relationship with imperialism, more specifically cultural imperialism. Further it would compel us to explore the nexus that the European integration process has with the colonial discourse. However, one should note that for major part, the postcolonial studies are ahistorical. This is so because it treats colonial discourse as a never changing, still continued in its original form whatever may be the historical context and conditions. The postcolonialists' anti-historical posturing has been attributed to their willing and sometimes overwhelming dependence on the post-structuralist philosophical tendencies.[34] This ahistorical tendency of postcolonialism has come under a severe criticism in recent times. When critically engaged with Said's Orientalism, Arif Dirlik brings the issue of historicity in postcolonialism to the ground:

> It is necessary to restore full historicity to our understanding of the past and the present, historicity not in the sense that Said uses 'historicism' but historicity that is informed by the complexity of everyday life, which accounts for what unites but, more importantly, for diversity in space and time... A thoroughgoing historicism subjects culture to the structures of everyday life, rather than erasing those structures by recourse to a homogenizing culturalism.[35]

He thus improvised the postcolonial theory by proposing two revised propositions: as a first proposition, he stressed the need to avoid all sorts of cultural homogenization and binary opposition: East / West; Orient / Occident; and North / South. And as a second proposal, he asked to concentrate on everyday life, its diversity in space and time, that is, the necessary historical change. By adding these two propositions, Dirlik was able to demonstrate that the discourse of orientalism was not the exclusive creation of the Europeans as Said has proposed earlier. On the other hand, for Dirlik, the oriental people were themselves active participants in the production and circulation of this discourse: "Where orientalism as articulated by Said is wanting, is in ignoring the 'Oriental's' participation in the unfolding of the discourse on the orient, which raises some questions about the location of the discourse and, therefore, its implications for power".[36]

Thus by revising Said's notion of orientalism by exposing the nature of the complicity of the Orientals in the very production of this discourse, what Dirlik called it as "self-orientalization of Oriental's",[37] he has inverted the question of power in Occident / Orient or North / South relations. While orientalist discourse was constructed by the Europeans to make Orientals powerless and subordinated, at the same time ironically the very same discourse was and is used by the Orientals, in turn, as a powerful tool against the West. Dirlik explained this ironic twist as "Orientalism, which earlier articulated a distancing of Asian societies from the Euro-American, now appears in the articulations of differences within a global modernity as Asian societies emerge as dynamic participants in a global capitalism".[38] His entire argument can be summed up like this: The capitalist modernity brought Europe make contacts with other peoples. And in this contact zones (he calls them as location) both Europeans and as well as the non-Europeans took active part in the production and circulation of a discourse known as Orientalism to make each one powerful in opposition to each other.

Though Dirlik's critical appraisal is appreciable, he has failed in his final conclusion to comprehend the subtle difference that exists in the operationalization of the oriental discourse. The Europeans used the oriental discourse to make non-Europeans powerless and colonized. To put it otherwise, the discourse was employed as a sort of offensive weapon in the hands of the Europeans. Whereas the self-orientalization of the Orientals was aimed to make them powerful in the face of intense European oppression; that is, it acted as a defensive tool in their fight against the colonialism. Then comes the question: how could it be possible to a discourse produced at a same location by two different actors in compliance with each other, be used by one as an offensive weapon and by the other as a defensive mechanism? Understanding this paradox, what I would rather call it as paradox of orientalism, has the key to our understanding of European integration in the postcolonial period.

I can attribute the failure of Dirlik in recognizing this paradox to his corresponding failure to historicize the location of the production of the orientalist discourse. According to Dirlik, the capitalist modernity is the site where orientalism was and is produced continuously by both the Europeans and non-Europeans. Is this capitalist modernity is an unchanging, static entity? Or does it have its own historicity? I believe that the capitalist modernity was itself historically evolved entity, which in turn bound to change in due course of history. It is only by capturing the historicity of capitalist modernity that one can understand the above discussed paradox of orientalism.

In the formal phase of colonialism, the Europeans produced and circulated the discourse of orientalism in universal scale; theirs is the classical paradigm of Europe Vs the rest. On the contrary, the non-European engagement with orientalism revolved in a particularistic mode. Its production and circulation was limited within their national boundaries. Its purpose was to differentiate the natives from their colonial masters and achieved their national liberation. In this sense, it had a limited and particularistic interest unlike the Europeans who aimed for universal conquering. But this has changed after the demise of colonialism. Now the Orientals have their own nation-state. With the newly found confidence and courage, these nations are now actively taking part in the capitalist modernity and project their own models as the ideal one to be emulated by others in contrast to the European model. Definitely today there are many contenders and competitors to Europe's claim to universal validity. On this assumption only Huntington envisages the current world situation as 'Clash of Civilizations'. Some scholars even proceed to think that the capitalist modernity itself gets changed and started coining different nomenclature to picture out this presumed shift: late capitalism, post-industrialism and post-modernism so on.

In this changed conditions Europe has but two options: to renew its old universalistic claim albeit with new sets of arguments and discourses; or to revert to the defensive tactics of the exact kind that the former colonized countries pursued during the colonial subjugation. That is to choose either universalism or particularism. I would prefer to call this 'either / or situation' of Europe in a more dramatic sense as 'Europe at the antithesis of culture and civilization'. This conceptual criterion has been well explained in detail in Chapter 1. It is in this context that the European integration has its role and relevance.

It has given Europe the much-needed moral and as well as material resources to boast of its supposed still valid universal claim to superiority. It has already started such a boasting by claiming that while the rest of the world has frozen within the category of nation and fight among themselves, Europe the vanguard of historical march is moving forward to post-national community. What Christopher Patten, European Commissioner for External Relations exhorted during his visit to New Delhi - "Europe, we are trying to create something unique, something that does not exist anywhere else in the world",[39] is a telling signal to the colonial mentality of projecting European integration as always a modular example to be emulated by others. Patten was even more forthright when he declared,

> The skills we developed in Europe to manage our own affairs jointly are relevant to a world that struggles to develop a framework to contain the passions of states. Sharing our experience of regional integration is therefore perhaps one of the most important international contributions that Europe can make. Our experience in pulling off this delicate trick may offer a valid and credible model for other regions in the world.[40]

In this sense it has been argued that Europe still has the potential of projecting itself as a universal model. On the other hand one can easily observe that the European integration is being used as a particularistic tactic, making its boundary strong enough to prevent any percolation of both men and ideas from the 'other world' to keep preserve its cultural identity and purity. Jacques Delors, the much-acclaimed former president of the European Commission once urged, "Europe must look itself economically, politically and culturally... The member states must also realize that the European area, the web of dialogue and cooperation we have woven between us, will enable us to regain our strength and hence our identity".[41]

Then why this contradiction? When we closely follow the history of the colonial discourse, we can discern two kinds of discoursing: the preservation of difference with superior/ inferior relationship; and the assertion of equality by the elimination of difference.[42] The entire modern history of Europe is the history of tactical deployment of either of these discourses. The choice of the deployment of any of these two discourses was determined by the contextual conditionality of the location where it has been deployed. This has been understood as the ambivalence of colonial discourse. In a sarcastic tone, Homi Bhabha calls it as "mimicry of Europe" in the oriental landscape.[43]

While Bhabha concentrates only on the strategic mimicry in the colonized space of the distant history, we can extend, in a more accurate sense, invert his arguments to the present historical circumstance of Europe, that is, European integration. One can, thus, capture the nexus that exists between the present European integration discourse and the earlier imperial discourse; and with economic, political and as well as cultural imperialism.

REFERENCES

1. Ashis Nandy, *The Intimate Enemy: Loss and Recovery of Self under Colonialism* (Delhi, 1983), p. xi.
2. P. Hulme quoted in Ania Loomba, *Colonialism/ Postcolonialism* (London, 1998), p.19. Emphasis original.

3. Talal Asad, "Anthropology and the Colonial Encounter", in Gerrit and Bruce Mannheim, ed., *The Politics of Anthropology: From Colonialism and Sexism, Towards a View from Below* (The Hague, 1979), p.93.
4. Katheleen Gough, "New Proposals for Anthropologists", *Current Anthropology*, vol. 9, no. 5, 1968, p. 403.
5. Dipesh Chakrabarty, "Postcoloniality and the Artifice of History, Who Speaks for 'Indian' Pasts ?", *Representation*, vol.37, Winter 1992, pp.1and 3.
6. Bill Ashcroft, Gareth Griffths and Helen Tiffin, ed., *The Empire Writes Back: Theory and Practice in Post-Colonial Literature* (London, 1989), p. 1.
7. Meenakshi Mukherjee, *Interrogating Post-Colonialism* (Delhi, 1993), p. 5.
8. S. Kaviraj, "On the Structures of Nationalist Discourse", in T.V. Sathyamurthy, ed., *State and Nation in the Context of Social Change* (Delhi, 1994), Vol. 1.
9. Gyan Prakash, ed., *After Colonialism: Imperial Histories and Postcolonial Displacements* (Princeton, New Jersey, 1995).
10. Partha Chatterjee, *Nation and Its Fragments: Colonial and Postcolonial Histories* (Delhi, 1994), p. 213.
11. Dipesh Chakrabarty, no. 5, p. 8.
12. For this line of argument refer, Ashis Nandy, no.1.
13. Gayatri Chakravorty Spivak, "Can the Subaltern Speak?", in Cary Nelson and Lawrence Grossberg, ed., *Marxism and the Interpretation of Culture* (Chicago, 1988).
14. Partha Chaterjee, no. 10, p. 13.
15. Partha Chaterjee, "Beyond the Nation? Or Within?", *Economic and Political Weekly*, January 4-11, 1994, pp. 30-34.
16. Jim George, *Discourses of Global Politics: A Critical (Re) Introduction to International Relations* (Boulder, 1994), p. 16.
17. Phillip Darby and A.J. Paolini, "Bridging International Relations and Postcolonialism", *Alternatives*, vol.19, no.3, Summer 1994, pp.371-97.
18. Ibid., p.375.
19. H.J. Margenthau, *Politics Among Nations: Struggle for Power and Peace* (Neon Alfred A. Knopf, 1978), edn. 5 .
20. Martin Wight, "Why is There no International Theory?", in Herbert Butterfield and Martin Wight, ed., *Diplomatic Investigations* (London, 1966), pp. 18-30.
21. Justin Rosenberg, *The Empire of Civil Society: A Critique of the Realist Theory of International Relations* (London, 1994).

22. Phillip Darby and A.J. Paolini, no. 17, p. 379.
23. Sankaran Krishna, "The Importance of Being Ironic: A Postcolonial View on Critical International Relations Theory", A Review Essay, *Alternatives*, vol. 18, no. 3, Summer 1993, p. 388.
24. Ibid., p. 405.
25. Phillip Darby, "Postcolonialism", in Phillip Darby, ed., *At the Edge of International Relations: Postcolonialism, Gender and Dependency* (London, 1997), p. 17.
26. Phillip Darby, "Introduction", in Phillip Darby, ed., no.25, p.4.
27. John Gallagher and Ronald Robinson, "The Imperialism of Free Trade", *The Economic History Review*, vol.6, no.1, 1953, p. 5.
28. For an elaborate analysis on this point see, Jacques Marseille, "The Phases of French Colonial Imperialism: Towards a New Paradigm", *Journal of Imperial and Commonwealth History*, vol.13, no.3, May 1985, pp.127-141.
29. For discussion on Linggadjat agreement refer, Abu Hanifah, *Tales of a Revolution* (Sydney, 1972), pp. 202-15.
30. Quoted in Gordon Martel, "Decolonization After Suez: Retreat or Rationalisation?", *Australian Journal of Politics and History*, vol. 46, no. 3, September 2000, p. 409.
31. On this point refer, John Kent, "Bevin's Imperialism and the Idea of Euro-Africa, 1945-49", in M.Dockhill, and J.W. Young, ed., *British Foreign Policy, 1945-56* (London, 1989), pp. 52-66. Again for an historical background of the Anglo-French cooperation see, John Kent, "Anglo-French Colonial Cooperation, 1939-49", *Journal of Imperial and Commonwealth History*, vol.18, no.1, Jan 1988, pp.55-82.
32. W.M.Roger Louis and Ronald Robinson, "The Imperialism of Decolonization", *Journal of Imperial and Commonwealth History*, vol. 22, no. 3, 1994, pp. 462-511. For related argument also refer, Catherine R. Schenk, "Decolonization and European Economic Integration: Free Trade Area Negotiations, 1956-58", *Journal of Imperial and Commonwealth History*, vol.24, no.3, September 1996, pp.444-63.
33. David Campbell, "Global Inscription: How Foreign Policy Constitute the United States", *Alternatives*, vol. 25, 1990. pp. 263-86.
34. For a brilliant analysis of the place of history in the post-structural theory refer, Derek Attridge, Geoff Bennington and Robert Young, ed., *Post-structuralism and the Question of History* (Cambridge, 1987).

35. Arif Dirlik, "Chinese History and the Question of Orientalism", *History and Theory*, vol.35, no.4, December 1996, p. 118.
36. Ibid., p. 112.
37. Ibid., p. 113.
38. Ibid., p. 108.
39. A written speech "The Role of the European Union on the World Stage", delivered by C.H. Christopher Patten, as part of Jean Monnet Lecture, in New Delhi, January 25, 2001 (European Commission in India) p. 2. http://europa.eu.int/
40. Ibid., pp. 3-4.
41. Delors quoted in the European Union's publicity booklet titled, "From Single Market to European Union" (Luxembourg, 1992), p.44.
42. For an excellent argument on this aspect see, T. Todorov, *The Conquest of America*, R. Howard, trans. (New York, 1987).
43. For him mimicry is one of the most elusive and effective strategies of colonial power and knowledge. For further reference see, Homi Bhabha, "Of Mimicry and Man: The Ambivalence of Colonial Discourse", in Philip Rice and Patricia Waugh, ed., *Modern Literary Theory: A Reader* (London, 1992), 2nd ed.

Bibliography

PRIMARY SOURCES

European Union Documents

Commission of the European Communities, Bulletin. 12, Clause. 2501, *Declaration on the European Identity* (Luxembourg: Office for Official Publication of the EC, 1973).

Commission of the European Communities, *Treaties Establishing the European Communities,* (abridged), (Luxembourg, 1983).

Commission of the European Communities, COM (84), 300/Final, *Television Without Frontiers: Green Paper on the Establishment of the Common Market for Broadcasting, especially by the Satellite and Cable* (Brussels, 1984).

Commission of the European Community, "The Communities Broadcasting Policy: Proposals for a Council Directive Concerning Broadcasting Activities", *Bulletin of the European Communities,* supplement 8/86 (Luxembourg, 1986).

Commission of the European Communities, *Annual Report 1987 of the Council for Cultural Co-operation* (Strasbourg, 1988).

Commission of the European Communities, COM (88), 331/Final, Bulletin of the EC, Supplement no.2, *A People's Europe: Communication from the Commission to the European Parliament* (Luxembourg, 1988).

Commission of the European Communities, European File. 4, *Towards a Large European Audiovisual Market* (Luxembourg, 1988).

Commission of the European Communities, European File. 6, *Books and Reading: A Cultural Challenge for Europe* (Brussels, 1989).

Commission of the European Communities, XXIII *General Report on the Activities of the European Communities 1989* (Luxembourg, 1990).

Commission of the European Communities, *Treaty on European Union Singed at Maastricht on 7 February* (abridged), (Luxembourg, 1992).

Commission of the European Communities, COM (92) 149, *New Prospect for Community Cultural Action* (Brussels, 1992).

Commission of the European Communities, CC.82/94/852, *Information Communication and Openness* (Brussels, 1994).

Commission of the European Communities, COM (94), 347, *Towards an Information Society in Europe* (Luxembourg, 1994).

Commission of the European Communities, COD 94/0188, *Proposal for European Parliament Council Decision Establishing a Program to Support Artistic and Cultural Activities Having a European Dimension: KALEIDOSCOPE-2000* (Brussels, 1994).

Commission of the European Communities, COD 94/0188, *Proposal for European Parliament Council Decision Establishing a Program to Support in the Field of Books and Readings: ARIANE* (Brussels, 1994).

Commission of the European Communities, COD 95/0190, *Proposal for European Parliament and Council Decision Establishing a Community Action Program in the Field of Cultural Heritage: RAPHAEL* (Brussels, 1994).

Commission of the European Community, "Treaty on European Union," in *European Union, Selected Instruments Taken from the Treaties*, Book I, Vol. I (Luxembourg, 1999).

"Report on European Union", by L. Tindermans, *Bulletin of the European Communities*, Supplement no. 1/76 (Luxembourg, 1976).

"Report on Europe Today: State of European Integration, 1980-1981", European Parliament Secretariat, Director-General for Research and Documentation (Luxembourg, 1981).

"A People's Europe: Report from the *ad hoc* Committee", by P. Adinnino, *Bulletin of the European Communities*, Supplement no.7, (Brussels, 1985).

"Report on a General System for the Recognition of Higher Education Diplomas", *Bulletin of the European Communities*, Supplement 8/85 (Luxembourg, 1985).

"Report on the Information Policy of the European Community", by G. Baget-Bozzo, *Bulletin of the European Communities*, DOC.A-111, (Brussels, 1986).

"Report on European Cultural Cooperation", by Gunther Muller, *Parliamentary Assembly of the Council of Europe*, Vol. 1, 3 February 1988, Doc. 5871.

"Report on European Cultural Co-operation", by M. Muller, submitted to *Parliamentary Assembly of the Council of Europe,* DOC. 5871 (Strasbourg: 19 April 1988).

"Report of the Secretary General on Problems of Education and Training in Europe", *Parliamentary Assembly of the Council of Europe,* Vol. 1, (Strasbourg: 12 April 1988), Doc.5864.

First Report of the Foreign Ministers submitted to The Heads of States and Government on 27 October 1970, in *European Political Co-operation* (Bonn, 1988).

Report submitted to the European Council, Lisbon on 24 June 1992, Europe and the Challenge of Enlargement, (Brussels, 1992).

A Citizen's Europe, A Report by P. Fontaine, Bulletin of the EC, DOC.C-017 (Brussels, 1991).

Report by the Think-Tank on the Audio-visual Policy in the European Union CC.83/94/733, (Brussels, 1994).

Memorandum from Mr. Ripa di Meana to the Commission, COM (92), X/ 9/87, *A Fresh Boost for Culture in the European Community,* (Brussels, 1992).

Resolution of the Ministers responsible for Cultural Affairs, meeting within the Council of 17 February 1986, *Official Journal,* No. C 044, 26.02.1986, Doc. 486Y0226(02).

Resolution of the Council and of the Ministers responsible for Cultural Affairs, meeting within the Council of 9 November 1987 on the promotion of translation of the works of European Culture", *Official Journal,* No. C309, 19.11.1987, Doc. 487Y1119(01).

Conclusion of the Ministers of Culture meeting within the Council of 12 November 1992 on guideline for Community Cultural Action, *Official Journal,* C.336, 19.12.1992, Doc. 492Y1219(01).

Draft Resolution of 4 April 1995 on Culture and Multimedia, *Official Journal,* C.247, 23.09.1995, Doc. 395Y0923(01).

Decision 1419/1999/EC of the European Parliament and of the Council of 25 May 1999 establishing a Community Action for the European Capital of Culture Event for the year 2005-2019, *Official Journal,* L.166, 01.07.1999, Doc. 399D1419

Council Resolution of 28 October 1999, "Integrating History into Community's Cultural Action", *Official Journal,* No. C.324, 12.11.1999, Doc. 3999Y1112(01).

Council Resolution of 25 July 1996 on Access to Culture for All, *Official Journal,* C.242, 21.08.1996, Doc. 396Y0821(01).

Decision No 508/2000/EC of the European Parliament and of the Council of 14 February establishing the Culture- 2000 Program, *Official Journal,* L.063, 10.03.2000, Doc. 300D0508.

Council Resolution of 26 June 2000 on the Conservation and

Enhancement of European Cinema Heritage, *Official Journal*, C.193, 11.07.2000, Doc. 300Y0711(01).

"Community Action in the Field of Tourism", Commission Communication to the Council transmitted on 31 January 1986, *Bulletin of the European Communities*, Supplement 4/86 (Luxembourg, 1986).

Dembour, Marie-Benedicte, "Harmonization and the Construction of Europe: Variation away from a Musical Theme", EU Working Paper, Law No. 96/4 (Florence: European University Institute, 1996).

Klaus-Dieter, Borchardt, European Integration: The Origins and Growth of the European Union (Luxembourg, 1995), edn.4.

Klaus-Dieter, Borchardt, *The Community of European Law* (Luxembourg, 2000).

Lejeune, G., "Culture in Europe", Commission of the European Communities, DG Research, Science and Education (Brussels: 1 March, 1978).

European Union's publicity booklet titled "How Does the European Union Work?" (Luxembourg, 1998), edn. 2.

European Union's publicity booklet titled, "Treaty of Amsterdam: What has changed in Europe?" (Luxembourg, 1999).

Memoirs, Official Speeches and Statements, Etc.

Adenauer, Konrad, *Memoirs*, Gainer, trans (London, 1969).

Communiqué of the Conference of the Heads of State and Government of the Member States of EC, The Hague, 2 December, 1969, in *European Political Co-operation* (Bonn, 1988).

de Gaulle, Charles, *Memoirs of Hope: Renewal and Endeavor* (New York, 1971)

Delors, J., Statement to the European Parliament on "Program of the Commission for 1986", *Bulletin of the European Community*, Supplement 1/86 (Luxembourg, 1986).

Kohl, Helmut, Statement to the *Bundestag*, 18 March 1987, published in, *European Political Cooperation* (Bonn, 1988), edn.5, p.378.

Mertz, Statement on behalf of the Luxembourg Presidency at the CSCE Forum, Budapest, 15 October 1985.

Papoutsis, Christos, *Culture and Tourism: Opportunities and Perspectives* (Luxembourg, 1986), Speech / 96 /52. http://www.europa.eu.int/

Reding, Viviane, " Which Cultural Policy for the European Union?", Speech Delivered to Conference of the world Association of Newspapers, Hanover, 1 June, 2000. http://www.europa.eu.int/

Reading, Viviane, "Which Cultural Policy for the European Union?", Speech Delivered to Conference of the World Association of Newspapers, Hanover, 1 June 2000. http://www.europa.eu.int/

Statement of the Conference of the Heads of States and Government of the EC, Paris Summit, 21 October 1972, in *European Political Co-operation* (Bonn, 1988).

SECONDARY SOURCES

Books

Akzin, Benjamin, *States and Nation* (Garden City, N.Y: Doubleday, 1966).

Albert, Michel, *Capitalism against Capitalism* (London: Whurr, 1993).

Anderson, Benedict, *Imagined Communities: Reflections on the Origins and Spread of Nationalism*, Revised edn. (London: Verso, 1991).

Ash, Timothy Garton., *In Europe's Name: Germany and the Divided Continent* (London: Vintage, 1994).

Ashcroft, Bill, Gareth Griffths and Helen Tiffin, ed., *The Empire Writes Back: Theory and Practice in Post-Colonial Literature* (London: Routledge, 1989).

Attridge, Derek, Geoff Bennington and Robert Young, ed., *Post-structuralism and the Question of History* (Cambridge: Cambridge University Press, 1987).

Axline, Andrew W., ed., *The Political Economy of Regional Cooperation: Comparative Case Studies* (London: Pinter, 1994).

Baechler, J., et. al. eds., *Europe and the Rise of Capitalism* (Oxford: 1988).

Bailey, J., *Social Europe* (London: Longman, 1992).

Bainbridge, Timothy, and Teasdale, Anthony, *The Penguin Companion to European Union* (Harmondsworth: Penguin, 1995).

Bajpai, Kanti P., and Harish C. Shukul, ed., *Interpreting World Politics* (New Delhi: Sage, 1995).

Baldwin, Richard, *Towards an Integrated Europe* (London: Centre for Economic Policy Research, 1994).

Barth, F., *Ethnic Group and Boundaries: The Social Organization of Cultural Difference* (London: Allen & Unwin, 1969).

Barzini, Luigi., *The Europeans* (London, 1986).

Bauman, Z., "From Pilgrim to Tourist - or a Short History of Identity", in Stuart Hall and Paul du Gay, eds., *Questions of Cultural Identity* (London: Sage, 1996), pp. 25-34.

Baylis, John, and Steve Smith, ed., *The Globalization of World Politics: An Introduction to International Relations* (New York: Oxford University Press, 1997).

Martin Holms, ed., *The Eurosceptical Reader* (London, 1996).

Beyme, Klaus Von, *Right-Wing Extremism in Europe* (London: Frank Cass, 1988).

Birch, Anthony H., *Nationalism and National Integration* (London, 1989).

Blaut, James M., *The National Question: Decolonizing the Theory of Nationalism* (London: Zed Books, 1987).

Blumler, J. G., *Television and Public Interest: Vulnerable Values in West European Broadcasting* (London: Sage Publication, 1992).

Boissevain, J., and J. Friedl, *Beyond the Community: Social Processes in Europe* (The Hague: University of Amsterdam, 1975).

Breuilly, J., *The State of Germany: The National Idea in the Making, Unmaking and Remaking of a Nation- State* (London, 1992).

Breuilly, John., *Nationalism and the State* (Chicago: Chicago University Press, 1985).

Brubaker, Rogers., *Citizenship and Nationhood in France and Germany* (Cambridge, Mass: Harvard University Press, 1992).

Bruno de Witte, "Cultural Linkages", in William Wallace, ed., *The Dynamics of European Integration* (London: Pinter Publishers, 1990).

Bryson, Lyman, and Others, ed., *Foundations of World Organizations: A Political and Cultural Appraisal, Eleventh Symposium* (New York, NY.: The Conference on Science, Philosophy and Religion, 1952).

Bull, H., *The Anarchical Society: A Study of Order in World Politics* (London: Macmillan, 1977).

Bull, Hedley, " The Revolt Against the West", in Hedley Bull, and Adam Watson, ed., *The Expansion of International Society* (Oxford: Clarendon Press, 1984), p. 217-28.

Burgess, Michael, *Federalism and European Union: The Building of Europe, 1950-2000* (London: Routledge, 2000).

Cafruny, Alan W, and Rosenthal, Glenda C., ed., *The State of the European Community, Vol.2: The Maastricht Debate and Beyond* (Boulder: Lynne Rienner, 1993).

Cash, William, *Against a Federal Europe: The Battle for Britain* (London: Duckworth, 1991).

Cecchini, Paolo, and Others, *The European Challenge 1992: The Benefits of a Single Market* (London: Aldershot, 1988).

Chaterjee, Partha, *The Nation and Its Fragments* (Delhi: Oxford University Press, 1994).

Chatterjee, Partha, *Nationalist Thought and Colonial World: A Derivative Discourse?* (Delhi: Oxford University Press, 1986).

Laue, Theodore H. Von., *The World Revolution of Westernization: The Twentieth Century in Global Perspective* (Oxford: Oxford

University Press, 1987).

Church, C.H., *European Integration Theory in the 1990s* (London: UNL / European Dossiers 33, 1996).

Cohen, A. P., *The Symbolic Construction of Identity* (London: Routledge, 1985).

Cooper, Robert, *The Post-Modern State and the World Order* (London: Demos, 1996).

Cowgill, A., *The Maastricht Treaty in Perspective* (Stroud: British Management Data Foundation, 1992).

Creighton, Colin, and Shaw, Martin, ed., The Sociology of War and Peace (London: Macmillan, 1987).

Curry, W.B., *The Case for Federal Union* (Hardmondsworth: Penguin, 1939).

Dahrendorf, R., *Whose Europe ? Competing Vision for 1992* (London: Institute for Economic Affair, 1989).

Dann, Otto., *Nation and Nationalism in Deutschland 1770-1990* (Munich: C.H. Beck, 1993).

Darby, Phillip, ed., *At the Edge of International Relations: Postcolonialism, Gender and Dependency* (London, N.Y.: Continuum, 1997).

De Porte, A.W., *Europe Between the Superpowers: The Enduring Balance* (London, 1979).

Dedman, M.J., *The Origins and Development of the European Union, 1945-95* (London: Routledge, 1996).

Deighton, A., *Building Postwar Europe: National Decision Making and European Institutions, 1948-63* (London: Macmillan, 1995).

Delanty, Gerard, *Inventing Europe* (London: Macmillan, 1995).

Denitch, Bogdan., *Ethnic Nationalism : The Tragic Death of Yugoslavia* (Minneapolis : University of Minnesota Press, 1994).

Derian Der, and Michael Shapiro, ed., *International / Intertextual Relations: Postmodern Readings of World Politics* (Lexington: Lexington Books, 1989).

Deutsch, Karl W., *Political Community and North Atlantic Area* (New Jersey: Princeton University Press, 1957).

Deutsch, Karl W., *The Analysis of International Relations* (Englewood Cliffs, N.J.: Prentice Hall, 1968).

Deutsch, Karl., *Nationalism and Social Communication* (Cambridge: MIT Press, 1953).

Duroselle, J., *Europe: A History of its People* (London: Viking, 1990).

Duroselle, J-P., "General de Gaulle's Europe and Jean Monnet's Europe", in C. Cosgrove and K. Twitchett, ed., *The New International Actors: The UN and the EEC* (London, 1970), p. 187-200.

Eisenstadt, S.N., *European Civilization in a Comparative Perspective: A Study in the Relations Between Culture and Social Structure* (Oslo: Norwegian University Press, 1987).

Elias, Norbert, *The Civilising Process: State Formation and Civilization*, trans. Edmund Jephocott (Oxford: Basil Blackwell, 1982).

Eliot, T.S., *Notes Towards the Definition of Culture* (London: Faber and Faber, 1948).

Evans, P., Rueschemeyer, D. and T. Skocpol, ed., *Bringing the State Back In* (Cambridge: Combridge University Press, 1985).

Featherstone, M., *Global Culture: Nationalism, Globalization and Modernity* (London: Sage Publication, 1990).

Featherstone, Mike, *Consumer Culture & Postmodernism* (London: Sage, 1991).

Franck, Andre Gunther, and Barry K. Gills, ed., *The World System: Five Hundred Years or Five Thousand?* (London, N.Y., 1993).

Fulbrook, Mary, ed., *National Culture and European History* (Boulder: Westview Press, 1993).

Fursdon, Edward, *The European Defense Community: A History* (London, 1980).

Gallacher, Tom, ed., *Nationalism in the Nineties* (Edinburgh: Edinburgh University Press, 1991).

Gay, P., *The Enlightenment: An Interpretation* (New York, NY.: Alfred A. Knopf, 1967).

Gellner, Ernest, *Culture, Identity and Politics* (Cambridge: Cambridge University Press, 1987).

Gellner, Ernest, *Nations and Nationalism* (Ithaca, N.Y.: Cornell University Press , 1983).

George, Jim, *Discourses of Global Politics: A Critical (Re) Introduction to International Relations* (Boulder, Colorado: Lynne Rienner, 1994).

George, S., *Politics and Policy in the European Community* (Oxford: Clarendon Press, 1985).

Andrew Gamble and Anthony Payne, ed., *Regionalism and World Order* (London, 1996).

Giddens, Anthony, *The Nation-State and Violence* (Cambridge: Polity, 1985).

Desmond Dinan, ed., *Encyclopedia of the European Union* (London, Routledge, 1998).

Gilpin, Robert, *The Political Economy of International Relations* (Princeton, NJ.: Princeton University Press, 1987).

Ginsburg, Norman, "Postmodernity and Social Europe", in John Carter, ed., *Postmodernity and the Fragmentation of Welfare State* (London: Routledge, 1998).

Goddard, V., and Others, *Anthropology of Europe: Contested Identities and Boundaries* (Oxford: Berge, 1995).

Goldberg, D.T., *Multiculturalism* (Oxford: Blackwell, 1994).

Gowan, Peter, and Perry Anderson, eds., *The Question of Europe* (London: Verso, 1997).

Grillo, Ralph, ed., *Nation and State in Europe: Anthropological Perspective* (London: Academic Press, 1980).

Hadjimichalis, Costis, and Sadler, David, ed., *Europe at the Margins: New Mosaics of Inequality* (New York: John Willey & Sons, 1995).

Hale, John, *The Civilization of Europe in the Renaissance* (London: Macmillan, 1994).

Hall, J. A., *Powers and Liberties: The Causes and Consequences of the Rise of the West* (Harmondsworth: Penguin, 1986).

Hall, S., "Introduction: Who Needs 'Identity'?" in Stuart Hall and Paul du Gay, ed., *Questions of Cultural Identity* (London: Sage, 1996).

Hall, Stuart, "The Question of Cultural Identity", in *The Polity Reader in Cultural Theory* (Cambridge: Polity Press, 1994), pp. 119-125.

Hall, Stuart, "The West and the Rest: Discourse and Power", in S. Hall, and B. Gieben, ed., *Formations of Modernity* (Cambridge: Open University Press, 1992), pp.275-320.

Hallstein, Walter, and Hans Barker, "European Economic Community", in C.D. Kering, ed., *Marxism, Communism and Western Society: A Comparative Encyclopedia* (New York: Herder and Herder, 1972), Vol. 3, pp. 228-38.

Halperin, William S., ed., *Essays in European Historiography* (Chicago: The University of Chicago Press, 1974).

Handle, Richard., "Is 'Identity' a Cross-Cultural Concept ?", in John Gillis, ed. *Commemorations: The Politics of National Identity* (Princeton, NJ.: Princeton University Press, 1994).

Harding, S., and Others, *Contrasting Values in West European Unity, Diversity, and Change* (London: Macmillan, 1986).

Stephen Graubard, ed., *A New Europe?* (Boston: Houghton Mifflin, 1964).

Hass, E.B., *Beyond Nationalism: Functionalism and International Organization* (Stanford, CA.: Stanford University Press, 1964).

Hass, E.B., *The Uniting of Europe: Political, Economic and Social Forces, 1950-1957* (Stanford, CA.: Stanford University Press, 1958).

Hass, E.B., *Web of Interdependence: The United States and International Organization* (Englewood Cliffs: Prentice-Hall, 1970).

Hass, E.B., *Nationalism, Liberalism, and Progress, Vol I: The Rise and Decline of Nationalism*, (Ithaca NY: Cornell University Press, 1997).

Heer, F., *The Intellectual History of Europe* (Garden City: Doubledey, 1968).

Heidrich, Joachim, *Changing Identities: The Transformation of Asian and African Societies under Colonialism* (Berlin: Verlag Das Arabische Buch, 1994).

Heseltine, Michael, *The Challenge of Europe* (London: Weidenfeld and Nicolson, 1989).

Hobsbawm, Eric, and Terence, Ranger, ed., *The Invention of Tradition* (Cambridge: Cambridge University Press, 1983).

Hobsbawm, Eric, *Nations and Nationalism Since 1780* (Cambridge: Cambridge University Press, 1990).

Hoffmann, Stanley, *The European Sisyphus: Essays on Europe 1964-1994* (Boulder, CO.: Westview, 1995).

Holland, M., *European Community Integration* (London: Pinter Publication, 1993).

Hopkins, Terence K., and Wallerstein, I., *The Age of Transition: Trajectory of the World System*, 1945-2025 (London: Zed Books, 1996).

Huntington, Samuel, *The Clash of Civilizations and Remaking of World Order* (New York: Simon and Schuster, 1996).

Jacobson, Harold K., *Networks of Interdependence: International Organizations and the Global Political System* (New York, NY.: Alfred A. Knopf, 1979).

Jordan, Glenn, and Weedon, Chris, *Cultural Politics: Class, Gender, Race and the Postmodern World* (Cambrige, MA.: Blackwell, 1995).

Jordan, T., *The European Cultural Area* (London: Harper, 1973).

Kennedy, Paul, *Europe and the Future: In Preparing for the 21st Century* (London: Harper collins, 1993).

Keohan, Robert, and Stanley Hoffman, ed., *The New European Community: Decision-Making and Institutional Change* (Boulder, 1991).

Keohane, Robert O., *After Hegemony: Cooperation and Discord in the World Political Economy* (Princeton, N.J.: 1984) p. 31.

Keohane, Robert O., and Joseph Nye, ed., *Power and Interdependence: World Politics in Transition* (Boston, 1977).

Keohane, Robert O., and Nye, Joseph Jr., *Transnational Relations and World Politics* (Cambridge: 1971).

Keohane, Robert O., Hoffman, Stanley, and Nye, Joseph Jr., *After the Cold War: International Institutions and State Strategies* (Cambridge, MA.: Harvard University Press, 1993).

Keylor, William R., *The Twentieth-Century World: An International History* (Oxford, New York, 1984).

Knopf, Hans-Joachim, *English Identity and European Integration: A Case of Non-Europeanization?* (Florence: European University Institute, 1997).

Kohn, Hans, *Nationalism: Its Meaning and History* (London: Anvil Books, 1965).

Krippendorff, E., *International Relations as a Social Science* (New Delhi: Manohar, 1982).

Krugman, Paul, *Pop Internationalism* (Cambridge: MIT Press, 1998).

Laffan, Brigid, and Others, *Europe's Experimental Union: Rethinking Integration* (London: Routledge, 2000).

Lankowski, ed., *Europe's Emerging Identity: Regional Integration Vs Opposition Social Movements in European Community* (Boulder: Lynne Reiner, 1995).

Leicester, G., "A Pragmatic Approach to the Construction of Europe", in M. Herrero de Minon and G. Leicester, *Europe: A Time for Pragmatism* (London: European Policy Forum, 1996).

Lewis, David W.P., *The Road to Europe: History, Institutions and Prospects of European Integration, 1945-1993* (New York, NY.: Peter Lang, 1994).

Linklater, Andrew, *Beyond Realism and Marxism: Critical Theory and International Relations* (London: Macmillan, 1990).

Lipgens, Walter, ed., *Documents on the History of European Integration, Vol.1: Continental Plans for European Union 1939-1945I,* (New York: Walter de Gruyter & Co, 1985).

Lipgens, Walter, ed., *Documents on the History of European Integration, Vol.2: Plans for European Union in Great Britain and in Exile, 1939-1945* (New York: Walter de Gruyter & Co, 1985).

Lipgens, Walter, ed., *Documents on the History of European Integration, Vol.3: The Struggle for European Union by Political Parties and Pressure Groups in Western European Countries, 1945-1950* (New York: Walter de Gruyter & Co, 1985).

Livezeanu, Irina., *Cultural Politics in Greater Romania: Regionalism, Nation Building, and Ethnic Struggle, 1918-1930* (Ithaca, N.Y. and London: Cornell University Press, 1995).

Lodge, J., *The European Community and the Challenge of the Future* (London: Pinter, 1989).

Loomba, Ania, *Colonialism/ Postcolonialism* (London: Routledge, 1998).

Lyons, F.S.L., *Internationalism in Europe, 1815-1914* (Leyden: A.W. Sythoff, 1963).

MacDonald, S., ed., *Inside European Identities* (Oxford: Berge, 1993).

Mandel, Ernest, *Europe Vs America: Contradictions of Imperialism* (New York, 1970).

Mann, M., *Sources of Social Power: The Rise of Classes* ***and Nation- States***

1760-1914 (Cambridge: Cambridge University Press, 1986).

McAllister, R., *From EC to EU* (London: Routledge, 1997).

McSweeney, Bill, ed., *Moral Issues in International Affairs: Problems of European Integration* (Basingstoke: Macmillan, 1998).

Mehrotra, L.L., "Why Regional Cooperation?", in L.L. Mehrotra, H.S. Chopra and Gert W. Kueck, ed., *SAARC 2000 and Beyond* (New Delhi: Manohar 1995), pp. 13-17.

Melkote, Rama S., *Regional Organizations: A Third World Perspective* (New Delhi: Sterling Publishers, 1990).

Michelman, H., and Soldatos, P., *European Integration: Theories and Approaches* (Lanham, MD.: University Press of America, 1994).

Middlemass, K., and Others, *Orchestrating Europe* (London: Fontana, 1995).

Mikkeli, Heikki, *Europe as an Idea and Identity* (Basingstoke: Macmillan, 1998).

Milward, Alan S., *The Reconstruction of Western Europe, 1947-51* (London: Methuen, 1984).

Milward, Alan S. and Others, ed., *The Frontier of National Sovereignty: History and Theory 1945-1992* (London: Routledge, 1994).

Milward, Alan S., *The European Rescue of the Nation State* (London: Routledge, 1992).

Mitrany, David, "The Prospect of Integration: Federal or Functional?", in Taylor and Groom, ed., *Functionalism: Theory and Practice in International relations* (London: University of London Press, 1975).

Mittleman, J.H., ed., *Globalization: Critical Reflections* (Boulder, London: Lynne Rienner, 1996).

David Held and Anthony McGrew, ed., *The Global Transformations Reader: An Introduction to the Globalization Debate* (Cambridge: Polity Press, 2000).

Mooers , C., The Making of Bourgeois Europe (London, 1991).

Morgenthau, H.J., *Politics Among Nations: The Struggle for Power and Peace* (New York: Alfred A. Knoff, 1961), edn.3.

Morley, David and Robins, Kevin, *Spaces of Identity: Global Media, Electronic Landscapes and Cultural Boundaries* (London: Routledge, 1995).

Mosse, George L., *Towards the Final Solution: A History of European Racism* (London: RKP, 1986).

Mourik, M. "European Cultural Co-operation", in A. Rijksbaron and Others, ed., *Europe from a Cultural Perspective: Historiography and Perceptions* (The Hague, 1987), pp.19-25.

Muir, Ramsay, *Nationalism and Internationalism: The Culmination of Modern History* (London: Constable & Company Ltd, 1916).

Murphy, Craig, and Tooze, Roger, ed., *The New International Political Economy* (Boulder: Lynne Rienner, 1991).

Musolff, Andreass, and others, ed., *Conceiving of Europe: Diversity in Unity* (Dartmouth: Aldershot, 1996).

Nash, June, " Anthropology of the Multinational Corporation", in Gerrit Huizer and Bruce Mannheim, ed., *The Politics of Anthropology: From Colonialism and Sexism, Towards a View from Below* (The Hague, Paris: Mouton Publishers, 1979).

Nelson, B.F., and Stubb, A., ed., *The European Union: Readings on the Theory and Practice of European Integration* (Boulder: Lynne Reinner, 1994).

Neufeld, Mark, *The Restructuring of International Relations Theory* (Cambridge: Cambridge University Press, 1995).

Nkrumah, Kwame, *Neo-Colonialism: The Last Stage of Imperialism* (New York: International Publishers, 1965).

Nye, Joseph S., ed., *International Regionalism: Readings* (Boston, 1968).

O'Neill, M., *The Politics of European Integration: A Reader* (London: Routledge, 1996).

Parkinson, M., and F. Bianchini., eds., *Cultural Policy and Urban Regeneration: The West European Experience* (Manchester: Manchester University Press , 1993).

Passerini, "From the Ironies of Identity to the Identities of Irony", in Anthony Pagden, ed., *The Idea of Europe: The Politics of Identity from Antiquity to the European Union* (Cambridge: Cambridge University Press, 2000).

Passerini, Luisa, "The Last Identification: Why Some of Us Would Like to Call Ourselves Europeans and What We Mean by This", in Bo Strath, ed., *Europe and the Other and Europe as the Other* (Brussels, 1999).

Patijin, S., ed., *Landmarks in European Unity* (London, 1970).

Paul Taylor and A.J. Groom, ed., *Functionalism: Theory and Practice in International Relations* (London: University of London Press, 1975).

Payne, Anthony, and Andrew Gamble, ed., *Regionalism and World Order* (London, 1996).

Peter M.R. Strike, ed., *European Unity in Context: The Interwar Period* (London, 1989).

Peterson, Spike K., ed., *Gendered States: Feminist (Re)vision of International Relations Theory* (Boulder: Lynne Reinner, 1992).

Pinder , J., *European Community : The Building of a Union* (Oxford: 1991).

Pinter, John, "European Citizenship: A Project In Need of Completion", in Colin Crouch and David Marquand, ed., *Reinventing Collective*

Action From the Global to the Social (Oxford, 1995).

Prakash, Gyan, ed., *After Colonialism: Imperial Histories and Postcolonial Displacements* (Princeton, New Jersey: Princeton University Press, 1995).

Preston, P.W., *Political / Cultural Identity: Citizens and Nations in a Global Era* (London: Sage, 1997).

Satish Saberwal, ed., *Towards a Cultural Policy* (Delhi: Vikas Publishing House, 1975).

Ray, Maghroori and Bennett Ramberg, ed., *Globalism versus Realism: International Relations' Third Debate* (Boulder, Colorado, 1982).

Rengger, Nick, and Mark Hoffman, "Modernity, Postmodernism and International Relations", in Joe Doherty, Elspeth Graham and Mo Malek, ed., *Postmodernism and the Social Sciences* (London: Macmillan, 1992), pp.127-47.

Rijksbaron, A., ed., *Europe from a Cultural Perspective* (Nijgh & Van Ditmar University press, 1987).

Risse, Thomas, Daniela Engelmann, Hans-Joachim Knopf, and Klaus Roscher, *To Euro or Not to Euro? The EMU and Identity Politics in the European Union* (Florence: European University Institute, 1998).

Risse, Thomas, *Between the Euro and the Deutsche Mark: German Identity and the European Union* (Washington DC: Center for German and European Studies, Georgetown University), 1997.

Roche, Maurice, "Rethinking Citizenship and Social Movements: Themes in Contemporary Sociology and Non-conservative Ideology", in Kate Nash, ed., *Readings in Contemporary Political Sociology* (Oxford: Blackwell, 2000).

Rosa, Allan, and Antola, Esko, ed., A Citizen's Europe: In Search of A New Order (London:Sage, 1995).

Rosamond, Ben, *Theories of European Integration* (London: Macmillan, 2000).

Rosenberg, Justin, *The Empire of Civil Society: A Critique of the Realist Theory of International Relations* (London: Verso, 1994).

Rougemont, Denis de, *The Meaning of Europe* (London: Sidwick & Kackson Ltd., 1963).

SAARC Vision Beyond the Year 2000 - Report of the SAARC Group of Eminent Persons Established by the Ninth SAARC Summit (Shipra: Delhi, 1999).

Said, Abdul A., ed., *Theory of International Relations: The Crisis of Relevance* (New Jersey: Prentice-Hall, 1968).

Said , E., *Orientalism* (Handsmondsworth : Penquin, 1978).

Said, Edward W., *Culture and Imperialism* (London: Chatto & Windus, 1993).

Schaffner, Christina, "The Concept of Europe: A Network of Metaphor", in David March, and Lisa Sato-Lee, ed., *Europe on the Move: Fusion or Fission*? (Finland: Sietar Europa, 1994), pp.117-25.

Schlesinger, Philip, "Europeanness: A New Cultural Battlefield?", in J. Hutchinson, and A.D. Smith, ed., *Nationalism* (Oxford: Oxford University Press, 1994), pp. 316-25.

Schlesinger, Philip, *Media, State and Nation: Political Violence and Collective Identities* (London, 1992).

Schmidt, Helmut, *A Grand Strategy for the West: The Anachronism of National Strategies in an Independent World* (London, 1985).

Scholte, J.A., "The Globalization of World Politics', in John Baylis and Steve Smith, ed., *The Globalization of World Politics: An Introduction to International Relations* (New York: OUP, 1997), pp. 14-29.

Servan-Schreiber, Jean-Jacques, *The American Challenge*, Ronald Steel, trans. (New York, 1979).

Seton-Watson, H., "What is Europe? Where is Europe?", in G . Schopflin and N. Woods, eds., *In Search of Central Europe* (London : Polity Presss, 1989).

Seton-Watson, Huge., *Nations and States* (Boulder, Colo. : Westview , 1977).

Shaw, Martin, *Global Society and International Relations: Sociological Concepts and Political Perspectives* (Cambridge: Polity Press, 1994).

Shore, Cris, "Metaphors of Europe: Integration and the Politics of Language", in Stephen Nugent and Cris Shore, ed., *Anthropology and Cultural Studies* (London: Pluto Press, 1997).

Shore, Cris, and Wright, Sue, "Policy, a New Field of Anthropology", in C. Shore and S. Wright, ed., *Anthropology of Policy: Critical Perspectives on Government and Power* (London: Routledge, 1997).

Skocpol, Theda, *States and Social Revolution* (Cambridge: Cambridge University Press, 1979).

Smith, Anthony D., *Theories of Nationalism* (London: Duckworth and Company Ltd , 1983).

Smith, Anthony D., *Nations and Nationalism in Global Era* (Cambridge: Polity Press, 1996).

Smith, Anthony D., *The Ethnic Origins of Nations* (Oxford : Basil Blackwell, 1986) .

Smith, Steve, "The Self-Images of a Discipline: A Genealogy of International Relations Theory", in Ken Booth and Steve Smith, ed., *International Relations Theory Today* (Cambridge, UK, 1995).

Spinelli, Alterio, "The Growth of the European Movement Since the Second World War", in Michael Holms, ed., *European Integration: Selected Readings* (Harmondsworth: Penguin, 1972), pp. 43-68.

Spivak, Gayatri Chakravorty, "Can the Subaltern Speak?", in Cary Nelson and Lawrence Grossberg, ed., *Marxism and the Interpretation of Culture* (Chicago: University of Illinois Press, 1988).

Stares, Paul B., ed., *The New Germany and the New Europe* (Washington DC: Brookings Institution, 1992).

Stirk, P., *The Making of the New Europe* (London: Grower : 1990) .

Stirk, Peter M.R., and Weigall, David, ed., *The Origins and Development of European Integration* (London: Pinter, 1999).

Stoler, Ann Lara, "Rethinking Colonial Categories: European Communities and the Boundaries of Rule", in Nicholas B. Dirks, ed., *Colonialism and Culture* (Ann Arbor, 1992).

Strik, P., ed., *European Unity in Context : The Interwar Period* (London : Pinter , 1989) .

Sugar, Peter, and Lela Gardner Noble, eds., *Nationalism in Eastern Europe* (Seattle : University of Washington Press, 1994) .

Swaan, De, "Notes on the Emerging Global Language System: Regional, National and Supranational", *Media, Culture and Society*, vol. 13, no. 3, pp. 311-324.

Sylvester, Christine, *Feminist Theory and International Relations in a Postmodern Era* (Cambridge: Cambridge University Press, 1993).

Taylor, C., *Sources of the Self : The Making of the Modern Identity* (Cambridge : Cambridge, 1989)

Taylor, Paul, *International Cooperation Today: The European and the Universal Pattern* (London: Elek, 1971).

Taylor, Paul and Groom, A.J.R., ed., *International Organization: A Conceptual Approach* (London: University of London, 1975).

Taylor, Paul, *The European Union in the 1990s* (Oxford: Oxford University Press, 1996).

Thampson , J.B., *Ideology and Modern Culture* (Cambridge : Polity Press, 1990).

Therborn, Goran, *European Modernity and Beyond: The Trajectory of European Societies, 1945-2000* (London: Sage, 1995).

Tilly, Charles H., *The Formation of Nation State in Western Europe* (New Jersey, NJ.: Princeton University Press, 1975).

Tilly, Charles., "Retrieving European Lives", in Oliver Zunz, ed., *Reliving the Past: The Worlds of Social History* (Chapell Hill: The University of North Carolina Press, 1985).

Todorov, T., *The Conquest of America*, R. Howard, trans. (New York: Harper Torch Books, 1987).

Tomlinson, John, *Globalization and Culture* (Oxford: Polity, 1999).

Trivedi, Harish and Mukherjee, Meenakshi, ed., *Interrogating Postcolonialism: Theory, Text and Context* (Shimla: Indian Institute of Advanced Study, 1996).

Urwin , D. and Rokkan, S., *Economy, Territory, and Identity: Politics of West European Peripheries* (London: Sage Publication, 1983).

Vaughan, Richard., *Twentieth Century Europe : Paths to Unity* (London, 1979).

Waever, Ole, "Imperial Metaphors: Emerging European Analogies to Pre-Nation State Imperial Systems", in Ola Tunander and Others, ed., *Geopolitics in Post-Wall Europe: Security, Territory and Identity* (London: Sage, 1997), pp. 59-93.

Wallace, H., *Europe : The Challenge of Diversity* (London : Royal Institute of International Affair, 1985).

Wallace, W., *Dynamics of European Integration* (London : Pinter, 1990).

Wallerstein, I., *Geopolitics and Geoculture: Essays on the Changing World-System* (Cambridge, Cambridge University Press, 1991).

Wallerstein, Immanual, *The Modern World System I, Capitalist Agriculture and the Origins of European World Economy in the Sixteenth Century* (London, N.Y.: 1974).

Webber, Jonathan, ed., *Jewish Identities in the New Europe* (London: Littman Library of Jewish Civilization, 1994).

William, W., *The Transformation of Western Europe* (London: Pinter, 1999).

Williams, Howards, *International Relations and the Limits of Political Theory* (London: Macmillan, 1996).

Wilson, H.T., *Tradition and Innovation: The Idea of Civilization as Culture and Its significance* (London: Routledge & Kegan Paul, 1984).

Wilson, T.M., and M.E. , Smith, *Cultural Change and the New Europe : Perspectives on the European Community* (Boulder: Westview, 1993).

Wistrich, E, *After 1992 : The United States of Europe* (London : Routledge, 1989).

Wolff, Larry, *Inventing Eastern Europe: The Map of Civilization on the Mind of the Enlightenment* (Standford, CA.: Standford university Press, 1994).

Woolf, Stuart, *Napoleon's Integration of Europe* (London : 1991).

Yalvac, Faruk, "The Sociology of the State and the Sociology of International Relations", in Michael Banks and Martin Shaw, ed., *State and Society in International Relations* (Hamel Hempstead: Harvester-Wheatsheaf, 1991).

Yasemin Nuhoglu Soysal, "Towards a Postnational Model of Membership in Europe", in Kate Nash, ed., *Readings in Contemporary Political Sociology* (Oxford, 2000).

Zurcher, Arnold J. *The Struggle to Unite Europe 1940-1958* (Westport, CT: Greenwood, 1975).

Articles

Archer, M.S., "Myth of Cultural Integration", *British Journal of Sociology*, vol.36, no.3, Sep 1985, pp.333-53.

Arnold, Hans., "Maastricht: The Beginning or End of a Development?", *Aussen Politik*, vol. 44, no. 3, 1993, pp. 271-80 .

Ashley, Richard "The Geo-political Space: Towards a Critical Social Theory of International Politics", *Alternative*, vol.12, 1987, pp.403-34.

Auruch, K., "Making Culture and Its Costs" , *Ethnic and Racial Studies*, vol. 15, no. 4, 1992, pp. 614-26 .

Bance , A., "The Idea of Europe : From Erasmus to Erasmus", *Journal of European Studies*, vol . 22 , no. 2, Spring 1997, pp.214-23.

Banchoff, T., "German Policy Towards the European Union: The Effects of Historical Memory", *German Politics*, vol. 6, no. 1, 1997, pp. 60-76.

Barry, Andrew, "The European Community and European Government: Harmonization, Mobility and Space", *Economy and Society*, vol. 22, no. 3, Aug 1993, pp. 314-328.

Bauman, Z., "On the Origin of Civilization: A Historical Note", *Theory, Culture and Society*, vol.1, no. 3, 1983, pp. 32-43.

Bhavanani, K.K., "Towards a Multicultural Europe ? : Race, Nation and Identity in 1992 and Beyond", *Feminist Review*, vol. 12, no. 45, Autumn 1993, pp. 30-45 .

Bonilla-Silva, Eduardo, " 'This is a White Country': The Racial Ideology of the Western Nations of the World-System", *Sociological Inquiry*, vol. 70, no. 2, Spring 2000, pp.188-214.

Bossenbrock, Martin, "The Living Tools of Empire: The Recruitment of European Soldiers for the Dutch Colonial Army, 1814-1909", *Journal of Imperial and Commenwealth History*, vol. 23, no. 1, Jan 1995, pp.26-53.

Bredow, Wilfred Von, "Post-post-nationalism: Unified Germany after the East-West conflict", *International Journal*, vol. 48, no. 3, June 1993, pp. 413-33.

Campbell, David "Global Inscription: How Foreign Policy Constitute the United States", *Alternatives*, vol.25, 1990, pp. 263-86.

Carrihers , M. , " Why Humans Have Culture?", *Man*, vol. 25, no. 2, pp. 189-207 .

Chakrabarty, Dipesh "Postcoloniality and the Artifice of History, Who Speaks for 'Indian' Pasts ?", *Representation*, vol.37, Winter 1992, pp.1-13.

Chaterjee, Partha "Beyond the Nation? Or Within?", *Economic and Political Weekly*, January 4-11, 1994, pp. 30-34.

Cichowski, Rachel A., "Western Dreams, Eastern Realities: Support of the European Union in Central and Eastern Europe", *Comparative Political Studies*, vol.33, no.10, Dec 2000, pp. 1243-1278.

Cox, Robert "Gramsci, Hegemony and International Relations: An Essay in Method", *Millenium: Journal of International Studies*, vol.12, no.2, 1983, pp. 269-291.

Daly, Kathleen, "Four Aspects of the Renaissance", *European History Quarterly*, vol.17, no.1, Jan 1987, pp. 79-85.

Darby, Phillip and A.J. Paolini, "Bridging International Relations and Postcolonialism" *Alternatives*, vol. 19, no. 3, Summer 1994, pp. 371-97.

Dashefsky, A., "And Search Goes On : The Meaning of Religio-Ethnic Identity and Identification", *Sociological Analysis*, vol. 33, no. 2, 1972, pp. 239-45.

Diligensky, Herman, " Interests of Civilization: Global Aspects", *Social Sciences*, vol. 14, no. 1, 1983, pp. 57-74.

Dirlik, Arif "Chinese History and the Question of Orientalism", *History and Theory*, vol. 35, no. 4, December 1996, pp.96-118.

Dogan, Mattei "Comparing the Decline of Nationalism in Western Europe: The Generational Dynamic", *International Social Science Journal*, May 1993, pp.177-98.

Dyke, Gretchen J. Van, and Others, " Stimulating Simulations: Making the European Union a Classroom Reality", *International Studies Perspective*, vol.1, no.2, Aug 2000, pp.145-59.

Eichenberg, R.C., and R.J. Dalton, "European Community: The Dynanics of Public Support for European Integration", *International Oranization*, vol. 47, no. 4, Autumn 1993, pp. 507-34.

Eisenstadt, S.N., "Cultural Tradition and Political Dynamics", *British Journal of Sociology*, vol.32, no.2, June 1981, pp. 155-81.

Emanuel, S., "Culture is Space: The European Cultural Channel", *Media, Culture and Society*, vol. 14, 1992, pp.281-99.

Ferrara, Alessandro, "The Paradox of Community", *International Sociology*, vol. 12, no. 4, Dec 1997, pp.395-408.

Ford , C., " Religion and Popular Culture in Modern Europe", *Journal of Modern History*, vol. 65, no. 1, March 1993, pp. 152-72 .

Friedman , J. , "Culture, Identity and World Process", *Review*, vol. 12, no. 1, Winter 1989, pp. 51-69.

Gallagher, John, and Robinson, Ronald, "The Imperialism of Free Trade", *The Economic History Review*, vol. 6, no. 1, 1953, pp. 1-15.

Gill, Stephen "Two Concepts of International Political Economy', *Review of International Studies*, vol.16, 1990, pp.369-81.

Grieco, J.M., "The Maastricht Treaty, Economic and Monetary Union, and the Neo-Realist Research Programme", *Review of International Studies*, vol. 21, no. 1, 1995, pp. 21-40.

Gurpreet Mahajan, "Reconsidering Postmodernism: What is New in the Old Lamp", *Economic and Political Weekly*, January 28, 1995, pp.45-52.

Habermas, J, "Yet Again: German Identity", *New German Critique*, no.52, Winter 1992, pp.22-34.

Hall, S., "Europe's Other Self", *Marxism Today*, August 1991, pp. 18-23.

Halliday, Fred., "A 'Crisis' of International Relations", *International Relations*, vol.8, Nov 1985, pp.398-412.

Halliday, Fred., "State and Society in International Relations: A Second Agenda", *Millenium*, vol.12, no.2, 1987, pp.215-29.

Hass, E.B., "Turbulent Fields and the Regional Integration", *International Organization*, vol.30, no.2, 1976, pp. 173-212.

Hassener, Pierre, " Europe Between United States and Soviet Union", *Government and Opposition*, vol.21, no.1, Winter 1986, pp.17-35.

Hilton, Paul, and Ilyin, Mikhail, "Metaphor in Political Discourse: The Case of the 'Common European House' ", *Discourse and Society*, vol.4, no.1, 1993, pp.7-31.

Hirst, Paul, and Thompson, Grahame, " The Problem of 'Globalization': International Economic Relations, National Economic Management and the Formation of the Trading Bloc", *Economy and Society*, vol.21, no.4, Nov 1992, pp. 357-96.

Hoffman, Stanley, "Obstinate or Obsolete? The Fact of the Nation State and the Case of Western Europe", *Daedalus*, no. 95, 1964, pp. 862-915.

Hoffman, Stanley, "The European Process at Atlantic Cross-Purpose", *Journal of Common Market Studies*, vol.3, 1965, pp. 85-101.

Holland, Robert, ed., " Emergencies and Disorder in the Empires after 1945", *Journal of Imperial and Commonwealth History*, Special Issue, vol. 21, no.3, September 1993.

Huntington, Samuel "The Lonely Superpower: The New Dimension of Power", *Foreign Affairs*, vol.78, no.2, pp.46-52.

Hurrell, A "Explaining the Resurgence of Regionalism in World

Politics", *Review of International Studies*, vol. 21, no. 4, 1995, pp. 14-32.

Kalmer, I., "Modern Concept of Culture", *Journal of History of Ideas*, vol.48, no.4, Oct -Dec 1987, pp.671-90.

Keohane Robert O. and Joseph S. Nye Jr., "Globalization: What is New? What is Not? (And So What?)", *Foreign Policy*, no.118, Spring 2000, pp. 104-112.

Klaic, Dragan, "Close Encounters: European Internationalism", *Theatre, Yale School of Drama*, vol.29, no.1, Winter 1999, pp.115-27.

Knapp , K. , "Common Market or Common Culture ?" , *European Journal of Education*, vol. 25, no. 1, 1990, pp. 56-60.

Krashodebski, Z., "Longing for Community : Phenomenological Philosophy of Politics and the Dilemmas of European Culture", *International Sociology*, vol. 8, no. 3, Sept. 1993, pp. 339-53.

Kratochwil, Friedrich, and Ruggie, John G., "International Organization: The State of the Art and the Art of the State", *International Organization*, vol. 40, 1986, pp. 753-75.

Krishna, Sankaran, "The Importance of Being Ironic: A Postcolonial View on Critical International Relations Theory", A Review Essay, *Alternatives*, vol. 18, no. 3, Summer 1993, pp. 388-393.

Lacapra, D., "Everyone a Mentalite Case? Transference and the 'Culture' Concept", *History and Theory*, vol. 23, no. 3, 1984, pp. 296-311.

Laszlo, F. , "Cultural Factors in Europe's Role in Inter-regional World Order", *Studies On Developing Countries*, vol. 1 , 1989, pp. 111-26.

Lee, O., "Observation on Anthropological Thinking about Culture Concept: Clifford Geertz and P. Bourdieu", *Berkeley Journal of Sociology*, vol. 33, 1988, pp. 115-30.

Lepsius, M. Rainer, "The Nation and Nationalism in Germany", *Social Research*, vol. 52, 1985, pp. 43-64.

Linklater, A. , "Problems of Community in International Relations", *Alternatives*, vol. 5, no. 2, Spring 1990, pp. 135-54 .

Lively, Jack, "The Europe of Enlightenment", *History of European Ideas*, vol. 1, no. 2, 1981, pp. 90-98.

Lotman, Yuri, "History of Culture: Movement in the Future", *Social Sciences*, vol.19, no.3, 1988, pp.136-54.

Lyon, David, "British Identity Cards: The Unpalatable Logic of European Membership?" *The Political Quarterly*, vol. 62, no. 3, 1991, pp. 377-385.

Mayhew, Anne, "Culture: Core Concept under Attack", *Journal of Economic Issues*, vol. 21, no. 2, June 1987, pp. 587-603.

Mercer, J., "Anarchy and Identity", *International Organization*, vol. 49, no. 2, 1995, pp. 229-252.

Moravcsik, Andrew, "Prefaces and Power in the European Community: A Liberal Intergovernmentalist Approach", *Journal of Common Market Studies*, vol.31, 1993, pp.473-524.

Morgan, Roger, "What Kind of Europe? The Need for a 'Grand Debate' ", *Government and Opposition*, vol. 35, no. 4, Autumn 2000, pp. 547-58.

Nelson, Benjamin, "Civilizational Complexes and Inter-Civilizational Encounters", *Sociological Analysis*, vol. 34, Summer 1873, pp.79-80.

Neumann, I.B., "Self and Other in International Relations", *European Journal of International Relations*, vol. 2, no. 2, 1996, pp. 139-174.

Newton, Scott, "Britain, the Sterling Area and European Integration, 1945-50", *Journal of Imperial and Commonwealth History*, vol. 13, no. 3, May 1985, pp. 163-82.

Norgaard, Asbjorn Sonne "Institutions and Postmodernity in IR: The 'New EC'", *Cooperation and Conflict*, vol. 29, no. 3, 1994, pp. 245-287.

Norton, W., "Humans, Lands and Landscape: A Proposal for Cultural Geography", *Canadian Geographer*, vol. 31, no. 1, Spring 1987, pp.21-29.

Nugent, N., "The Deepening and Widening of the European Community: Recent Evolution, Maastricht and Beyond", *Journal of Common Market Studies*, vol. 30, no. 3, 1992, pp. 311-328.

Oommen, T.K. "Reconciling Equality and Pluralism", *The Hindu*, April 28, 2001, p.10.

Pieterse, Jan Nederveen, "Fictions of Europe", *Race & Class*, vol. 32, no. 3, Jan-March 1991, pp. 5-10.

Rattansi, Ali, "Postcolonialism and Its Discontents", *Economy and Society*, vol.26, no.4, Nov 1997, pp. 480-500.

Richard Falk, "Regionalism and World Order After the Cold War", *Australian Journal of International Affairs*, vol. 49, May 1995, pp. 1-15.

Rosow, Stephen J. , "Forms of Internationalization : Representations of Western Culture on a Global Scale" , *Alternatives*, vol.5, no.3 , Summer 1990, pp.287-302 .

Ruggie, John "Territoriality and Beyond: Problematizing Modernity in International Relations", *International Organization*, vol.47, no.1, 1994, pp. 143-44.

Schenk, Catherine R., "Decolonization and European Economic Integration: The Free Trade Area Negotiations, 1956-58", *Journal of Imperial and Commonwealth History*, vol.24, no.3, Sep 1996, pp. 446-63.

Schlesinger, Philip "Wishful Thinking: Cultural Politics, Media, and Collective Identities in Europe", *Journal of Communication*, vol.43, no.2, Spring 1993, pp. 6-17.

Schneider, G., and L.E. Cedferman, "Change of Tide in European Political Cooperation: A Limited Information Model of European Integration", *International Organization* , vol.8, no.4, Autumn 1994, pp.633-62 .

Schudson, M., "How Culture Works?: Perspectives from Media Studies on Efficacy of Symbols", *Theory and Society*, vol.18, no.2, March 1989, pp.153-80 .

Scot, Alan, "Bureaucratic Revolutions and Free Market Utopias" *Economy and Society*, vol. 25, no.1, Feb 1996, pp. 89-110.

Seglow, Jonathan, "Universals and Particulars: The Case of Liberal Cultural Nationalism", *Political Studies*, vol.46, no.5, 1998, pp.963-77.

Shachleton , M. , "European Community Between Three Ways of Life : A Cultural Analysis" , *Journal of Common Market Studies* , vol.29, no.6, December 1991, pp. 575-602 .

Shore, C., "Inventing the People's Europe: Critical Approaches to European Community 'Cultural Policy'", *Man*, vol.28, no.4, December 1993, pp.779-800 .

Smith, A.D. "The Nation: Invented, Imagined, Reconstructed?" *Millenium*, vol.13, no.2, 1991, pp. 200-217.

Smith, A.D., "National Identity and the Idea of European Unity", *International Affairs*, vol.68, no.1, 1992, pp. 55-76.

Strange, Susan "International Economics and International Relation: A Case of Mutual Neglect", *International Affairs*, April 1970, pp. 304-15.

Suny, Roland Grigor, "Ambiguous Categories: States, Empires, and Nations", *Post-Soviet Affairs*, vol. 1, no. 2, 1995, pp. 185-96 .

Swidler, A., "Culture in Action. Symbols and Strategies", *American Sociological Review*, vol. 51, no. 2, 1986, pp. 273-286.

Taylor, Paul, "The Politics of European Communities: The Confederal Phase", *World Politics*, vol.28, 1975, pp.336-66.

Tempelman, Sasja, "The Janus Face of Community: The Rationality of Group Identification and Exclusion", Review Article, *Mershon International Studies Review*, vol.40, 1996, pp. 119-121.

Tombs, Robert, "Europe in Love, Love in Europe", *Times Literary Supplement*, 6 August 1999.

Tylor, W.H, "Educating British Children for European Citizenship", *European Journal of Education* , vol.28, no.4, 1994, pp.437-44 .

Urbany, Rene, "Europe, We Are Fighting for What?", *World Marxist*

Review, vol.28, no.1, Jan 1985, pp. 16-23.

Verdery, Katherine, "Wither 'Nation' and 'Nationalism' ?", *Daedalus*, vol . 122, no. 3, 1993, pp. 37-46 .

Webber, F, "From Ethnocentrism to Euroracism", *Race & Class*, vol. 32, no. 3, 1991, pp. 7-19.

Williams, Glyndwr, "Savage Noble and Ignoble: European Attitudes Towards the Wider World before 1800", *Journal of Imperial and Commenwealth History*, vol. 6, no. 3, 1996, pp. 332-354.

Wodak, Ruth, "The Rise of Racism: An Austrian or a European Phenomenon?" *Discourse & Society*, vol. 11, no. 1, Jan 2000, pp. 5-16.

Zerilli, Linda M.G., "This Universalism Which is not One", *Diacritics*, Review Article, Summer 1998, pp. 3-19.

Index

Aberystwyth, 9
Acheson, 140
Adenauer, Konrad, 138–9
Adinnino Committee, 153, 156, 174–6, 199
Afghanistan, Soviet Invasion of, 151
Afrcia, 219, 226
Agnelli, Giovanni, 111
Alexander, Macedonian, 108
Algerian Militant Nationalism, 141
Alison, Walter, 110
Allied Powers, 8
America, 26, 64, 112, 133–5
American Hegemony, 30
Amsterdam Treaty, 157–8
Anderson, Perry, 52, 120, 194
Angell, Norman, 99
Anglo-American Tradition, 46
Annales School, 89
Aquinas, Thomas, 106
Arab-Israeli War, 18
Arendt, Hannah, 103
Aron, Robert, 111
Asad, Talat, 211
Ashley, Richard, 36
Asia, 140, 219
  Minor, 61
Asian Solidarity, 47
Athenian Democracy, 99
Atlantic Alliance, 19
Augustine, 105
Austro-Hungarian Monarchy, 17

Babel, Tower of, 11
Baget-Bozzo Committee, 192
Balance of Power, Concept of, 6
Bandug Conference, Spirit of, 47
Barker, Ernest, 110
Barry, Andrew, 130
Beethoven, 201
Belgium, 142
Benelux Agreement, 138
Berlin, 4, Blockade, 137
Bevin, Ernest, 226
Beyen, John William, 141
Bhabha, 231
Bildung, Concept of, 91–2
Bismark, 165
Black Africa, 65
Blant, 81
Bonn, 145
Brailford, 9
Brandel, 98
Brandt, Willy, 147
Brazzaville Conference, 225
Brelton Wood System, 133, 149, Collapse of, 18
Bremen European Council Summit, 151
Briffault, Robert, 111

Britain, 23, 39, 46, 63, 91–2, 111, 133–4, 139, 146, 149–50, 152, 170, 225
British Hegemony, 23
  Imperialism, Experience of, 223
  Liberal School, 6
Brubacker, 41
Brussels, 170
  Summit, 151
  Treaty, 134
Bryce, Lord, 8
Burges Speech, 154

Cabiatti, Attilio, 111
Caesar, Augustus, 97
Campbell, David, 36, 221, 227
Canada, 151, 195
Cannig, George, 63
Carolingian Empire, Emergence of, 106
Ceccnini, Paolo, 154
Chabral, Amilcar, 80
Chakraborty, Dipesh, 211
Charlemagne, 98, 106, 127
Chatterjee, Partha, 217
China, 69
Christianity, 104
Churchill, Winston, 115, 133–4
Cinematograph Committee, 84
Civilization, 39, 89–90, 92–93, 96
  Clash of, 40, 230
Cold War, 47, 99, 128, 132, 135, 152
  Condition, 20, 48–9
Collective Identity, Formation of, 44
Colombo, Emilio, 152
Colonial Rule, 47
Colonialism, 215 Aspect of, 209
Common European Home, 153
  Market, Achievement of, 3
  Racism, 45
Communication, 17, 44
Communism, 39
Communist Ideology, 6
  Informantion Bureau, 137
Community Cultural Action, New Prospects for, 184
Comte, August, 69
Cooper, Richard, 19
Copenhagen Report, 149, 172
Copernican Revolution, 71
Coudenhone-Kalergi, Count, 110
Critical International Relation Theory, 31
Culture, 90, 93, 95–6, 182
Cultural Revolution, 171,
  Policy, 180–1, 184
Curry, W B, 99
Czardom, Collapse of, 9
Czechoslovakia, Soviet Invasion of, 137

Dahrendorf, 143, 148–9
Dante, 106–8
Darby, Phillip, 221
Daudien, Arnaud, 111
Davignon Report, 1489
De Gaulle, 143–6
Deleuze, 102
Delors, Jacques, 154, 175, 184, 231
De Monarchia, 108
Denmark, 145
De Porte, 130–2
Dependency, Theory of, 27
Derian, D K, 36, 221
Descartian Cartesian Approach, 111
De Swaan, 194
Deutsch, 17–8, 31
Dien Bien Phu, 141
Dillon, Michael, 221
Dirlik, 228–9
Dooge Committee, 153

Dube, 180
Dublin, 155
Dumont, Louise, 96
Dunne, Timothy, 11
Duroselle, 198

East-West Confrontation, 132
  Division, Collapse of, 34
Economic Recession, 98
Edward, 80–1
Elias, Norbert, 96
Empty Chair Crisis, 145
England, 17, 63
Europa, 60,62
Europe, 12, 13, 15, 26, 30, 38–9
  Expansion of, 38, 42–5, 60–1, 63–4, 66–9, 88–9, 106, 110, 112–4, 129, 149, 198, 207–8
  Existence of, 98
  Origins of, 60
Eurpean Coal and Steel
  Community Treaty, 110
  Community, 35, 51
  Flag, 200
  Integration, 6, 11, 17–8, 20, 25, 33, 37, 39, 41–2, 45, 67, 127, 132, 135, 165, 167
  Process, 35,
  theory, 15
  Payment Union, 136
  Recovery Program, 136
  Monetary System, 151, 156
  Economic Community, 51
  Parliament, 124
  Union, 1–3, 42, 44–5, 49–51, 120, 122, 132
  Formation, 4
  Report on, 150

Facism, Rise of, 64
Facist Resistant Movement, 84
Fagen, 20
Falk, Richard, 35
Fanon, 80–1
Featherstone, 37
Febvre, Lucien, 89–90
Federal Policy, 14 System 11
  Union Movement, 111
Federici, Silvia, 93
First World War, 5, 8, 22, 47, 108–9, 128, 132
Foreign Policy, 46 Relations, American Council of, 9
Foucher, Michael, 64
Founchet Plan, 145
France, 50, 89, 91–2, 115, 134, 138–9, 144, 146-7, 150–1, 155, 225
Frank, Gunther, 29
Free India, 47
French Cultural Hegemony, 91
  Imperialism, 92
  Revolution, 91
Frency, Henri, 114
Freund, Sigmund, 94
Fukuyama, 39
Fulton, 133
Future World Order, Wilsonia visit of, 9

Gallagher, 223–4
Gamble, 22–3
General Agreements of Trade and Tariff, 133
Genscher, Dietrich, 152
George, Jim, 8–9
George, Stephen, 143, 149
German Nationalism, 6
  Romantic Movement, 92
  Unification, 165
Germany, 8–9, 13, 23, 31, 50, 90–2, 147, 150–2, 155
  Problem of National Solidarity of, 12

Gidden, Anlhony, 32
Gills, 29
Giplin, Robert, 21, 30
Giscard' Estaing, Valery, 150
Global Capitalism, 36
Globalization, 33, 35–6, 50
  Concept of, 41
  Drive, Part of, 2
  Study of, 33
Gorbachev, 153
Gossman, Lionel, 93–4
Gottmann, 62
Gough, Kathleen, 211
Grand Design, 146, 225
Great Depression, 18
Greater Europe, 64
Greece, 99–100
Greek, 93–4
  Civilization, 65
Groom, 46
Grotians, 23

Hague Summit, 148
Halliday, Fred, 32
Hallstein, Walter, 145
Hamreal Report, 150
Hampson, Norman, 97
Hansen, 16
Hass, Ernest, 15–7, 24, 31, 48, 127
Hegel, 72, 76, 101
Hegemonic Stability, Decline of, 31
Hegemony, Concept of, 21
Heller, Agness, 69–76
Helsinki Conference, 151
Herder, 92
Herodotus, 62
Hitler, 109, 112
Hoffman, 16–7, 146, 148, 150
Holland, 129–30, 140, 144, 147
Huntington, Samuel, 39–40, 230
Hurrell, 2

Independence, Geographical Concept of, 2 Theory of, 220
Imperialism, 223, Critique of, 10
Imperialist England, 81
India, 46–8, 51, 69, 84, 214
Indian National Congress, 46 Liberation Movements, 47
Indo-China War, 47, 141
Industrial Revolution, 90
Interdependence, 21 Condition of, 19–20, 22 Emergence Mode of, 23
Intergovernmental Summit, 134–5
International Affairs, British Royal Institute of, 9, 39
  Anarchy, 4
  Monetary Fund, 133
  Peace Carnegie, Endorcement for, 9
  Political Economy, 4, 19
International Relations, 1, 4–5, 11, 18, 21, 31, 35–6, 40, 45–6, 97, 179, 218, 220–1
  Development of, 46
  History of, 7
  Legitimacy to, 4
  Objective Law of, 12
  Subject matter, 3
  System, Political Aspect of, 27
Internationalism, Concept of, 12
Interparadigm Debate, 4
Iranian Islamic Revolution, 151
Ireland, 17
Italy, 152

Jameson, Frederick, 81
Japan, 23, 26, 31, 112, 144
Jerusalem, 70
Joad, C E M, 99
Johnson, Douglas, 98
Justice, International Court of, 9

Kaleidoscope, 186
Kant, 98
Kafz, 194
Kautsky, 25
Kennan, George, 135–6
Kennedy, John, 146
Keohane, Robert, 19–20, 23–4, 33, 149, 220
Keylor, 133, 136, 140, 142
Kiernan, V G, 77–8
Kissinger, 99
Kluckhohn, 92
Kluke, 113
Kohl, Helmut, 153–5
Korean War, 140
Kothari, Rajni, 180
Krasner, 23
Krippendorff, 31
Krishna, Sankaran, 221
Kroeber, 92

League of Nations, 10
  Brainchild of, 12
  Formation of, 9
Lenin, 10, 25, 112
Leviathan State, 10
Liberal Internalism, 11–12
Liberalism, Theoretical Percinct of, 9
Liebes, 194
Linggajat Agreement, 225
Lipgens, Walts, 109, 128
London, 135 Report, 174
Louis, 226
Lumier Project, 193
Luxembourg Report, 149, 171

Maastricht, 155 Treaty, 41, 126, 155–8, 166, 176, 178–9, 184
Mann, 70
Marcilius, 106
Marshall, George, 136
Marx, 10, 69,
Marx-Lenin Approach, 26
Mennell, Stephen, 93
Messina, 141
Mexico, 175
Milan European Council Meeting, 153
Milward, Alan, 13, 130–1, 159
Mitrany, David, 14–5
Mittrand, Francois, 153
Modelski, 38
Modern Lebanon, 60
Monnet, Jean, 17, 138–9, 141, 150, 170
Morgenthau, 11–3, 219
Morleau-Ponty, 67, 69, 76
Mukherjee, Meenakshi, 214
Multiculturalism, Era of, 44
Multipolarity, Emergence of, 31
Mutual Independence, Degree of, 1

Nandy, Ashis, 209
Napoleon, 108, 127
Nash, June, 43
Nationalism, Bankruptcy of, 110
  Birth of, 96
  Obsolescence of, 10
Nazi Empire, 109
  Resistant Movement, 114
Nehru, Jawaharlal, 46–7
Netherlands, 141
New Intenational Economic Order, 18, World Order, 132
Nietzsche, 102
Non-Alignment Movement, 46
Norgaard, 36–7
North Atlantic Treaty Organisation, 137
Nye, Joseph, 1, 19–20, 24, 33, 220

Ode to joy, 201

Ordre Nouveau, 111
Orientalism, Discourse of, 228
Oomen, T K, 51

Pan-Europe Movement, 110
Papoutsis, Christes, 200
Paris, 67, 138 Summit, 149, 171
Pattern, Christopher, 230
Payne, 22
Peloponeasian War, 99
Plato, 72
Pleven Plan, 140
Political Unification, 6
Poluralism, 51
Post-Modernism, 36–7
Power of Hitler, Rise of, 9
Power Politics, Balance of, 48
  System, Balance of, 8–9
Prebisch, Paul, 27
Prussia, 92
Puchala, 20

Rana, A R, 48
Raphael Program, 185
Reading, Viviane, 182, 188
Reagan, 151
Regional Integration theory, Obsolenscence, 17
Regionalism, 1–2, 34, Emergence of, 22 Role of, 35
Resistance Movement, 134
Robinson, 223–4, 226
Rome Treaty, 142–3, 145, 153–4, 168, 174, 199
Roosevelt, 132–3
Rossi, Ernesto, 114
Ruggie, John, 36–7
Rundell, John, 93
Russell, 104
Russia, 9, 63
  October Revolution, 112

SAARC, 48–9
Said, Edward, 81, 226, 228
Scheal, Walter, 149, 171
Scheler, Max, 95
Schengen Agreement, 155
Schiller, 92
Schlesinger, Philip, 43, 194
Schuman, Robert, 115, 138
  Plan, 136, 208
Second World War, 3, 25, 67, 115, 127–8, 132, 137, 167, 225
  Consequences of, 207
Shapiro, Michael, 36, 221
Shaw, Martin, 33
Shore, Cris, 42–3, 200
Simmel, 95
Simon, 60
Single European Act, 176
Skocpol, Theda, 32
Social Sceinces, 91
  Rise of, 69
Socialist Revolution,
  Need for, 25
Sonderweg, 65
Soviet Threat, 19,
  Union, 12, 63, 130, 132, 135–7, 140, 150–1
South Asia, 48–51
Spaak, Henry, 17, 142
Spengler, Oswald, 65, 95
Spinelli, Alferid, 114–5, 134–5, 153
Spofford Jr., Charles B, 84
State System, 36
Steiner, 179
Strange, Susan, 18–9, 24
Strategic Defence Inititative, 152
Streit, Clarence, 10–1

Taylor, 76, 78
Thatcher, Margaret, 152, 154
Third Debate, 4, 31,

World, 51, 221
Thomson, E D, 82
Thueydides, 100
Tindaman, 150
Report, 156, 173–4
Totalitarianism, Ganeology of, 99
Toynbee, Arnold, 39, 64–5
Traditional Isolationist Policy, 134
Transnational Relations and World Politics, 19
Truman Doctrine, 135
Turkey, 61, 64
Tyros, 60

United Europe, 16
Untied Nations, 49, 132, 136–7, 139–40
Charter, 137
United States, 13, 22–3, 46, 49, 130, 132, 134, 150–1, 227

Valery, Paul, 68, 76
Vandenberg, 137
Vernon, Raymond, 19–20
Versailles Treaty, 132
Vienna Congress, 134, 142
Vietnam, 147
Debacle, 18

Walker, Martin, 64
Wallerstein, Immanual, 27–30
Waltzian Neo-Realists, 20
War and Peace, Issue of, 4
War, Causes of, 10
Recurrence of, 6
Clautwizian, idea of, 8
Warsaw Treaty Pact, 137
Weber, Alfred, 96
Weber, Max, 69, 95–6
Weimer Republic, Collapse of, 9
Wells, H G, 8–9, 99
Weltan Schaung, 71
Werner Plan, 148, 151
West Germany, 139, 154
Westphalia, 37
Western Europe, 2–3, 18, 23, 51, 98, 136, 138–9, 146, 165, 171
Williams, Raymond, 90
Wilson, Harold, 150
Wisonian Vision, 109
Woolf, Eric, 110
Working Peace System, 14
World Economy, 29–30
Economic Crisis, 150
Politics, Future of, 33

Xenophobic Tendency, 45

Yalta and Postdam Conference, 132
Young, Oran, 27